ALSO BY UCADIA

Pactum De Singularis Caelum
Pactum De Singularis Christus
Pactum De Singularis Islam
Pactum De Singularis Spiritus

Maxims of Divine Law
Maxims of Natural Law
Maxims of Cognitive Law
Maxims of Bioethics Law
Maxims of Ecclesiastical Law
Maxims of Positive Law
Maxims of Sovereign Law
Maxims of Fiduciary Law
Maxims of Administrative Law
Maxims of Economic Law
Maxims of Monetary Law
Maxims of Civil Law
Maxims of Criminal Law
Maxims of Education Law
Maxims of Food & Drugs Law
Maxims of Urban Law
Maxims of Company Law
Maxims of Technology Law
Maxims of Trade & Intellectual Property Law
Maxims of Security Law
Maxims of Military Law
Maxims of International Law

MISSALE CHRISTUS
SECUNDUS

Proper of Heroes and Saints

Official English First Edition

By
UCADIA

Missale Christus – Secundus: ***Proper of Heroes and Saints*** Official English First Edition. Copyright © 2009-2020 UCADIA. All Rights reserved in Trust.

No part of this book may be reproduced, or stored in a retrieval system, or transmitted in any form or by any means electronic, mechanical, photocopying, recording or otherwise, without the express and authentic written permission of the Publisher or the Universal Ecclesia of One Christ.

The Publisher disclaims any liability and shall be indemnified and held harmless from any demands, loss, liability, claims or expenses made by any party due or arising out of or in connection with any differences between previous non-official English drafts and this Official English First Edition.

A party that threatens, makes or enacts any demand or action, against this publication or the Publisher hereby acknowledge they have read this disclaimer and agree with this binding legal agreement and irrevocably consent to Ucadia or the Universal Ecclesia of One Christ and its competent forums as being the original and primary Jurisdiction for resolving any such issue of fact and law.

Published by Ucadia Books Company, a Delaware stock corporation (File Number 6779670)
901 N Market St #705 Wilmington Delaware 19801.
First edition.

UCADIA® is a US Registered Trademark in trust under Guardians and Trustees Company protected under international law and the laws of the United States.

ISBN 978-1-64419-067-8

Pactum De Singularis Caelum
Covenant of One Heaven

Article 134 (Supreme Sacred Gifts & Rites)

Supreme Sacred Gifts and Rites of Heaven shall be the customary rules, standards and procedures whereby the Thirty-Three (33) Sacred Gifts of Heaven are properly administered and dispensed by qualified and authorised persons, in accord with the most sacred Covenant.

"Missal of Christ" (*Missale Christus*) shall be the original and primary sacred text containing the necessary rubrics, canons, sacramentaries, votives, invocations, instructions and orders for the proper conduct and proceeding of Sacred Liturgy of the Universal Rites of One Christ. The conduct of all sacramentaries concerning the thirty-three Sacraments and Extra-Sacramental Rites and Rubrics of Heaven shall be in accord with the Missal of Christ (Missale Christus).

Pactum De Singularis Christus
Covenant of One Christ

Article 14 (Missale Christus)

Universal Ecclesia of One Christ shall fulfil its sanctifying function through the Sacred Liturgy, being the rightful exercise of the presbyterial function entrusted to it by Christ. Within the Sacred Liturgy, the sanctification of humanity is perfected through visible signs and effected in a competent manner proper to each sign. Through the Sacred Liturgy, the worship of God and the Divine Creator of Heaven and Earth is conducted by the united Members of the Living Body of One Christ.

In accord with Article 134 (*Supreme Sacred Gifts and Rites*) of the most sacred Covenant *Pactum De Singularis Caelum*, The Missal of Christ (*Missale Christus*) shall be the original and primary sacred text containing the necessary rubrics, canons, sacramentaries, votives, invocations, instructions and orders for the proper conduct and proceeding of Sacred Liturgy of the Universal Rites of One Christ.

The conduct of all Sacramentals and Extra-Sacramentals of Heaven is in accord with the Missal of Christ (*Missale Christus*).

The Missal of Christ (*Missale Christus*) shall be divided into three (3) sacred books:-

(i)   Proper of Life & Mysteries; and

(ii) Proper of Days of Heroes & Saints; and

(iii) Proper of Sacraments, Rites & Prayers.

MISSALE CHRISTUS
SECUNDUS
PROPER OF HEROES & SAINTS
CONTENTS

Title I: Proper of Heroes & Saints

I.I – Proper of Heroes & Saints	15
I.II – Common Concepts of Saints	16
I.III – Formal Norm of Saints	17

Title II: Patron Saints of Peoples & Regions

II.I – Patron Saints of Regions	19
II.II – Patron Saints of the Americas	19
II.III – Patron Saints of Europa	19
II.IV – Patron Saints of Africa	20
II.V – Patron Saints of Asia	20
II.VI – Patron Saints of Arabia & Middle East	20
II.VII – Patron Saints of Oceania	20
II.VIII – Patron Saints of Antarctica	20

Title III: Patron Saints and Heroes of Nations

III.I – Patron Saints and Heroes of Nations	21
III.II – Patron Saints of Nations of the Americas	22
III.III – Patron Saints of Nations of Europa	24
III.IV – Patron Saints of Nations of Africa	26
III.V – Patron Saints of Nations of Asia	27
III.VI – Patron Saints of Nations of Arabia & Middle East	28
III.VII – Patron Saints of Nations of Oceania	29

Title IV: Patron Saints of Causes

IV.I – Patron Saints of Causes	31

Title V: Prayers and Intercessions Attributed to Saints

V.I – Prayers and Intercessions Attributed to Saints	33

Title VI: Relics and Venerated Objects of Saints

VI.I – Relics and Venerated Objects of Saints	35

Title VII: Consecrated Objects Dedicated to Saints
    VII.I – Consecrated Objects Dedicated to Saints 37

Title VIII: Mass Dedicated to Saint
    VIII.I – Mass Dedicated to Saint 39

Title IX: Proper of January
    IX.I – January 2 (Basil the Great, Gregory Nazianzen) 41
    IX.II – January 4 (Elizabeth Ann Seton) 42
    IX.III – January 5 (John Neumann) 43
    IX.IV – January 6 (André Bessette, Abdallah Qara'ali) 44
    IX.V – January 7 (Raymond of Penyafort) 45
    IX.VI – January 13 (Hilary of Poitiers) 46
    IX.VII – January 17 (Anthony of Egypt) 47
    IX.VIII – January 20 (Eusebius of Esztergom) 49
    IX.IX – January 21 (Agnes of Rome) 50
    IX.X – January 23 (Vincent of Saragossa) 50
    IX.XI – January 24 (Francis de Sales) 51
    IX.XII – January 25 (Conversion of St Paul) 52
    IX.XIII – January 26 (Timothy and Titus) 53
    IX.XIV – January 27 (Angela Merici) 54
    IX.XV – January 28 (Charles the Great – Charlamagne) 55
    IX.XVI – January 31 (John Bosco, Menno Simons) 56

Title X: Proper of February
    X.I – February 3 (Blaise of Sebasle) 59
    X.II – February 5 (Agatha of Sicily) 59
    X.III – February 6 (Paul Miki and Companions) 60
    X.IV – February 7 (Cornelius the Centurion) 62
    X.V – February 8 (Jerome Emiliani) 63
    X.VI – February 10 (Scholastica of Nursia) 64
    X.VII – February 11 (Our Lady of Lourdes) 65
    X.VIII – February 14 (Cyril and Methodius) 66
    X.IX – February 17 (Holy Founders of the Servite Order) 66
    X.X – February 18 (Martin Luther) 67

X.XI – February 21 (Peter Damian, John Henry Newman) 68

X.XII – February 23 (Polycarp) 71

X.XIII– February 24 (Matthias the Apostle) 72

X.XIV – February 25 (Jacob Hutter) 72

X.XV – February 27 (Constantine the Great) 73

Title XI: Proper of March

XI.I – March 1 (Katharine Drexel) 75

XI.II – March 2 (John and Charles Wesley) 75

XI.III – March 4 (Gerasimus of Jordan, Casimir Jagiellon) 76

XI.IV – March 7 (Thomas Aquinas) 78

XI.V – March 8 (John of God) 79

XI.VI – March 9 (Frances of Rome) 80

XI.VII – March 17 (Patrick of Ireland) 80

XI.VIII – March 18 (Cyril of Jerusalem) 81

XI.IX – March 19 (Joseph Spouse of the Blessed) 82

XI.X – March 21 (Thomas Cranmer) 83

XI.XI – March 23 (Gregory the Illuminator, Turibius of Mogrovejo) 84

XI.XII – March 31 (Our Lady of the Southern Cross) 86

Title XII: Proper of April

XII.I – April 2 (Francis of Paola) 87

XII.II – April 4 (Martin Luther King Jr, Isidore) 87

XII.III – April 5 (Vincent Ferrer) 90

XII.IV – April 7 (John Baptist de la Salle) 90

XII.V – April 11 (Stanislaus of Szczepanów) 91

XII.VI – April 13 (Martin I) 92

XII.VII – April 21 (Anselm of Canterbury) 93

XII.VIII – April 23 (George of England) 93

XII.IX – April 24 (Fidelis of Sigmaringen) 94

XII.X – April 25 (Mark the Evangelist) 95

XII.XI– April 28 (Peter Chanel) 96

XII.XII – April 29 (Catherine of Siena) 97

XII.XIII – April 30 (Pius V) 97

Title XIII: Proper of May

    XIII.I – May 1 (Joseph the Worker, Our Lady of Eternal Russia) 99

    XIII.II – May 2 (Athanasius of Alexandria) 100

    XIII.III – May 3 (Philip and James) 101

    XIII.IV – May 4 (Damien de Veuster) 102

    XIII.V – May 5 (Our Lady of Europe) 103

    XIII.VI – May 12 (Nereus and Achilleus) 104

    XIII.VII – May 13 (Our Lady of Fatima) 104

    XIII.VIII – May 14 (Matthias the Apostle) 105

    XIII.IX – May 15 (Isidore the Farmer) 106

    XIII.X – May 18 (John I) 107

    XIII.XI – May 20 (Bernardine of Siena) 107

    XIII.XII – May 21 (Christopher Magallanes and Companions) 108

    XIII.XIII– May 22 (Rita of Cascia) 109

    XIII.XIV – May 23 (Nicolaus Copernicus and Johannes Kepler) 110

    XIII.XV – May 25 (Bede the Venerable) 111

    XIII.XVI – May 26 (Philip Neri) 111

    XIII.XVII – May 27 (John Calvin) 112

    XIII.XVIII – May 30 (Joan of Arc) 113

Title XIV: Proper of June

    XIV.I – June 1 (Justin Martyr) 115

    XIV.II – June 2 (Marcellinus and Peter) 115

    XIV.III – June 3 (Charles Lwanga and Companions) 116

    XIV.IV – June 4 (Francis Caracciolo) 117

    XIV.V – June 5 (Boniface) 118

    XIV.VI – June 6 (Norbert of Xanten) 119

    XIV.VII – June 9 (Ephrem the Syrian) 119

    XIV.VIII – June 11 (Barnabas the Apostle) 120

    XIV.IX – June 13 (Anthony of Padua) 121

    XIV.X – June 19 (Romuald of Ravenna) 122

    XIV.XI – June 21 (Aloysius Gonzaga) 123

XIV.XII – June 22 (Paulinus of Nola) 123

XIV.XIII – June 24 (The Nativity of Saint John the Baptist) 124

XIV.XIV – June 27 (Cyril of Alexandria, Joseph Smith Jr.) 125

XIV.XV – June 28 (Irenaeus of Lyon) 127

XIV.XVI – June 29 (Apostles Peter and Paul) 128

XIV.XVII – June 30 (First Martyrs of the Church of Rome) 129

Title XV: Proper of July

XV.I – July 1 (Junípero Serra) 131

XV.II – July 3 (Thomas the Apostle) 131

XV.III – July 4 (Elizabeth of Portugal, Our Lady of Liberty & Charity) 132

XV.IV – July 5 (Anthony Zaccaria) 134

XV.V – July 6 (Jan Hus, Maria Goretti) 135

XV.VI – July 9 (Augustine Zhao Rong and Companions) 136

XV.VII – July 11 (Benedict of Nursia) 137

XV.VIII – July 13 (Henry the Exuberant) 138

XV.IX – July 15 (Bonaventure) 139

XV.X – July 16 (Our Lady of Mount Carmel) 140

XV.XI – July 18 (Camillus de Lellis) 140

XV.XII – July 20 (Apollinaris of Ravenna) 141

XV.XIII – July 21 (Lawrence of Brindisi) 142

XV.XIV – July 22 (Mary Magdalene) 143

XV.XV – July 23 (Bridget of Sweden) 144

XV.XVI – July 24 (Thomas a Kempis, Sharbel Makhluf) 146

XV.XVII – July 25 (James the Apostle) 147

XV.XVIII – July 26 (Joachim and Anne) 147

XV.XIX – July 29 (Martha) 148

XV.XX – July 30 (Peter Chrysologus) 149

XV.XXI – July 31 (Ignatius of Loyola) 150

Title XVI: Proper of August

XVI.I – August 1 (Alphonsus Liguori) 153

XVI.II – August 2 (Eusebius of Vercelli) 153

XVI.III – August 4 (John Vianney) 154

XVI.IV – August 7 (Sixtus II, Pope, and Companions) 155

XVI.V – August 8 (Dominic de Guzmán) 156

XVI.VI – August 9 (Teresa Benedicta of the Cross) 156

XVI.VII – August 10 (Lawrence of Rome) 157

XVI.VIII – August 11 (Clare of Assisi) 158

XVI.IX – August 12 (Jane Frances de Chantal, Florence Nightingale) 159

XVI.X – August 13 (Pontian and Hippolytus) 161

XVI.XI – August 14 (Maximilian Kolbe) 162

XVI.XII – August 16 (Stephen of Hungary) 162

XVI.XIII – August 19 (John Eudes) 163

XVI.XIV – August 20 (Bernard of Clairvaux) 164

XVI.XV – August 21 (Pius X) 165

XVI.XVI – August 22 (Our Lady of Asia) 165

XVI.XVII – August 23 (Rose of Lima) 166

XVI.XVIII – August 24 (Bartholomew the Apostle) 167

XVI.XIX – August 25 (Louis the Saint) 168

XVI.XX – August 27 (Monica of Numidia) 168

XVI.XXI – August 28 (Augustine of Hippo, John Smyth) 169

Title XVII: Proper of September

XVII.I – September 1 (Gregory the Great) 171

XVII.II – September 2 (Our Lady of Harmony of Heaven & Earth) 171

XVII.III – September 5 (Teresa of Calcutta) 172

XVII.V – September 9 (Peter Claver) 174

XVII.V – September 13 (John Chrysostom) 174

XVII.VI – September 16 (Cornelius and Cyprian) 175

XVII.VII – September 17 (Robert Bellarmine) 176

XVII.VIII – September 19 (Januarius of Benevento) 177

XVII.IX – September 20 (Andrew Kim Tae-gon and Companions) 178

XVII.X – September 21 (Matthew the Apostle and Evangelist) 178

XVII.XI – September 23 (Pio of Pietrelcina) 179

XVII.XII – September 25 (Cosmas and Damian) 180

XVII.XIII – September 26 (Paul VI) 181

XVII.XIV – September 27 (Vincent de Paul) 182

XVII.XV – September 28 (Wenceslaus of Bohemia) 183

XVII.XVI – September 29 (Archangels Michael, Gabriel and Raphael) 184

XVII.XVII – September 30 (Jerome, George Whitefield) 185

Title XVIII: Proper of October

XVIII.I – October 1 (Thérèse of Lisieux) 187

XVIII.II – October 2 (The Holy Guardian Angels) 187

XVIII.III – October 4 (Francis of Assisi) 188

XVIII.IV – October 6 (Bruno of Cologne, William Tyndale) 189

XVIII.V – October 9 (Denis of Paris and Companions) 191

XVIII.VI – October 10 (John XXIII) 192

XVIII.VII – October 14 (Callistus I) 193

XVIII.VIII – October 15 (Teresa of Ávila) 194

XVIII.IX – October 16 (Hedwig of Silesia) 195

XVIII.X – October 17 (Ignatius of Antioch) 195

XVIII.XI – October 18 (Luke the Evangelist) 196

XVIII.XII – October 19 (Jean de Brébeuf) 197

XVIII.XIII – October 20 (Paul of the Cross) 198

XVIII.XIV – October 22 (Pope John Paul II the Great) 199

XVIII.XV – October 23 (John of Capistrano) 200

XVIII.XVI – October 24 (Anthony Mary Claret) 201

XVIII.XVII – October 25 (Our Lady of Universal Wisdom & Light) 202

XVIII.XVIII – October 27 (Armand Jean le Bouthillier de Rancé) 203

XVIII.XIX – October 28 (Apostles Simon and Jude) 203

XVIII.XX – October 30 (John Wyclif) 204

Title XIX: Proper of November

XIX.I – November 1 (All Saints Day) 205

XIX.II – November 3 (Martin de Porres) 205

XIX.III – November 4 (Charles Borromeo) 206

XIX.IV – November 10 (Leo the Great) 207

XIX.V – November 11 (Martin of Tours) 207

XIX.VI – November 12 (Josaphat Kuntsevych) 208

XIX.VII – November 13 (Frances Xavier Cabrini) 209

XIX.VIII – November 15 (Albert the Great) 210

XIX.IX – November 16 (Margaret of Scotland) 211

XIX.X – November 17 (Elizabeth of Hungary) 211

XIX.XI – November 22 (Cecilia) 212

XIX.XII – November 23 (Clement I) 213

XIX.XIII – November 24 (John Knox, Andrew Dung-Lac) 214

XIX.XIV – November 25 (Catherine of Alexandria) 215

XIX.XV – November 28 (Our Lady of Africa) 216

XIX.XVI – November 30 (Andrew the Apostle) 217

Title XX: Proper of December

XX.I – December 3 (Francis Xavier) 219

XX.II – December 4 (John Damascene) 220

XX.III – December 6 (Nicholas of Myra) 221

XX.IV – December 7 (Ambrose of Milan) 221

XX.V – December 9 (Juan Diego Cuauhtlatoatzin) 222

XX.VI – December 11 (Damasus I) 223

XX.VII – December 12 (Our Lady of Guadalupe) 224

XX.VIII – December 13 (Lucy of Syracuse) 225

XX.IX – December 14 (John of the Cross) 226

XX.X – December 16 (Adelaide of Italy) 227

XX.XI – December 21 (Peter Canisius) 227

XX.XII – December 23 (John of Kanty) 228

XX.XIII – December 26 (Stephen) 229

XX.XIV – December 27 (John the Apostle) 229

XX.XV – December 29 (Thomas Becket) 230

Title XXI: Notes

XXI.I – Notes 233

Title XXII: Tables

XXII.I – Tables 235

Title I: Proper of Heroes and Saints

I.I – PROPER OF HEROES AND SAINTS

1. **The Wealth and Strength of Christian Life** rests not simply with its age or ubiquity, but with those faithful witnesses of each and every generation willing to dedicate their lives to defend the true teachings of Christ and our Divine Creator. Those we variously call heroes, saints and martyrs.

    Proper of Heroes and Saints

    No one is called by the Divine Creator or Christ to have to sacrifice their lives for the good of the Universal Ecclesia. Such an act without deeper purpose or meaning, would necessarily contradict the firm teachings of Christ himself concerning the true nature of the Divine Creator.

    Christ chose to live, die and rise from death precisely to end all forms of blood and ritual sacrifice; and to instil a liturgy and knowledge of love, mercy and respect of the wonders of life and the Divine Creator. Yet life and the presence of free will creates challenges and trials for each generation to make sound decisions. Sometimes, through periods of willing ignorance and forgetfulness, great evil rises up and threatens the future survival of families, communities and even civilisation itself.

    It Is midst these moments of crisis and darkness, that many people cry out for help and guidance. It is precisely these times and cycles in history that the community of the Universal Ecclesia of One Christ has been blessed by so many willing to rise above and demonstrate through their Christian faith such heroic action and selfless courage.

2. The purpose of the **Proper of Heroes and Saints** is to ensure that all members of the People of God can identify and connect with historic and contemporary heroes, saints and martyrs of the faith of their own culture, regions and communities.

    Purpose of Proper of Heroes and Saints

    In being able to identify with authentic historic figures that once walked the same streets and toiled in the same buildings and fields, it is a Divine hope that the faith of all members of the People of God may be renewed and strengthened through the Universal Ecclesia of One Christ: That nothing is impossible. That people have overcome even the most harrowing of circumstances. That the Divine Creator is always present and emanating love, compassion and an earnest dialogue with every soul, even if such knowledge may be obscured or even diminished due to the circumstances of life. Most significantly, that the spirit of Christ lives through the lives of many people all around us and within us.

I.II – COMMON CONCEPT OF SAINTS

1. A "saint" in the eyes of most people is commonly understood to mean a person recognised as having an exceptional degree of holiness or closeness to God through the teachings of Christ. Thus, not every Saint may be regarded as having lived a pious life, but every Saint is necessarily accepted as being close to God and Christ.

   Common Concept of Saints

   As a consequence, the lives of many people historically honoured and venerated as saints may seem considerably less pious and holy in their actions, but for clear signs of Divine connection or inspiration.

   Similarly, there are those rare people in life that men and women recognise as exemplifying the very essence of holiness and sacred austerity, yet may never be known outside their community or country, much less officially recognised as a saint.

   These seeming anomalies arise from the natural tensions and perspectives of everyday culture, the history of the various Christian denominations and the evolution of church rules and doctrines.

2. The history of all Christian denominations are literally founded upon the reverence and memory of Saints and Heroes of the Faith. During the earliest formation of the Churches, the first followers frequently were forced to meet in secret places, catacombs, cemeteries and secluded places where the remains of the first martyrs and faithful were usually entombed. Over time, the first formal dedicated structures for worship were often founded upon notable sites of martyrdom and the graves of great saints.

   Historic Understanding of Saints in Teachings of the Church

   So rich is the history of Christianity of generations of heroes, martyrs and saints, that within a few centuries there were more recognised saints than days of the year or churches within the community. Historic churches and structures subsequently came to be named by the title (*titulus in Latin*) of the name of the most notable saint buried within its structure.

   Consequently, the doctrine and rules of many Christian denominations sought to codify the means whereby people were formally recognised as "saints" so that permission to revere someone through public veneration became restricted to only those servants of God whom the authority of the Church recorded in the list of the saints or the blessed.

   Such restrictions, while initially well intended, did give rise to certain periods of misuse by those entrusted to honour the history and memories of the Christian churches. Thankfully, this is no longer the case and those recognised as worthy of reverence through public veneration are genuinely merited as being recorded in the list of the saints.

3. The teachings and words of Christ are clear concerning the nature of holiness and those close to God and the Divine Creator. All who enter Heaven are saints. Furthermore, all those who willingly accept and receive the Holy Sacraments as entrusted to the Universal Ecclesia are sanctified as authentic members of the People of God.

    Teachings of Christ and the Divine Creator concerning Saints

    The word saint itself is derived from the ancient word *sanctus* meaning sanctified and holy. Therefore, if one were to accept the Revelations of Jesus Christ on their word, all who are blessed to receive the authentic Holy Sacraments of the Universal Ecclesia of One Christ are legitimate and valid candidates for sainthood, even if in life they struggle from time to time to live up to the enormity of such unmerited Divine Gifts and Actions bestowed upon them.

    Such revelations do not necessarily diminish the efficacy of the teachings and rules of each Christian denomination. Instead, the words and teachings of Christ reinforce the necessity of a united system of recognition that those esteemed by the Universal Ecclesia as meriting reverence through public veneration as being records in the list of the saints. They must be choices that sustain, inspire, nurture, unite and empower all the People of God, wherever they may live across Planet Earth and the Solar System.

    It is wholly inadequate and an affront against the teachings and Revelations of Christ himself if those candidates elevated to the status and reverence of sainthood are selected purely upon one region or one culture or one ethnicity of planet Earth.

    Saints have existed and continue to exist in all four directions of the globe. Therefore, it is a solemn obligation of the Universal Ecclesia of Christ to fulfil its mission to honour the teachings and Revelations of Christ in celebrating the saints, heroes and martyrs of all people and all regions and causes.

I.III – FORMAL NORM OF SAINTS

1. Article 67 (*Regnum*) of the most sacred Covenant *Pactum De Singularis Caelum* formally defines a "Saint" as

    Formal Norm of Saints

    > "a departed soul of one of the present twelve (12) higher order life forms presently nominated to the Divina, also known as the Divine Mind who the living community of one of the twenty-four (24) Star Systems also nominated to the Divina believe is

worthy of such nomination."

Article 67 further defines a Saint as "the supreme Regional Spiritual Collective leader" of a region of Heaven known as a **Regnum**, holding such position for a term not exceeding one hundred and twenty eight (128) Earth based years.

Article 22 of the most sacred Covenant defines:

> "A total of one hundred and forty-four thousand (144,000) saints of office are to be elected by the combined Members of the three (3) great faiths of One Christ, One Islam and One Spirit Tribe on behalf of planet Earth for a period of one hundred and twenty-eight (128) years at an official celebration known as the Great Conclave of One Heaven. Saints that have been re-elected three (3) times are to be known as Holy Saints and ineligible to hold further office except Great Spirit. Only Holy Saints may be eligible to be elected by the Living Members of One Heaven to the Offices of Apostle, or Consul or Augustus."

The terms of defining the eligibility and formality of the office of Saint is vested through the most sacred Covenant *Pactum De Singularis Christus* and the proper authority of the norms and precepts of the Universal Ecclesia of One Christ.

4. The old doctrine concerning the "communion of saints" whereby a spiritual solidarity was asserted to exist only between certain Christian Persons on Earth and certain Spiritual Beings in Heaven, to the exclusion of other Christian and Jewish members and Spiritual Beings, is wholly incompatible, out-of-date and contrary to the Divine Mandate of Christ as instituted through the most sacred Covenants *Pactum De Singularis Caelum* and *Pactum De Singularis Christus*.

    The term "communion of saints" is licit to continue in perspective of the Universal Ecclesia of One Christ and all living and departed persons, when it is respected as a description of the union between departed members and the living members constituting the Living Body of Christ.

[margin: Narrow Perspective of Communion of Saints no longer valid]

Title II: Patron Saints of Peoples and Regions

II.I – PATRON SAINTS OF PEOPLES AND REGIONS

1. A hero (or heroine) is commonly recognised as a person who, in the face of danger overcomes adversity, through feats of ingenuity, courage or strength of character. In Ancient Greek (hērōs) the word literally means "protector" or "defender". The notion and ideal of the "hero" has played a central role in the culture of every human civilisation since the beginning of time.

   Each and every generation has been entertained and enthralled by the feats of heroes; and looked to establish their own meaning and identity through the discovery and veneration of their own contemporary exemplars. Heroes have been the main focal character of teaching and learning, art, music, literature and sacred scripture.

   The Christian tradition is similar to cultural traditions that existed prior to the coming of Christ, in the central importance of the hero to the Divine Story of Humanity. To Christians, Christ is *the ultimate hero*, overcoming the greatest adversity of isolation, humiliation and death to transform the very structure of Heaven and Earth through a New Covenant of Love Mercy and Redemption.

   Patron Saints of Peoples and Regions

2. A Patron Saint is one who has been assigned by a venerable tradition, or chosen by election, as a special intercessor with God and the proper advocate of a particular locality, and is honoured by clergy and people with a special form of religious observance. It is the proper authority of the Universal Ecclesia, with the heads of all Christian congregations for each region that determines and ratifies Patron Saints.

   The notion of Patron Saint

3. All major geographic regions and oceans are blessed and dedicated to at least one male and one female saint.

   Patron Saints of Regions

II.II – PATRON SAINTS OF THE AMERICAS

1. The Patron Saints of the Americas Region are:-

   (i) Our Lady of the Americas (December 12th); and

   (ii) Saint Peter Claver (September 9th).

   Patron Saints of the Americas

II.III – PATRON SAINTS OF EUROPA

1. The Patron Saints of the European Region are:-

   (i) Our Lady of Europe (May 5th); and

   (ii) Saint Francis of Assisi (October 4th).

   Patron Saints of Europa

II.IV – PATRON SAINTS OF AFRICA

1. The Patron Saints of the Africa Region are:-
    (i) Our Lady of Africa (November 28ᵗʰ); and
    (ii) Saint Augustine of Hippo (August 28ᵗʰ).

Patron Saints of Africa

II.V – PATRON SAINTS OF ASIA

1. The Patron Saints of the Asia Region are:-
    (i) Our Lady of Asia (August 22ⁿᵈ); and
    (ii) Saint Francis Xavier (December 3ʳᵈ).

Patron Saints of Asia

II.VI – PATRON SAINTS OF ARABIA & MIDDLE EAST

1. The Patron Saints of the Arabian and Middle East Region are:-
    (i) Our Lady of Mount Carmel (July 6ᵗʰ); and
    (ii) Saint Anthony of Egypt (January 17ᵗʰ).

Patron Saints of Arabia & Middle East

II.VII – PATRON SAINTS OF OCEANIA

1. The Patron Saints of the Oceania Region are:-
    (i) Our Lady of the Southern Cross (March 3ʳᵈ); and
    (ii) Saint Damien de Veuster (May 4ᵗʰ).

Patron Saints of Oceania

II.VIII – PATRON SAINTS OF ANTARCTICA

1. The Patron Saints of the Antarctica Region are:-
    (i) Our Lady of the Snows (August 5th); and
    (ii) Saint John Bosco (January 31ˢᵗ).

Patron Saints of Antarctica

Title III: Patron Saints and Heroes of Nations

III.I – PATRON SAINTS AND HEROES OF NATIONS

1. All Nations on Planet Earth recognised by the Universal Ecclesia of One Christ are blessed and bestowed with one primary saint known as the Patron Saint of the Nation, being either male or female in aspect. A Nation may then have individual saints venerated and chosen for particular states or regions within the Nation.

    A Patron Saint of a Nation is one who has been assigned by a venerable tradition, or chosen by election, as a special intercessor with God and the proper advocate of a particular nation state, and is honoured by clergy and people with a special form of religious observance. It is the proper authority of the Universal Ecclesia, with the heads of all Christian congregations for each region that determines and ratifies Patron Saints of Nations.

    Patron Saints & Heroes of Nations

2. Where a Nation State has not yet confirmed a specific saint as its Primary Patron Saint, the Universal Ecclesia, with consultation with Christian congregations may elect the Regional Patron Saint to be recognised for the time being as the Patron of the Nation. However, this decision must be reviewed every eight years to determine if a suitable candidate unique for the nation may be selected.

    Patron Saint of Region as Saint of Nation if Primary Patron Saint not yet elected

3. The Universal Ecclesia of One Christ reserves its plenary authority to nominate Patron Saints for Nations, where it deems that such a Patron is in the best interests of healing, unifying and promoting the Divine Mission of New Evangelisation for all Christians. To this end, four (4) Special Nominations are decreed:

    Special Nominations of Patron Saints for Nations

    (i) **Our Lady of Liberty and Charity** (July 4) as the Patron Saint of the United States of America, reflecting both the popular acclamation of the people of the Nation to the veneration of Lady Liberty; and the deep connection of the people of the United States to Christian values of charity and support for other nations; and

    (ii) **Our Lady of Harmony of Heaven and Earth** (Sept. 2) as the Patron Saint of the Peoples Republic of China, reflecting the ancient values and traditions of the Chinese People and the unique character of Chinese philosophy in the synthesis of institutions and ideals to achieve harmony and grace within the family and the community; and

    (iii) **Our Lady of Universal Wisdom and Light** (Oct. 25) as the Patron Saint of India, honouring the most ancient traditions of the region and its historic place in the formation of deep philosophical thought and understanding of the cosmos and of the relationship in life to all things; and

(iv) **Our Lady of Eternal Russia** (May 1) as the Patron Saint of Russia, honouring the resolute faith, trials and sacrifices of the people of Russia; and their abiding love for their homeland and cultural history and continuing achievements.

III.II – PATRON SAINTS OF NATIONS OF THE AMERICAS

1. The Patron Saints of the Nations of the Americas Region shall be:-

Patron Saints of Nations of the Americas

   (i) Anguilla (Our Lady of the Americas); and

   (ii) Antigua and Barbuda (Our Lady of the Americas); and

   (iii) Argentina (Our Lady of Luján); and

   (iv) Aruba (Our Lady of the Americas); and

   (v) Bahamas (Our Lady of the Americas); and

   (vi) Barbados (Andrew the Apostle); and

   (vii) Belize (Our Lady of the Americas); and

   (viii) Bermuda (Our Lady of the Americas); and

   (ix) Bolivia (Our Lady of Copacabana); and

   (x) Brazil (Our Lady of Aparecida); and

   (xi) Canada (Jean de Brébeuf); and

   (xii) Cayman Islands (Our Lady of the Americas); and

   (xiii) Chile (Teresa of Los Andes); and

   (xiv) Colombia (Our Lady of Chiquinquirá); and

   (xv) Costa Rica (Our Lady of the Angels); and

   (xvi) Cuba (Our Lady of Charity); and

   (xvii) Dominica (Our Lady of the Americas); and

   (xviii) Dominican Republic (Our Lady of Altagracia); and

   (xix) Ecuador (Mariana de Jesús de Paredes); and

   (xx) El Salvador (Our Lady of the Americas); and

   (xxi) Falkland Islands (Our Lady of the Americas); and

Title III: Patron Saints and Heroes of Nations

(xxii) French Guiana (Our Lady of the Americas); and

(xxiii) Grenada (Our Lady of the Americas); and

(xxiv) Guadeloupe (Our Lady of Guadeloupe); and

(xxv) Guatemala (Our Lady of Rosary); and

(xxvi) Guyana (Our Lady of the Americas); and

(xxvii) Haiti (Our Lady of Perpetual Succor); and

(xxviii) Honduras (Our Lady of Suyapa); and

(xxix) Jamaica (Our Lady of the Blue Mountains); and

(xxx) Martinique (Our Lady of the Americas); and

(xxxi) Mexico (Our Lady of Guadalupe); and

(xxxii) Montserrat (Our Lady of the Americas); and

(xxxiii) Nicaragua (James the Greater); and

(xxxiv) Panama (Our Lady of the Americas); and

(xxxv) Paraguay (Our Lady of Caacupé); and

(xxxvi) Peru (Rose of Lima); and

(xxxvii) Puerto Rico (Our Lady of Providence); and

(xxxviii) Saint Kitts and Nevis (Nevis); and

(xxxix) Saint Lucia (Lucia); and

(xl) Saint Pierre and Miquelon (Peter); and

(xli) Saint Vincent and the Grenadines (Vincent); and

(xlii) Suriname (Our Lady of the Americas); and

(xliii) Trinidad and Tobago (Our Lady of the Americas); and

(xliv) Turks and Caicos Islands (Our Lady of the Americas); and

(xlv) United States (Our Lady of Liberty and Charity); and

(xlvi) Uruguay (Our Lady of the Thirty-Three); and

(xlvii) Venezuela (Our Lady of Coromoto).

III.III – PATRON SAINTS OF NATIONS OF EUROPA

1. The Patron Saints of the Nations of the European Region shall be:-

    (i) Albania (Our Lady of Good Counsel); and

    (ii) Andorra (Our Lady of Meritexll); and

    (iii) Armenia (Gregory the Illuminator); and

    (iv) Austria (Leopold the Good); and

    (v) Belarus (Cyril of Turov); and

    (vi) Belgium (Joseph the Worker); and

    (vii) Bosnia and Herzegovina (Elijah); and

    (viii) Bulgaria (Cyril and Methodius); and

    (ix) Croatia (Joseph the Worker); and

    (x) Cyprus (Margaret of Antioch); and

    (xi) Czech Republic (Wenceslaus of Bohemia); and

    (xii) Denmark (Ansgar); and

    (xiii) Estonia (Our Lady of Europe); and

    (xiv) Faroe Islands (Olav the Holy); and

    (xv) Finland (Henry of Uppsala); and

    (xvi) France (Joan of Arc); and

    (xvii) Georgia (George of Lydda); and

    (xviii) Germany (Archangel Michael); and

    (xix) Gibraltar (Our Lady of Europe); and

    (xx) Greece (Panagia); and

    (xxi) Greenland (Our Lady of Europe); and

    (xxii) Hungary (Stephen of Hungary); and

    (xxiii) Iceland (Thorlac Thorhallsson); and

    (xxiv) Ireland (Patrick); and

    (xxv) Israel (Archangel Michael); and

Patron Saints of Nations of Europe

(xxvi) Italy (Francis of Assisi); and

(xxvii) Kosovo (Our Lady of Europe); and

(xxviii) Latvia (Our Lady of Europe); and

(xxix) Liechtenstein (Our Lady of Europe); and

(xxx) Lithuania (Casimir); and

(xxxi) Luxembourg (Cunigunde of Luxemburg); and

(xxxii) Macedonia (Our Lady of Europe); and

(xxxiii) Malta (Our Lady of the Assumption); and

(xxxiv) Moldova (Our Lady of Europe); and

(xxxv) Monaco (Devota); and

(xxxvi) Montenegro (Our Lady of Europe); and

(xxxvii) Netherlands (Plechelm); and

(xxxviii) Norway (Olaf II); and

(xxxix) Poland (Our Lady of Częstochowa); and

(xl) Portugal (Our Lady of Fátima); and

(xli) Romania (Our Lady of Europe); and

(xlii) Russia (Our Lady of Eternal Russia); and

(xliii) San Marino (Marinus); and

(xliv) Serbia (Sava); and

(xlv) Slovakia (Our Lady of Sorrows); and

(xlvi) Slovenia (Joseph); and

(xlvii) Spain (Our Lady of Europe); and

(xlviii) Sweden (Birgitta of Sweden); and

(xlix) Switzerland (Nicholas of Flue); and

(l) Ukraine (Josaphat); and

(li) United Kingdom (Andrew the Apostle).

III.IV – PATRON SAINTS OF NATIONS OF AFRICA

1. The Patron Saints of the Nations of the African Region shall be:-

    (i)   Angola (Immaculate Heart of Mary); and

    (ii)   Benin (Our Lady of Africa); and

    (iii)   Botswana (Our Lady of Africa); and

    (iv)   Burkina Faso (Our Lady of Africa); and

    (v)   Burundi (Our Lady of Africa); and

    (vi)   Cameroon (Our Lady of Africa); and

    (vii)   Cape Verde (Our Lady of Africa); and

    (viii) Central African Republic (Our Lady of Africa); and

    (ix)   Chad (Our Lady of Africa); and

    (x)   Comoros (Our Lady of Africa); and

    (xi)   Democratic Republic of the Congo (Our Lady of Africa); and

    (xii)   Equatorial Guinea (Our Lady of Africa); and

    (xiii) Ethiopia (Frumentius); and

    (xiv)   Gabon (Our Lady of Africa); and

    (xv)   Gambia (Our Lady of Africa); and

    (xvi)   Ghana (Our Lady of Africa); and

    (xvii) Guinea (Our Lady of Africa); and

    (xviii) Guinea-Bissau (Our Lady of Africa); and

    (xix)   Ivory Coast (Our Lady of Africa); and

    (xx)   Kenya (Our Lady of Africa); and

    (xxi)   Lesotho (Our Lady of Africa); and

    (xxii) Liberia (Our Lady of Africa); and

    (xxiii) Madagascar (Vincent de Paul); and

    (xxiv) Malawi (Our Lady of Africa); and

    (xxv)   Mali (Our Lady of Africa); and

Patron Saints of Nations of Africa

Title III: Patron Saints and Heroes of Nations

(xxvi) Mauritius (Saint Louis); and

(xxvii) Mayotte (Our Lady of Africa); and

(xxviii) Mozambique (Our Lady of Africa); and

(xxix) Namibia (Our Lady of Africa); and

(xxx) Niger (Our Lady of Africa); and

(xxxi) Nigeria (Patrick); and

(xxxii) Republic of the Congo (Our Lady of Africa); and

(xxxiii) Réunion (Our Lady of Africa); and

(xxxiv) Rwanda (Christ the King); and

(xxxv) Saint Helena (Helena); and

(xxxvi) São Tomé and Príncipe (Our Lady of Africa); and

(xxxvii) Senegal (Our Lady of Africa); and

(xxxviii) Seychelles (Our Lady of Africa); and

(xxxix) Sierra Leone (Our Lady of Africa); and

(xl) Somalia (Our Lady of Africa); and

(xli) South Africa (George); and

(xlii) South Sudan (Our Lady of Africa); and

(xliii) Swaziland (Our Lady of Africa); and

(xliv) Tanzania (Our Lady of Africa); and

(xlv) Togo (Our Lady of Africa); and

(xlvi) Uganda (Our Lady and Uganda Martyrs); and

(xlvii) Zambia (Our Lady of Africa); and

(xlviii) Zimbabwe (Our Lady of Africa).

III.V – PATRON SAINTS OF NATIONS OF ASIA

1. The Patron Saints of the Nations of the Asia Region shall be:- *Patron Saints of Nations of Asia*

   (i) Bangladesh (Our Lady of Asia); and

   (ii) Bhutan (Our Lady of Asia); and

- (iii) Brunei (Our Lady of Asia); and
- (iv) Cambodia (Joseph); and
- (v) China (Our Lady of Harmony of Heaven and Earth); and
- (vi) Hong Kong (Our Lady of Harmony of Heaven and Earth); and
- (vii) India (Our Lady of Universal Life and Wisdom); and
- (viii) Indonesia (Our Lady of Perpetual Help); and
- (ix) Japan (Archangel Michael & Holy Martyrs of Japan); and
- (x) Laos (Our Lady of Asia); and
- (xi) Macau (Our Lady of Harmony of Heaven and Earth); and
- (xii) Malaysia (Our Lady of Asia); and
- (xiii) Maldives (Our Lady of Asia); and
- (xiv) Mongolia (Our Lady of Asia); and
- (xv) Myanmar (Our Lady of Asia); and
- (xvi) Nepal (Our Lady of Asia); and
- (xvii) North Korea (Our Lady of Asia); and
- (xviii) Philippines (Our Lady of Asia); and
- (xix) Singapore (Francis Xavier); and
- (xx) South Korea (Our Lady of Asia); and
- (xxi) Sri Lanka (Our Lady of Asia); and
- (xxii) Taiwan (Our Lady of Harmony of Heaven and Earth); and
- (xxiii) Thailand (Our Lady of Asia); and
- (xxiv) Vietnam (Archangel Michael & Holy Martyrs of Vietnam).

III.VI – PATRON SAINTS OF NATIONS OF ARABIA & MIDDLE EAST

1. The Patron Saints of the Nations of the Arabian & Middle East Region shall be:-

    - (i) Afghanistan (Our Lady of Mount Carmel); and
    - (ii) Algeria (Cyprian of Carthage); and
    - (iii) Azerbaijan (Bartholemew the Apostle); and

Patron Saints of Nations of Arabia & Middle East

(iv)   Bahrain (Our Lady of Mount Carmel); and

(v)   Djibouti (Our Lady of Mount Carmel); and

(vi)   Egypt (Mark the Evangelist); and

(vii)   Eritrea (Our Lady of Mount Carmel); and

(viii)   Iran (Maruthas); and

(ix)   Iraq (Abraham); and

(x)   Jordan (John the Baptist); and

(xi)   Kazakhstan (Our Lady of Mount Carmel); and

(xii)   Kuwait (Our Lady of Mount Carmel); and

(xiii)   Kyrgyzstan (Our Lady of Mount Carmel); and

(xiv)   Lebanon (Our Lady of Lebanon); and

(xv)   Libya (Augustine of Hippo); and

(xvi)   Mauritania (Our Lady of Mount Carmel); and

(xvii)   Morocco (Our Lady of Mount Carmel); and

(xviii) Oman (Our Lady of Mount Carmel); and

(xix)   Pakistan (Francis Xavier); and

(xx)   Palestinian Territory (Our Lady of Palestine); and

(xxi)   Qatar (Our Lady of Mount Carmel); and

(xxii)   Saudi Arabia (Our Lady of Mount Carmel); and

(xxiii) Sudan (Josephine Bakhita); and

(xxiv)   Syria (Barbara); and

(xxv)   Tajikistan (Our Lady of Mount Carmel); and

(xxvi)   Tunisia (Our Lady of Mount Carmel); and

(xxvii) Turkey (John the Apostle); and

(xxviii) Turkmenistan (Our Lady of Mount Carmel); and

(xxix)   United Arab Emirates (Our Lady of Unity of Faiths); and

(xxx)   Uzbekistan (Our Lady of Mount Carmel); and

(xxxi)   Western Sahara (Our Lady of Mount Carmel); and

(xxxii) Yemen (Our Lady of Mount Carmel).

III.VII – PATRON SAINTS OF NATIONS OF OCEANIA

1. The Patron Saints of the Nations of the Oceanic Region shall be:-

    (i) American Samoa (Our Lady of the Southern Cross); and

    (ii) Australia (Mary of the Cross Mackillop); and

    (iii) Cocos Islands (Our Lady of the Southern Cross); and

    (iv) Cook Islands (Our Lady of the Southern Cross); and

    (v) East Timor (Our Lady of Fátima); and

    (vi) Fiji (Saint Peter the Apostle); and

    (vii) French Polynesia (Our Lady of the Southern Cross); and

    (viii) Guam (Our Lady of Camarin); and

    (ix) Kiribati (Our Lady of the Southern Cross); and

    (x) Marshall Islands (Our Lady of the Southern Cross); and

    (xi) Micronesia (Our Lady of the Southern Cross); and

    (xii) Nauru (Our Lady of the Southern Cross); and

    (xiii) New Caledonia (Our Lady of the Southern Cross); and

    (xiv) New Zealand (Our Lady of the Southern Cross); and

    (xv) Niue (Our Lady of the Southern Cross); and

    (xvi) Northern Marianas (Our Lady of the Southern Cross); and

    (xvii) Palau (Our Lady of the Southern Cross); and

    (xviii) Papua New Guinea (Archangel Michael); and

    (xix) Samoa (Our Lady of the Southern Cross); and

    (xx) Solomon Islands (Archangel Michael); and

    (xxi) Tokelau (Our Lady of the Southern Cross); and

    (xxii) Tonga (Our Lady of the Southern Cross); and

    (xxiii) Tuvalu (Our Lady of the Southern Cross); and

    (xxiv) Vanuatu (Our Lady of the Southern Cross).

Patron Saints of Nations of Oceania

Title IV: Patron Saints of Causes

IV.I – PATRON SAINTS OF CAUSES

1. **Dedicating prayers** concerning a cause to a particular Saint is as old as the church. It reflects both a practical Christian history as well as ancient practices that have existed since the first human civilisations.

    The Universal Ecclesia of One Christ and its associated churches have a rich history of variety in those who chose to listen to the call of Christ and accept a life of mission and service of others. Doctors, bakers, millers, farmers, soldiers, kings, queens, teachers, weavers, midwives and many other occupations are represented among the venerated halls of Saints. In acknowledging such skills in life dedicated to the faith, it has made sense for generations of the Christian faithful that such Saints have an affinity to certain occupations and causes.

    In terms of universal cultural history of human civilisation, the practice of invoking certain spiritual and celestial beings for help on causes has deep root in human culture. In pre-Christian communities there is a rich history of invoking specific beings for specific causes; and indeed in attributing certain chronic problems to negative beings. During his Mission, Christ sought to allay such fears and superstitions as a weaker connection between Heaven and Earth and God and the Divine Creator. Christ encouraged the faithful to focus their prayers to our Heavenly Father, aided by the intercession of the saints and not the other way around. However, Christ did not condemn the people for their deep seated historical beliefs in prayers for causes.

    <small>Patron Saints of Causes</small>

2. Consistent with the Magisterium of Christ and His Divine Word, the Universal Ecclesia of One Christ and the authority of all associated denominations are forbidden from officially endorsing the assignment of Patron Saints for Causes. However, this does not preclude the passive tolerance for such cultural tradition.

    Instead, the churches are tasked with the delicate and important mission concerning the veneration of Saints in ensuring that such cultural traditions are not exploited by individuals or groups to their own ends, or that a practice of veneration of one or more Saints corrupts to the point of directly opposing the Living Word of Christ.

    Simply, the Living Body of Christ can never actively endorse practices that contradict the Living Word of Christ that God and the Divine Creator are the ultimate destination for all prayers and that Saints only assist in the intercession of causes and are not the primary focus for worship.

    <small>Assignment of Patron Saints of Causes</small>

Title V: Prayers and Intercessions Attributed to Saints

V.I – PRAYERS AND INTERCESSIONS ATTRIBUTED TO SAINTS

1. The Intercession of the Saints through correct prayer and practice is a widely held practice among the Congregations and Churches of the Universal Ecclesia of One Christ. It logically follows from key examples accounted during the Ministry of Christ such as the presence of Moses and Elijah during the Transfiguration, as well as historic examples within the Psalms of appropriate intercession through prayer.

    Prayers and Intercessions Attributed to Saints

    Authentic Christian Prayer of Intercession is distinct and wholly different to the notion of "summonsing a spirit", that is rightly forbidden as practice within the most sacred Covenants *Pactum De Singularis Caelum* and *Pactum De Singularis Christus*.

    In the first instance, authentic prayers of intercession do not offend Heaven, nor breach the Divine maxims of Law in making demands, threats or extortion against spiritual beings. Instead, an authentic prayer of intercession is firstly a humble petition and request.

    In the second instance, an authentic prayer of intercession never attempts to invoke a spiritual being onto the ground plane of physical reality of this world, as such an act openly defies the Divine Teachings of Christ and is a grave offence against the laws of Heaven as explicitly defined by the most sacred Covenants *Pactum De Singularis Caelum* and *Pactum De Singularis Christus*. Such unlawful attempts that are akin to necromancy are an affront against Heaven and the spirits in question and have no lawful, legal or spiritual effect, no matter what the claimed ancient provenance of such invocations.

    In the third instance, an authentic prayer of intercession never places the spirit as the final arbitrator of Divine Grace, Mercy or Miraculous Intercession. As Christ himself made clear, it is our Heavenly Father and God, not a Saint or spirit that is the final Divine Authority.

2. Christ fully understood the history and enormous attraction of ancient non-Christian practices of praying to local spiritual beings for intervention. Christ knew that people find it harder to focus in their mind such vast concepts as God and the Divine Creator, compared to an ancient spiritual being for some specific cause. Yet the Mission of Christ demanded that people be enlightened to the true source of power and revelation and not be beguiled or disappointed by the false idols placed before people.

    Prayers within the Living Liturgy of Christ

    To this end, Christ ensured that the Living Liturgy be the proper place for honouring and petitioning Saints. That whilst separate prayers to saints is licit, in any formal gathering of the faithful, the formula of any petitions for intercession must be in the context of authorised Liturgy and not locally or generally developed customs.

Title VI: Relics and Venerated Objects of Saints

TITLE VI.I – RELICS AND VENERATED OBJECTS OF SAINTS

1. **The Customary and Traditional Rite** of placing relics of martyrs or other saints under a fixed Altar is permitted to be preserved within those Customary and Traditional Rites that deem such ancient tradition as absolutely necessary, in accord with the sacred Covenant *Pactum De Singularis Christus* and associated norms and precepts. However, in all other instances, no bones or relics or bodies are to be buried within or beneath Altars.

    Relics and Venerated Objects of Saints

    Furthermore, the practice of displaying sacred images in churches for the reverence of the faithful is to remain in effect. Nevertheless, they are to be exhibited in moderate number and in suitable order so that the Christian people are not confused nor occasion given for inappropriate devotion.

2. By its intrinsic authority, all valid and legitimate relics must be registered and certified by proper authority of the Universal Ecclesia of One Christ and the authority of its denominations. An object venerated as a holy relic or object of importance concerning a Saint shall have no legitimacy, nor force or effect unless the sacred object in question is properly registered.

    Registration, Validity and Administration of Sacred Relics

    The Universal Ecclesia of One Christ shall maintain a central register, representing its plenary authority in all such matters and a second register shall be maintained by the relevant diocese or traditional rite and community claiming the right to hold and protect the said sacred relic.

3. It is absolutely forbidden to sell a Holy Relic, or to arbitrarily alienate or seize a Holy Relic.

    Forbiddence to Sell or Alienate Records of Relic

4. The Universal Ecclesia of One Christ reserves the absolute and final right of investigation and arbitration concerning the legitimacy and validity of any claimed Holy Relic or Sacred Artefact, with due respect and care to the confidence of the faithful of a particular community or region who may hold great esteem in such objects.

    Investigation of Authenticity

    Above all, the proper authority of the Universal Ecclesia must balance the principles of faith, protecting it from the temptations of corruption, versus the practical and real needs of local communities of faithful.

    If in the event that a claimed relic is denied registration and thus denied legitimacy, the Universal Ecclesia must ensure that the proper authority of any related Traditional Rite and local authority is given the proper grounds and juridic process of appeal and fair justice. Furthermore, if circumstances demand such a denial, due to clear evidence of forgery, intentional deception, trickery, corruption or other illicit acts, then the proper authorities must be especially sensitive to restoring any damage to the confidence and faith of the local community.

5. The Universal Ecclesia of One Christ reserves the absolute and final right of appeal and arbitration concerning any dispute between bodies, congregations or churches and the claim to any Holy Relics.   *Dispute over Relics*

    In all cases where the separate claims of two or more parties demonstrate sufficient custom, tradition and devotion, the proper authority of the Universal Ecclesia of One Christ must not award sole rights to the disputed relic to one side, thus injuring the history and custom of the other, even if the circumstances of acquiring the Holy Relic may have been without due authority or legitimacy at the time. Instead, an award of years not greater than eight years shall be allocated whereby each party shall be permitted a period of control and veneration of the previous relics in dispute.

Title VII: Consecrated Objects Dedicated to Saints

VII.I – CONSECRATED OBJECTS DEDICATED TO SAINTS

1. The possession of consecrated objects by the faithful as an expression of earnest reverence to the faith and history of Christianity is an accepted and licit tradition. From the earliest days, Christians manufactured, acquired or adopted symbols as outward signs and assistance for their faith. The most notable of these being such items as the symbol of the cross, figures of Christ, or Mother Mary or other Saints and the Holy Rosary.

    Consecrated Objects Dedicated to Saints

    Unlike the challenges facing the Universal Ecclesia of One Christ and its propely authorised denominations concerning the official endorsement of any formal veneration of Saints for causes, the proper systems of consecration, registration, certification, authentication of consecrated objects for personal use by the faithful is a fundamental obligation of its Divine Mandate in accord with the most sacred Covenants *Pactum De Singularis Caelum* and *Pactum De Singularis Christus*.

    Absolutely no object, whether it be an icon, cross, figure, rosary, medal, picture, sticker, clothing, painting, certificate, or any other form of Christian devotion is permitted to be given, with or without compensation, without the proper authority or license of registration to the local valid place of worship, the diocese or traditional rite that holds jurisdiction and the Universal Ecclesia of One Christ itself.

    The gift or sale of objects of Christian devotion without the proper proof of consecration, registration, certification and authentication is a serious offence against the local Christian Community, and its diocese or traditional authority and the Body of Christ in general. The Universal Ecclesia and its propely authorised denominations reserve the right to prosecute each and every proven case either through its own ecclesial competent forums, or with assistance from secular and law enforcement authorities to prosecute such acts as criminal offences.

2. To assist the Christian faithful, the Living Body of Christ recognises the help and assistance that physical objects of a devotional and consecrated nature may bring for personal use. The Universal Ecclesia is therefore tasked with the Mission of being eternally vigilant that members of the community of Christ are educated and competent in their focus and prayers that such objects be only an assistance and not to be a devotion in itself; and against the potential misuse and corruption of such earnest devotion by sordid acts of profiteering and misrepresentation.

    The principle of proper registration

    Consequently, to guard against sordid and wicked acts impeding the genuine intentions of the faithful, the Universal Ecclesia and its properly authorised denominations shall mandate that all objects of devotion for personal or community use are first properly registered, manufactured, consecrated, certified and distributed by valid license in accord the norms and precepts of the Church and its congregations.

The Universal Ecclesia and its properly authorised denominations shall allow sufficient time for all existing objects of devotion to be properly registered, or re-consecrate as needed, so as to avoid any concern by the faithful.

Thereafter, an object of devotion that is devoid of the proper documentation of registration, consecration and certification is therefore without validity and anyone found culpable of attempting to sell or give such objects shall be potentially liable for ecclesial offences as well as the enforcement of civil or criminal offences.

3. To ensure that the sanctity of consecrated places is not defiled, it is absolutely forbidden to offer, with or without compensation, authorised and properly registered consecrated objects within the main space of sacred places of worship.

    Offer of Consecrated Objects

    However, the provision of such consecrated objects through annexes and entrances or buildings near or adjoining such spaces is licit, providing such displays neither impede the free entrance of the faithful nor make any form of condition of entry to compensate by purchasing one or more valid consecrated objects.

    Any local community or authority or body that defies such conditions and seeks to pollute those sacred places assigned to their trust shall have all licenses and rights to the offer of such valid and legitimately registered consecrated objects revoked for a suitable period of penalty.

4. Properly consecrated objects for personal and community use may never be sold for profit. Instead, they may be offered either free, or on condition of minimum compensation accounting for the cost of manufacture, registration and display.

    Fees for Registration of Consecrated Objects

    The Mandatory Fees for Registration at the Universal Ecclesia level are never permitted to be higher than ten percent of the base cost of manufacturing and displaying the item. Similarly, the Mandatory Fees for Registration at the Diocese or Traditional Community level are never permitted to be higher than twenty percent of the base cost of manufacturing and displaying the item.

Title VIII: Mass Dedicated to Saint

VIII.I – MASS DEDICATED TO SAINT

1. A mass may be dedicated to a Saint or Hero if they are listed within the Proper of a month within the *Proper of Saints and Heroes*, or permitted under the rules of a consecrated community or traditional and customary rite.

    Mass Dedicated to Saint

    The Universal Ecclesia of One Christ and its properly authorised congregations do not permit the dedication of Masses to persons under the title of Saint, unless it conforms to the rules as stated.

    Dedications and memorials concerning deceased members of the Christian Community are well expressed and defined within the Proper of Sacraments, Rites and Prayers and the Proper of Life and Mysteries.

2. For a Saint or Hero listed within the *Proper of Saints and Heroes,* a Tripartite Mass Form is used, with the following specific elements defined in relation to the Saint or Hero:

    Elements of Proper of Months

    (i)   Entrance Antiphon; and

    (ii) Living Testimony and Living Gospel; and

    (iii) Offertory Antiphon; and

    (iv) Prayer Over the Offerings; and

    (v)   Communion Antiphon; and

    (vi) Prayer After Communion.

Title IX: Proper of January

IX.I – JANUARY 2

1. Saints Basil the Great and Gregory Nazianzen,   January 2
Bishops and Doctors of the Church
Memorial

Entrance Antiphon   Psalm 1:1

Blessed is the person who does not guide his steps by ill counsel, or turn aside where transgressors walk, or, where scornful souls gather, sit down to rest

Living Testimony: Basil the Great

Who are the greedy? Those who are not satisfied with what suffices for their own needs. Who are the robbers? Those who take for themselves what rightfully belongs to everyone. And you, are you not greedy? Are you not a robber? The things you received in trust as a stewardship, have you not appropriated them for yourself? Is not the person who strips another of clothing called a thief? And those who do not clothe the naked when they have the power to do so, should they not be called the same? The bread you are holding back is for the hungry, the clothes you keep put away are for the naked, the shoes that are rotting away with disuse are for those who have none, the silver you keep buried in the earth is for the needy. You are thus guilty of injustice toward as many as you might have aided, and did not.

Living Gospel: Basil the Great

We must try to keep the mind in tranquillity. For just as the eye which constantly shifts its gaze, now turning to the right or to the left, now incessantly peering up and down, cannot see distinctly what lies before it, but the sight must be fixed firmly on the object in view if one would make his vision of it clear, so too man's mind when distracted by his countless worldly cares cannot focus itself distinctly on the truth.

Offertory Antiphon

O God and Divine Creator, who gave light to your Church by the example and teaching of the Bishops Saints Basil and Gregory, grant that in humility we may learn your truth and practice it faithfully in charity. Through our Lord Jesus Christ, your Son, who lives and reigns with you in the unity of the Holy Spirit, one God, for ever and ever.

Missale Christus | Proper of Heroes & Saints

Prayer over the Offerings

May God and the Divine Creator accept and sanctify these humble gifts as symbols of the genuine personal offerings we make in commemoration of Basil the Great and Gregory Nazianzen. Through Christ our Light and Saviour.

Communion Antiphon   1 Cor 1: 23-24

We proclaim Christ crucified; Christ, the power of God and the wisdom of God.

Prayer after Communion

Heavenly Father and God of all Creation, we give thanks for the nourishment of your heavenly gifts of the Bread and Fruits of Eternal Spiritual Life. May our earnest participation together in commemoration of Basil the Great and Gregory Nazianzen bring forth favourable blessings upon our lives, our community and your Holy Apostolic Universal Ecclesia.

IX.II – JANUARY 4

1.   **Elizabeth Ann Seton,** Religious   January 4

Memorial

Entrance Antiphon   Psalm 2: 10-11

Princes, take warning; learn your lesson, you that rule the world. Tremble, and serve the Lord, rejoicing in his presence, but with awe in your hearts.

Offertory Antiphon

O God and Divine Creator, who bestowed Saint Elizabeth Ann Seton with a burning zeal to know your truths, grant that we may always seek you with diligent love and find you in daily service with sincere faith. Through our Lord Jesus Christ, your Son, who lives and reigns with you in the unity of the Holy Spirit, one God, for ever and ever.

Prayer over the Offerings

May God and the Divine Creator accept and sanctify these humble gifts as symbols of the genuine personal offerings we make in commemoration of Elizabeth Ann Seton. Through Christ our Light and Saviour.

Communion Antiphon   Jn 6: 51

I am the living bread from heaven, says the Lord. Whoever eats this bread will live for ever; the bread I shall give is my flesh for the life of the world.

Prayer after Communion

Heavenly Father and God of all Creation, we give thanks for the nourishment of your heavenly gifts of the Bread and Fruits of Eternal Spiritual Life. May our earnest participation together in commemoration of Elizabeth Ann Seton bring forth favourable blessings upon our lives, our community and your Holy Apostolic Universal Ecclesia.

IX.III – JANUARY 5

1. **John Neumann,** Bishop January 5
Memorial

Entrance Antiphon Psalm 3: 4

Lord, thou art my champion, thou art the pride that keeps my head erect. I have but to cry out to the Lord, and my voice reaches his mountain sanctuary, and there finds hearing.

Offertory Antiphon

O God and Divine Creator, who called Bishop Saint John Neumann to shepherd with charity and pastoral service your people in America, grant us through his intercession, the continued vibrant and vital education of our youth and the strength of love of the Christian family. That, as we continue to foster the Christian education of youth are strengthened by the witness of brotherly love,
we may constantly increase the family of your Church. Through our Lord Jesus Christ, your Son, who lives and reigns with you in the unity of the Holy Spirit, one God, for ever and ever.

Prayer over the Offerings

May God and the Divine Creator accept and sanctify these humble gifts as symbols of the genuine personal offerings we make in commemoration of John Neumann. Through Christ our Light and Saviour.

Communion Antiphon Mt 19: 29

Everyone who has given up home, brothers, or sisters, father or mother, wife or children or property for my sake will receive many times as much and inherit everlasting life.

Prayer after Communion

43

Heavenly Father and God of all Creation, we give thanks for the nourishment of your heavenly gifts of the Bread and Fruits of Eternal Spiritual Life. May our earnest participation together in commemoration of John Neumann bring forth favourable blessings upon our lives, our community and your Holy Apostolic Universal Ecclesia.

IX.IV – JANUARY 6

1. **André Bessette,** Religious — January 6
Memorial

Entrance Antiphon — Psalm 3: 4-6

Whenever I call on his name, the Lord will hear me. Repent, and transgress no more; take thought, as you lie awake, in the silence of your hearts. Offer self-sacrifices with due observance, and put your trust in the Lord.

Offertory Antiphon

O God and Divine Creator, who gave your servant, Saint André Bessette, a great devotion to Saint Joseph and a special commitment to the poor and afflicted, grant us through his intercession, the courage and faith to follow his example of prayer and love and so come to share with him in your glory. Through our Lord Jesus Christ, your Son, who lives and reigns with you in the unity of the Holy Spirit, one God, for ever and ever.

Prayer over the Offerings

May God and the Divine Creator accept and sanctify these humble gifts as symbols of the genuine personal offerings we make in commemoration of André Bessette. Through Christ our Light and Saviour.

Communion Antiphon — 1 Peter 1:15

But as he who called you is holy, you also be holy in all your conduct.

Prayer after Communion

Heavenly Father and God of all Creation, we give thanks for the nourishment of your heavenly gifts of the Bread and Fruits of Eternal Spiritual Life. May our earnest participation together in commemoration of André Bessette bring forth favourable blessings upon our lives, our community and your Holy Apostolic Universal

Ecclesia.

2. **Abdallah Qara'ali**
Founder of Lebanese Maronite Order

January 6

Ordinary

Entrance Antiphon — Psalm 3: 4-6

Whenever I call on his name, the Lord will hear me. Repent, and transgress no more; take thought, as you lie awake, in the silence of your hearts. Offer self-sacrifices with due observance, and put your trust in the Lord.

Offertory Antiphon

O God and Divine Creator, who gave your servant, Abdallah Qara'ali, a special commitment to the poor and afflicted in Lebanon, grant us through his intercession, the courage and faith to follow his example of prayer and love and so come to share with him in your glory. Through our Lord Jesus Christ, your Son, who lives and reigns with you in the unity of the Holy Spirit, one God, for ever and ever.

Prayer over the Offerings

May God and the Divine Creator accept and sanctify these humble gifts as symbols of the genuine personal offerings we make in commemoration of Abdallah Qara'ali. Through Christ our Light and Saviour.

Communion Antiphon — John 3:16

For God so loved the world, that he gave his only Son, that whoever believes in him should not perish but have eternal life.

Prayer after Communion

Heavenly Father and God of all Creation, we give thanks for the nourishment of your heavenly gifts of the Bread and Fruits of Eternal Spiritual Life. May our earnest participation together in commemoration of Abdallah Qara'ali bring forth favourable blessings upon our lives, our community and your Holy Apostolic Universal Ecclesia.

IX.V – JANUARY 7

1. **Raymond of Penyafort,** Priest

January 7

Memorial

Entrance Antiphon — Psalm 3: 9

From the Lord all deliverance comes; let thy blessing,

Lord, rest upon thy people.

Offertory Antiphon

O God and Divine Creator, who adorned the Saint Raymond with virtue of outstanding mercy and compassion for transgressors and for captives, grant us through his intercession, that we be free of the bonds of fear, regret and isolation so that we may carry out in freedom of spirit your Divine Mission of Salvation. Through our Lord Jesus Christ, your Son, who lives and reigns with you in the unity of the Holy Spirit, one God, for ever and ever.

Prayer over the Offerings

May God and the Divine Creator accept and sanctify these humble gifts as symbols of the genuine personal offerings we make in commemoration of Raymond of Penyafort. Through Christ our Light and Saviour.

Communion Antiphon 1 John 4

Beloved, let us love one another, for love is from God, and whoever loves has been born of God and knows God.

Prayer after Communion

Heavenly Father and God of all Creation, we give thanks for the nourishment of your heavenly gifts of the Bread and Fruits of Eternal Spiritual Life. May our earnest participation together in commemoration of Raymond of Penyafort bring forth favourable blessings upon our lives, our community and your Holy Apostolic Universal Ecclesia.

IX.VI – JANUARY 13

1. **Hilary**, Bishop and Doctor of the Church   January 13
Memorial

Entrance Antiphon Psalm 7: 8-9

All the nations will gather about thee, if thou will come back to thy throne and rule them, the Lord judging the nations!

Living Gospel: Hilary of Poitiers

Many are kept within the pale of the church by the fear of God; yet they are tempted all the while to worldly faults by the allurements of the world. They pray, because they are afraid; they sin, because it is their will. The fair hope of future life makes them call themselves Christians; the allurements of present pleasure make them act like heathen. They do not abide in ungodliness, because they hold the name of God in honour; they are not godly because they follow after things contrary to godliness.

Offertory Antiphon

O God and Divine Creator, who inspired Bishop Saint Hilary by your truth and vision, grant that we may be constantly committed to knowing and pronouncing your truth. Through our Lord Jesus Christ, your Son, who lives and reigns with you in the unity of the Holy Spirit, one God, for ever and ever.

Prayer over the Offerings

May God and the Divine Creator accept and sanctify these humble gifts as symbols of the genuine personal offerings we make in commemoration of Hilary of Poitiers. Through Christ our Light and Saviour.

Communion Antiphon — Psalm 1: 2-3

One who ponders the Divine maxims of Law of the Lord day and night shall yield fruit in due season.

Prayer after Communion

Heavenly Father and God of all Creation, we give thanks for the nourishment of your heavenly gifts of the Bread and Fruits of Eternal Spiritual Life. May our earnest participation together in commemoration of Hilary of Poitiers bring forth favourable blessings upon our lives, our community and your Holy Apostolic Universal Ecclesia.

IX.VII – JANUARY 17

1. **Anthony the Great,** Abbot — January 17

Memorial

Entrance Antiphon — Psalm 9: 2-3

Lord, I give thee all the thanks of my heart, recounting thy wonderful doings; glad and triumphant in thee, I will sing psalms to thy name, O God most high.

Living Testimony: St Anathasius Life of St Anthony

Whoever hammers a lump of iron, first decides what he is going to make of it, a scythe, a sword, or an axe. Even so we ought to make up our minds what kind of virtue we want to forge or we labour in vain.

Living Gospel: St Anthony the Great

I am going the way of my fathers, as the Scripture says, for I see myself called by the Lord. Be you wary and undo not your long service of God, but be earnest to keep your strong purpose, as though you were but now beginning. You know the demons who plot against you, you know how savage they are and how powerless; therefore, fear them not. Let Christ be as the breath you breathe; in Him put your trust. Live as dying daily, heeding yourselves and remembering the counsels you have heard from me. … So do you also be earnest always to be in union first with the Lord and then with the Saints, that after death, they also may receive you into everlasting tabernacles as known friends. Ponder these things, and mean them.

Offertory Antiphon

O God and Divine Creator, who called Abbot Saint Anthony to serve you by a wondrous way of life in the desert, grant us through his intercession, that learning to deny ourselves, we may always love you above all things. Through our Lord Jesus Christ, your Son, who lives and reigns with you in the unity of the Holy Spirit, one God, for ever and ever.

Prayer over the Offerings

May God and the Divine Creator accept and sanctify these humble gifts as symbols of the genuine personal offerings we make in commemoration of Anthony of Egypt. Through Christ our Light and Saviour.

Communion Antiphon

Mt 19: 21

If you would be perfect, go, sell what you have, give to the poor, and follow me, says the Lord.

Prayer after Communion

Heavenly Father and God of all Creation, we give thanks for the nourishment of your heavenly gifts of the Bread and Fruits of Eternal Spiritual Life. May our earnest participation together in commemoration of Anthony of Egypt bring forth favourable blessings upon our lives, our community and your Holy Apostolic Universal Ecclesia.

Title IX: Proper of January

IX.VIII – JANUARY 20

1.   **Eusebius of Esztergom**, Priest and Hermit   January 20
Founder of Order of Saint Paul the First Hermit (Pauline Fathers)
Memorial

Entrance Antiphon   Psalm 10: 2

My trust is in the Lord.

Offertory Antiphon

O God and Divine Creator, who gave such courage and strength of faith to your Saint Eusebius of Esztergom, grant us through his intercession, that we may make progress by communion in the faith and by worthy service. Through our Lord Jesus Christ, your Son, who lives and reigns with you in the unity of the Holy Spirit, one God, for ever and ever.

Prayer over the Offerings

May God and the Divine Creator accept and sanctify these humble gifts as symbols of the genuine personal offerings we make in commemoration of Saint Eusebius of Esztergom. Through Christ our Light and Saviour.

Communion Antiphon   1 Peter 1:15

But as he who called you is holy, you also be holy in all your conduct.

Prayer after Communion

Heavenly Father and God of all Creation, we give thanks for the nourishment of your heavenly gifts of the Bread and Fruits of Eternal Spiritual Life. May our earnest participation together in commemoration of Saint Eusebius of Esztergom bring forth favourable blessings upon our lives, our community and your Holy Apostolic Universal Ecclesia.

Missale Christus | Proper of Heroes & Saints

IX.IX – JANUARY 21

1. **Agnes of Rome**, Virgin and Martyr January 21
Patron of Girls
Memorial

Entrance Antiphon Psalm 11: 8

The Lord is just, and just are the deeds he loves.

Offertory Antiphon

O God and Divine Creator, who chooses what is weak in the world to confound the strong, grant us through the intercession of your beloved martyr Saint Agnes, that we may have the fortitude to follow her constancy in the faith. Through our Lord Jesus Christ, your Son, who lives and reigns with you in the unity of the Holy Spirit, one God, for ever and ever.

Prayer over the Offerings

May God and the Divine Creator accept and sanctify these humble gifts as symbols of the genuine personal offerings we make in commemoration of Agnes of Rome. Through Christ our Light and Saviour.

Communion Antiphon Lk 22: 28-30

It is you who have stood by me in my trials; and I confer a kingdom on you, says the Lord, that you may eat and drink at my table in my kingdom.

Prayer after Communion

Heavenly Father and God of all Creation, we give thanks for the nourishment of your heavenly gifts of the Bread and Fruits of Eternal Spiritual Life. May our earnest participation together in commemoration of Agnes of Rome bring forth favourable blessings upon our lives, our community and your Holy Apostolic Universal Ecclesia.

IX.X – JANUARY 23

1. **Vincent of Saragossa**, Deacon and Martyr January 23
Memorial

Entrance Antiphon Psalm 15: 4-5

He admonishes the reprobate, keeping his reverence for such as respect God, and are true, come what may, to his pledged word; And who lend without usury, and take no bribe to condemn the innocent. They who so live will stand firm for ever.

Offertory Antiphon

O God and Divine Creator, grant us through the intercession of your Martyr Saint Vincent the same courage so that our hearts may possess the Divine Love and Compassion that enabled him to triumph over all bodily torments. Through our Lord Jesus Christ, your Son, who lives and reigns with you in the unity of the Holy Spirit, one God, for ever and ever.

Prayer over the Offerings

May God and the Divine Creator accept and sanctify these humble gifts as symbols of the genuine personal offerings we make in commemoration of Vincent of Saragossa. Through Christ our Light and Saviour.

Communion Antiphon — Lk 22: 28-30

It is you who have stood by me in my trials; and I confer a kingdom on you, says the Lord, that you may eat and drink at my table in my kingdom.

Prayer after Communion

Heavenly Father and God of all Creation, we give thanks for the nourishment of your heavenly gifts of the Bread and Fruits of Eternal Spiritual Life. May our earnest participation together in commemoration of Vincent of Saragossa bring forth favourable blessings upon our lives, our community and your Holy Apostolic Universal Ecclesia.

IX.XI – JANUARY 24

1. Francis de Sales, Bishop and Doctor of the Church — January 24
Memorial

Entrance Antiphon — Psalm 16: 1

Keep me safe, Lord; I put my trust in thee.

Living Testimony of Bishop Jean-Pierre Camus on St Francis de Sales

Have patience with every one, but especially with yourself. You learn to speak by speaking, to study by studying, to run by running, to work by working; and just so you learn to love God and man by loving. All those who think to learn in any other way deceive themselves.

Living Gospel: St. Francis de Sales

When your heart roams or gets distracted lead it back very gently, softly putting it close to its Master; and even if you spend your whole hour doing nothing except gathering up your heart quite calmly and putting it close to Our Lord, and even if your heart does nothing except turn away as soon as you have led it back, your hour will have been very well spent.

Offertory Antiphon

O God and Divine Creator, who for the salvation of souls willed that the Bishop Saint Francis de Sales become all things to all, grant us through his intercession, that we may always display the same gentleness of charity in the service of our neighbour. Through our Lord Jesus Christ, your Son, who lives and reigns with you in the unity of the Holy Spirit, one God, for ever and ever.

Prayer over the Offerings

May God and the Divine Creator accept and sanctify these humble gifts as symbols of the genuine personal offerings we make in commemoration of Francis de Sales. Through Christ our Light and Saviour.

Communion Antiphon *(Psalm 1: 2-3)*

One who ponders the Divine maxims of Law of the Lord day and night shall yield fruit in due season.

Prayer after Communion

Heavenly Father and God of all Creation, we give thanks for the nourishment of your heavenly gifts of the Bread and Fruits of Eternal Spiritual Life. May our earnest participation together in commemoration of Francis de Sales bring forth favourable blessings upon our lives, our community and your Holy Apostolic Universal Ecclesia.

IX.XII – JANUARY 25

1. Conversion of Paul The Apostle — *January 25*
Memorial

Entrance Antiphon *(Psalm 16: 8)*

I keep my eyes always on the Lord. With him at my right hand, I will not be shaken.

Living Testimony: Paul to Corinthians *(1 Corinthians 12:4-11)*

Now there are diversities of gifts, but the same Spirit. And there are differences of administrations, but the same Lord. And there are diversities of operations, but it is the same God which worketh all in all.

Living Gospel: Paul   *Romans 13:8*

Owe no man any thing, but to love one another: for he that loveth another hath fulfilled the law. For this, Thou shalt not commit adultery, Thou shalt not kill, Thou shalt not steal, Thou shalt not bear false witness, Thou shalt not covet; and if there be any other commandment, it is briefly comprehended in this saying, namely, Thou shalt love thy neighbour as thyself.

Offertory Antiphon

O God and Divine Creator, who taught the whole world through the preaching of the blessed Apostle Paul, grant us through his intercession, that we may come nearer to you, through his example and conversion and be a true witness to your Divine Mission of Salvation for all peoples. Through our Lord Jesus Christ, your Son, who lives and reigns with you in the unity of the Holy Spirit, one God, for ever and ever.

Prayer over the Offerings

May God and the Divine Creator accept and sanctify these humble gifts as symbols of the genuine personal offerings we make in commemoration of the Conversion of St Paul. Through Christ our Light and Saviour.

Communion Antiphon   *Gal 2: 20*

I live by faith in the Son of God, who has loved me and given himself up for me.

Prayer after Communion

Heavenly Father and God of all Creation, we give thanks for the nourishment of your heavenly gifts of the Bread and Fruits of Eternal Spiritual Life. May our earnest participation together in commemoration of the Conversion of St Paul bring forth favourable blessings upon our lives, our community and your Holy Apostolic Universal Ecclesia.

IX.XIII – JANUARY 26

1.   **Timothy and Titus**, Bishops   January 26

Memorial

Missale Christus | Proper of Heroes & Saints

Entrance Antiphon   Psalm 16: 11

Thou will shew me the way of life, make me full of gladness in thy presence; at thy right hand are delights that will endure for ever.

Offertory Antiphon

O God and Divine Creator, who adorned Saints Timothy and Titus with apostolic virtues, grant us through their intercession, that living justly and devoutly we may be examples in our own time and communities of your heavenly promise. Through our Lord Jesus Christ, your Son, who lives and reigns with you in the unity of the Holy Spirit, one God, for ever and ever.

Prayer over the Offerings

May God and the Divine Creator accept and sanctify these humble gifts as symbols of the genuine personal offerings we make in commemoration of Timothy and Titus. Through Christ our Light and Saviour.

Communion Antiphon   Mk 16: 15; Mt 28: 20

Go into all the world, and proclaim the Gospel. I am with you always, says the Lord.

Prayer after Communion

Heavenly Father and God of all Creation, we give thanks for the nourishment of your heavenly gifts of the Bread and Fruits of Eternal Spiritual Life. May our earnest participation together in commemoration of Timothy and Titus bring forth favourable blessings upon our lives, our community and your Holy Apostolic Universal Ecclesia.

IX.XIV – JANUARY 27

1.   **Angela Merici**, Virgin   January 27

Entrance Antiphon   Psalm 17: 6

I cry to thee, the God who ever hearest me; turn thy ear towards me, and listen to my plea.

Offertory Antiphon

O God and Divine Creator, grant us through the intercession of your beloved Saint Angela that we might follow her in life her lessons of charity and prudence and hold fast to your Divine teachings. Through our Lord Jesus Christ, your Son, who lives and reigns with you in the unity of the Holy Spirit, one God, for ever and ever.

Prayer over the Offerings

> May God and the Divine Creator accept and sanctify these humble gifts as symbols of the genuine personal offerings we make in commemoration of Angela Merici. Through Christ our Light and Saviour.

Communion Antiphon — 1 Peter 1:15

> But as he who called you is holy, you also be holy in all your conduct.

Prayer after Communion

> Heavenly Father and God of all Creation, we give thanks for the nourishment of your heavenly gifts of the Bread and Fruits of Eternal Spiritual Life. May our earnest participation together in commemoration of Angela Merici bring forth favourable blessings upon our lives, our community and your Holy Apostolic Universal Ecclesia.

IX.XV – JANUARY 28

1. Charles the Great (Charlamagne) — January 28

Memorial

Entrance Antiphon — Psalm 18:3

> The Lord is my rock, my fortress and my savior; my God is my rock, in whom I find protection. He is my shield, the power that saves me, and my place of safety.

Living Testimony about Charlamagne: Walahfrid (9th C.)

> Charles was the keenest of all kings to seek out and support wise men so that they might philosophise with all delight. Almost all of the kingdom entrusted to him by God was so foggy and almost blind, but he made it luminous with the new ray of knowledge, almost unknown to this barbarous land, with God lighting the way so it could see.

Living Gospel: Charlamagne (9th C.)

> Right action is better than knowledge; but in order to do what is right, we must know what is right. Be humble and good to one another; be faithful to your lords. Husbands should love their wives and speak no rude word to them. Make us eternal truths receive, And practice all that we believe. Give us thyself, that we may see The Father and the Son, by thee.

Offertory Antiphon

> O God and Divine Creator, who inspired the Pippins to

devote themselves to a life of chivalry and piety as exemplified by your knight and sovereign Charlamagne, grant that we might be humble in our dealings with others and to live according to your code of civil virtue. Through our Lord Jesus Christ, your Son, who lives and reigns with you in the unity of the Holy Spirit, one God, for ever and ever.

Prayer over the Offerings

May God and the Divine Creator accept and sanctify these humble gifts as symbols of the genuine personal offerings we make in commemoration of Charles the Great. Through Christ our Light and Saviour.

Communion Antiphon — Micah 5:4

And he shall stand and shepherd his flock in the strength of the Lord, in the majesty of the name of the Lord his God.

Prayer after Communion

Heavenly Father and God of all Creation, we give thanks for the nourishment of your heavenly gifts of the Bread and Fruits of Eternal Spiritual Life. May our earnest participation together in commemoration of Charles the Great bring forth favourable blessings upon our lives, our community and your Holy Apostolic Universal Ecclesia.

IX.XVI – JANUARY 31

1. **John Bosco**, Priest — January 31
Founder of Salesians Congregation and Organisation
Memorial

Entrance Antiphon — Psalm 18: 47

Blessed be the living Christ who is my refuge, praised be the Divine Creator who delivers me!

Offertory Antiphon

O God and Divine Creator, who raised up Saint John Bosco to be a trusted father and teacher to the young, grant us through his intercession, that we may serve you in trust and honour in the protection and education of the children of our community. Through our Lord Jesus Christ, your Son, who lives and reigns with you in the unity of the Holy Spirit, one God, for ever and ever.

Prayer over the Offerings

May God and the Divine Creator accept and sanctify these humble gifts as symbols of the genuine personal offerings we make in commemoration of John Bosco. Through Christ our Light and Saviour.

Communion Antiphon — Micah 5:4

And he shall stand and shepherd his flock in the strength of the Lord, in the majesty of the name of the Lord his God.

Prayer after Communion

Heavenly Father and God of all Creation, we give thanks for the nourishment of your heavenly gifts of the Bread and Fruits of Eternal Spiritual Life. May our earnest participation together in commemoration of John Bosco bring forth favourable blessings upon our lives, our community and your Holy Apostolic Universal Ecclesia.

2. Menno Simons
Co-Founder of Anabaptist Movements of Universal Ecclesia

January 31

Memorial

Entrance Antiphon — Psalm 18:47

Blessed be the living Christ who is my refuge, praised be the Divine Creator who delivers me!

Offertory Antiphon

O God and Divine Creator, who inspired Menno Simons to seek and discover a deeper love and understanding of your most important sacraments, grant that might never be afraid to read and listen to your Divine Word and Mission. Through our Lord Jesus Christ, your Son, who lives and reigns with you in the unity of the Holy Spirit, one God, for ever and ever.

Prayer over the Offerings

May God and the Divine Creator accept and sanctify these humble gifts as symbols of the genuine personal offerings we make in commemoration of Menno Simons. Through Christ our Light and Saviour.

Communion Antiphon — Galatians 5:22

But the fruit of the Spirit is love, joy, peace, patience, kindness, goodness, faithfulness,

Prayer after Communion

Heavenly Father and God of all Creation, we give thanks for the nourishment of your heavenly gifts of the Bread

and Fruits of Eternal Spiritual Life. May our earnest participation together in commemoration of Menno Simons bring forth favourable blessings upon our lives, our community and your Holy Apostolic Universal Ecclesia.

Title X: Proper of February

X.I – FEBRUARY 3

1.   **Blaise of Sebasle,** Bishop and Martyr   February 3
Memorial

Entrance Antiphon   Psalm 19: 8

The Lord's perfect law, how it brings the soul back to life; the Lord's unchallengeable decrees, how they make the simple learned!

Offertory Antiphon

O God and Divine Creator, grant us through the example of your beloved physician, bishop and martyr Saint Blaise, that they may use our talents in this life to best help our community in your name. Through our Lord Jesus Christ, your Son, who lives and reigns with you in the unity of the Holy Spirit, one God, for ever and ever.

Prayer over the Offerings

May God and the Divine Creator accept and sanctify these humble gifts as symbols of the genuine personal offerings we make in commemoration of Saint Blaise. Through Christ our Light and Saviour.

Communion Antiphon   Lk 2: 30-31

My eyes have seen your salvation, which you prepared in the sight of all the peoples.

Prayer after Communion

Heavenly Father and God of all Creation, we give thanks for the nourishment of your heavenly gifts of the Bread and Fruits of Eternal Spiritual Life. May our earnest participation together in commemoration of Saint Blaise bring forth favourable blessings upon our lives, our community and your Holy Apostolic Universal Ecclesia.

X.II – FEBRUARY 5

1.   **Agatha of Sicily,** Virgin and Martyr   February 5
Memorial

Entrance Antiphon   Psalm 19: 8

The Lord's perfect law, how it brings the soul back to life; the Lord's unchallengeable decrees, how they make the simple learned!

Missale Christus | Proper of Heroes & Saints

Offertory Antiphon

O God and Divine Creator, grant us through the intercession of your beloved martyr Saint Agatha, the courage to hold firm to our virtue and faith in you, even in the face of oppression. Through our Lord Jesus Christ, your Son, who lives and reigns with you in the unity of the Holy Spirit, one God, for ever and ever.

Prayer over the Offerings

May God and the Divine Creator accept and sanctify these humble gifts as symbols of the genuine personal offerings we make in commemoration of Saint Agatha. Through Christ our Light and Saviour.

Communion Antiphon — Lk 22: 28-30

It is you who have stood by me in my trials; and I confer a kingdom on you, says the Lord, that you may eat and drink at my table in my kingdom.

Prayer after Communion

Heavenly Father and God of all Creation, we give thanks for the nourishment of your heavenly gifts of the Bread and Fruits of Eternal Spiritual Life. May our earnest participation together in commemoration of Saint Agatha bring forth favourable blessings upon our lives, our community and your Holy Apostolic Universal Ecclesia.

X.III – FEBRUARY 6

1. **Paul Miki and companions** — February 6

Memorial

Entrance Antiphon — Psalm 19: 9

How plain are the duties that Christ enjoins, the treasure of man's heart; how clear is the commandment the Lord gives, the enlightenment of man's eyes!

Living Testimony: Martyrdom of St. Paul Miki and Companions

Paul Miki, saw himself standing now in the noblest pulpit he had ever filled. To his "congregation" he began by proclaiming himself a Japanese and a Jesuit. He was dying for the Gospel he preached. He gave thanks to God for this wonderful blessing and he ended his "sermon" with these words: "As I come to this supreme moment of my life, I am sure none of you would suppose I want to deceive you. And so I tell you plainly: there is no way to be saved except the Christian way. My religion teaches me to pardon my enemies and all who have offended me. I do gladly pardon the Emperor and all who have sought my death. I beg them to seek baptism and be Christians themselves."

Living Gospel: Paul Miki — Paul Miki

The only reason for my being killed, is that I have taught the doctrine of Christ. I thank God it is for this reason that I die. I believe that I am telling the truth before I die. I know you believe me and I want to say to you all once again – ask Christ to help you become happy. I obey Christ. After Christ's example, I forgive my persecutors. I do not hate them. I ask God to have pity on all and I hope my blood will fall on my fellow men as a fruitful rain.

Offertory Antiphon

O God and Divine Creator, who called upon Paul Miki and his companions to be an inspiration of courage and faith for every person of faith, grant us through his intercession, that we might demonstrate the same courage of commitment to your Divine Mission of Unity of your Church and with all peoples and cultures. Through our Lord Jesus Christ, your Son, who lives and reigns with you in the unity of the Holy Spirit, one God, for ever and ever.

Prayer over the Offerings

May God and the Divine Creator accept and sanctify these humble gifts as symbols of the genuine personal offerings we make in commemoration of Paul Miki and his companions. Through Christ our Light and Saviour.

Communion Antiphon — Lk 22: 28-30

It is you who have stood by me in my trials; and I confer a kingdom on you, says the Lord, that you may eat and drink at my table in my kingdom.

Prayer after Communion

Heavenly Father and God of all Creation, we give thanks for the nourishment of your heavenly gifts of the Bread and Fruits of Eternal Spiritual Life. May our earnest participation together in commemoration of Paul Miki and his companions bring forth favourable blessings upon our lives, our community and your Holy Apostolic Universal Ecclesia.

X.IV – FEBRUARY 7

1.   **Cornelius the Centurion**   February 7

Memorial

Entrance Antiphon   Psalm 20: 2-3

The Lord listen to us in our time of need, the power of the Divine Creator be thy protection! May he send us aid from his holy place and watch over us.

Living Testimony: Acts 10: 1-8

There was, at Caesarea, a centurion named Cornelius, belonging to what is called the Italian cohort, a pious man who worshipped the true God, like all his household, gave alms freely to the people, and prayed to God continually. He, about the ninth hour of the day, had a vision, in which he clearly saw an angel of God come in and address him by his name. What is it, Lord? he asked, gazing at him in terror. And he answered, Thy prayers and alms-deeds are recorded on high in God's sight And now he would have thee send men to Joppa, to bring here one Simon, who is surnamed Peter; he lodges with a tanner, called Simon, whose house is close to the sea; thou wilt learn from him what thou hast to do. So the angel visitor left him, and thereupon he summoned two of his servants, and one of the soldiers who were in attendance on him, a man of piety; he told them all that had passed, and sent them on their way to Joppa.

Living Gospel: Cornelius the Centurion   Acts 10: 30-32

Three days ago, at this very time, I was making my afternoon prayer in my house, when suddenly I saw a man standing before me, in white clothes, who said to me, Cornelius, thy prayer has been heard, thy almsdeeds have won remembrance in God's sight. Thou art to send to Joppa, and summon thence that Simon who is also called Peter; he is lodging with a tanner called Simon, close to the sea. I lost no time, therefore, in sending for thee, and thou hast done me a favour in coming. Now thou seest us assembled in thy presence, ready to listen to whatever charge the Lord has given thee.

Offertory Antiphon

O God and Divine Creator, who spoke to the piety and faith of Cornelius in vision, grant us the same fortitute to honour the duty to your Divine Mission, even if the conditions of life sometimes presents obstacles, distractions and challenges. Through our Lord Jesus Christ, your Son, who lives and reigns with you in the unity of the Holy Spirit, one God, for ever and ever.

Prayer over the Offerings

May God and the Divine Creator accept and sanctify these humble gifts as symbols of the genuine personal offerings we make in commemoration of Cornelius. Through Christ our Light and Saviour.

Communion Antiphon — John 3:16

For God so loved the world, that he gave his only Son, that whoever believes in him should not perish but have eternal life.

Prayer after Communion

Heavenly Father and God of all Creation, we give thanks for the nourishment of your heavenly gifts of the Bread and Fruits of Eternal Spiritual Life. May our earnest participation together in commemoration of Cornelius bring forth favourable blessings upon our lives, our community and your Holy Apostolic Universal Ecclesia.

X.V – FEBRUARY 8

1. **Jerome Emiliani** — February 8
Founder of the Somaschi Fathers
Memorial

Entrance Antiphon — Psalm 20: 5-6

May he grant thee what thy heart desires, crown thy hopes with fulfilment. So may we rejoice at thy deliverance, rallied in the name of the Lord our God.

Offertory Antiphon

O God and Divine Creator, who called on Saint Jerome Emiliani to be a father and guide to orphans and troubled children, grant, through his intercession, that we may at all times continue to protect the innocence and well being of all vulnerable children and preserve faithfully the right of all children to be raised in a loving home. Through our Lord Jesus Christ, your Son, who lives and reigns with you in the unity of the Holy Spirit, one God, for ever and ever.

Prayer over the Offerings

May God and the Divine Creator accept and sanctify these humble gifts as symbols of the genuine personal offerings we make in commemoration of Saint Jerome. Through Christ our Light and Saviour.

Communion Antiphon 1 Peter 1:15

But as he who called you is holy, you also be holy in all your conduct.

Prayer after Communion

Heavenly Father and God of all Creation, we give thanks for the nourishment of your heavenly gifts of the Bread and Fruits of Eternal Spiritual Life. May our earnest participation together in commemoration of Saint Jerome bring forth favourable blessings upon our lives, our community and your Holy Apostolic Universal Ecclesia.

X.VI – FEBRUARY 10

1. **Scholastica of Nursia**, Virgin February 10
Founder of Benedictine Nuns
Memorial

Entrance Antiphon Psalm 21: 2-3

Lord, in your protection, well may we triumph in thy saving power! Never a wish in our hearts have you disappointed, never a prayer on our lips denied.

Offertory Antiphon

O God and Divine Creator, grant us through his intercession of your beloved Saint Scholastica, that we might follow her example and serve you with pure love and happily receive the fruits of what comes from loving you. Through our Lord Jesus Christ, your Son, who lives and reigns with you in the unity of the Holy Spirit, one God, for ever and ever.

Prayer over the Offerings

May God and the Divine Creator accept and sanctify these humble gifts as symbols of the genuine personal offerings we make in commemoration of Saint Scholastica. Through Christ our Light and Saviour.

Communion Antiphon 1 Peter 1:15

But as he who called you is holy, you also be holy in all your conduct.

Prayer after Communion

Heavenly Father and God of all Creation, we give thanks for the nourishment of your heavenly gifts of the Bread and Fruits of Eternal Spiritual Life. May our earnest participation together in commemoration of Saint Scholastica bring forth favourable blessings upon our lives, our community and your Holy Apostolic Universal Ecclesia.

X.VII – FEBRUARY 11

1. **Our Lady of Lourdes** — February 11
Memorial

Entrance Antiphon — Psalm 21: 8

One who stands firm, trusting in the Lord; the favour of the most High is with them.

Offertory Antiphon

O God and Divine Creator, grant us through the intercession of our Divine Mother Mary as Our Lady of Lourdes, that we may rise up and be cured of our disabilities and illnesses of faith. Through our Lord Jesus Christ, your Son, who lives and reigns with you in the unity of the Holy Spirit, one God, for ever and ever.

Prayer over the Offerings

May God and the Divine Creator accept and sanctify these humble gifts as symbols of the genuine personal offerings we make in commemoration of Our Lady of Lourdes. Through Christ our Light and Saviour.

Communion Antiphon — Galatians 5:22

But the fruit of the Spirit is love, joy, peace, patience, kindness, goodness, faithfulness.

Prayer after Communion

Heavenly Father and God of all Creation, we give thanks for the nourishment of your heavenly gifts of the Bread and Fruits of Eternal Spiritual Life. May our earnest participation together in commemoration of Our Lady of Lourdes bring forth favourable blessings upon our lives, our community and your Holy Apostolic Universal Ecclesia.

X.VIII – FEBRUARY 14

1.   **Cyril and Methodius**   February 14

Memorial

Entrance Antiphon   Psalm 23:4

Even though I walk through the valley of the shadow of death, I fear no evil, for you are with me; your rod and your staff, they comfort me.

Offertory Antiphon

O God and Divine Creator, who enlightened the Slavic peoples through the brothers Saints Cyril and Methodius, grant us through their intercession, that our hearts may grasp the words of your Divine Teaching that there are many rooms in your house, but only one Universal Ecclesia, and perfect through us a people of one accord united in true faith to your Divine Word. Through our Lord Jesus Christ, your Son, who lives and reigns with you in the unity of the Holy Spirit, one God, for ever and ever.

Prayer over the Offerings

May God and the Divine Creator accept and sanctify these humble gifts as symbols of the genuine personal offerings we make in commemoration of Cyril and Methodius. Through Christ our Light and Saviour.

Communion Antiphon   Mk 16: 20

The disciples went forth and preached the Gospel, while the Lord worked with them, confirming the word through accompanying signs.

Prayer after Communion

Heavenly Father and God of all Creation, we give thanks for the nourishment of your heavenly gifts of the Bread and Fruits of Eternal Spiritual Life. May our earnest participation together in commemoration of Cyril and Methodius bring forth favourable blessings upon our lives, our community and your Holy Apostolic Universal Ecclesia.

X.IX – FEBRUARY 17

1.   **The Seven Holy Founders of the Servite Order**   February 17

Founders of Servite Order

Memorial

Title X: Proper of February

Entrance Antiphon — Psalm 25: 1

All my heart goes out to thee, O Lord my God.

Offertory Antiphon

O God and Divine Creator, who inspired Bonfilius, Bonajuncta, Bartolomeus, Hugh, Manettus, Sostene and Alexius to a greater life of sanctification and the preaching of the Good News of Christ through greater devotion and service of our Mother Mary, grant through their intercession, the sanctification and support of all members of the Servite Order so that they may continue to serve your Divine Mission and your Divine Word. Through our Lord Jesus Christ, your Son, who lives and reigns with you in the unity of the Holy Spirit, one God, for ever and ever.

Prayer over the Offerings

May God and the Divine Creator accept and sanctify these humble gifts as symbols of the genuine personal offerings we make in commemoration of Holy Founders of the Servite Order. Through Christ our Light and Saviour.

Communion Antiphon — 1 Peter 1:15

But as he who called you is holy, you also be holy in all your conduct.

Prayer after Communion

Heavenly Father and God of all Creation, we give thanks for the nourishment of your heavenly gifts of the Bread and Fruits of Eternal Spiritual Life. May our earnest participation together in commemoration of Holy Founders of the Servite Order bring forth favourable blessings upon our lives, our community and your Holy Apostolic Universal Ecclesia.

X.X – FEBRUARY 18

1. **Martin Luther** — February 18

Founder of Lutheran Congregations of Universal Ecclesia

Memorial

Entrance Antiphon — Psalm 25: 4-5

Shew me thy ways, O Lord; teach me thy paths. Lead me in thy truth, and teach me: for thou art the God of my salvation.

Living Gospel: Martin Luther — Martin Luther

For in the true nature of things, if we rightly consider,

every green tree is far more glorious than if it were made of gold and silver. Our Lord has written the promise of resurrection, not in books alone, but in every leaf in springtime. Faith is a living, daring confidence in God's grace, so sure and certain that a man could stake his life on it a thousand times. If he have faith, the believer cannot be restrained. He betrays himself. He breaks out. He confesses and teaches this gospel to the people at the risk of life itself. All who call on God in true faith, earnestly from the heart, will certainly be heard, and will receive what they have asked and desired.

Offertory Antiphon

O God and Divine Creator, who tasked Martin Luther with a difficult and unpopular mission to weed out the lukewarm and those who had gone astray from your faith, grant that we might be inspired to be faithful and courageous to your mission of unity through right actions and right intentions of all Christian Faiths to your Living Body through the Universal Ecclesia. Through our Lord Jesus Christ, your Son, who lives and reigns with you in the unity of the Holy Spirit, one God, for ever and ever.

Prayer over the Offerings

May God and the Divine Creator accept and sanctify these humble gifts as symbols of the genuine personal offerings we make in commemoration of Martin Luther. Through Christ our Light and Saviour.

Communion Antiphon — John 3:16

For God so loved the world, that he gave his only Son, that whoever believes in him should not perish but have eternal life.

Prayer after Communion

Heavenly Father and God of all Creation, we give thanks for the nourishment of your heavenly gifts of the Bread and Fruits of Eternal Spiritual Life. May our earnest participation together in commemoration of Martin Luther bring forth favourable blessings upon our lives, our community and your Holy Apostolic Universal Ecclesia.

X.XI – FEBRUARY 21

1. **Peter Damian,** Bishop and Doctor of the Church — February 21
Memorial

Title X: Proper of February

Entrance Antiphon — Psalm 26: 12

On sure ground my feet are set; where his people gather I will join in blessing the Lord's name.

Living Testimony: Peter Damian

Consolation is already within your reach, if your good sense has not been dulled. My son, come to the service of God.

Living Gospel: Peter Damian — Peter Damian

By hammering gold, the smith beats out the dross. The sculptor files metal to reveal a shining vein underneath. The potter's furnace puts vessels to the test. And the fire of suffering tests the mettle of just men. The apostle James echoes this thought: Think it a great joy, dear brothers and sisters, when you stumble onto the many kinds of trials and tribulations.

Offertory Antiphon

O God and Divine Creator, grant us through the teaching and example of your Bishop Saint Peter Damian, that we put nothing before the teachings of Christ and remain ardent in the service of your Universal Ecclesia according to your Divine Works. Through our Lord Jesus Christ, your Son, who lives and reigns with you in the unity of the Holy Spirit, one God, for ever and ever.

Prayer over the Offerings

May God and the Divine Creator accept and sanctify these humble gifts as symbols of the genuine personal offerings we make in commemoration of Peter Damian. Through Christ our Light and Saviour.

Communion Antiphon — Psalm 1: 2-3

One who ponders the Divine maxims of Law of the Lord day and night shall yield fruit in due season.

Prayer after Communion

Heavenly Father and God of all Creation, we give thanks for the nourishment of your heavenly gifts of the Bread and Fruits of Eternal Spiritual Life. May our earnest participation together in commemoration of Peter Damian bring forth favourable blessings upon our lives, our community and your Holy Apostolic Universal Ecclesia.

2.   **John Henry Newman, Cardinal**   February 21
Memorial

Missale Christus | Proper of Heroes & Saints

Entrance Antiphon
Psalm 26: 12

On sure ground my feet are set; where his people gather I will join in blessing the Lord's name.

Living Testimony: John Henry Newman

Lead, Kindly Light, amidst th'encircling gloom, Lead Thou me on! The night is dark, and I am far from home, Lead Thou me on! Keep Thou my feet; I do not ask to see The distant scene; one step enough for me.

Living Gospel: John Henry Newman
John Henry Newman

God knows what is my greatest happiness, but I do not. There is no rule about what is happy and good; what suits one would not suit another. And the ways by which perfection is reached vary very much; the medicines necessary for our souls are very different from each other. Thus God leads us by strange ways; we know He wills our happiness, but we neither know what our happiness is, nor the way. We are blind; left to ourselves we should take the wrong way; we must leave it to Him.

Offertory Antiphon

O God and Divine Creator, who showed us the path of an elightened and peaceful shepherd through John Henry Newman, grant us the humility and the persistence to continue to learn and strengthen our faith. Through our Lord Jesus Christ, your Son, who lives and reigns with you in the unity of the Holy Spirit, one God, for ever and ever.

Prayer over the Offerings

May God and the Divine Creator accept and sanctify these humble gifts as symbols of the genuine personal offerings we make in commemoration of John Henry Newman. Through Christ our Light and Saviour.

Communion Antiphon
Micah 5:4

And he shall stand and shepherd his flock in the strength of the Lord, in the majesty of the name of the Lord his God.

Prayer after Communion

Heavenly Father and God of all Creation, we give thanks for the nourishment of your heavenly gifts of the Bread and Fruits of Eternal Spiritual Life. May our earnest participation together in commemoration of John Henry Newman bring forth favourable blessings upon our lives, our community and your Holy Apostolic Universal

Ecclesia.

X.XII – FEBRUARY 23

1.   **Polycarp,** Bishop and Martyr   February 23

Memorial

Entrance Antiphon   Psalm 27: 4

May I dwell in the house of the Lord all the days of my life, to behold the beauty of the Lord, and to enquire in his temple.

Offertory Antiphon

O God and Divine Creator, who was pleased to give the Bishop Saint Polycarp a place in the company of the Martyrs, grant, through his intercession, that, sharing with him in the chalice of Christ, we may rise through the Holy Spirit to eternal life. Through our Lord Jesus Christ, your Son, who lives and reigns with you in the unity of the Holy Spirit, one God, for ever and ever.

Prayer over the Offerings

May God and the Divine Creator accept and sanctify these humble gifts as symbols of the genuine personal offerings we make in commemoration of Polycarp. Through Christ our Light and Saviour.

Communion Antiphon   Lk 22: 28-30

It is you who have stood by me in my trials; and I confer a kingdom on you, says the Lord, that you may eat and drink at my table in my kingdom.

Prayer after Communion

Heavenly Father and God of all Creation, we give thanks for the nourishment of your heavenly gifts of the Bread and Fruits of Eternal Spiritual Life. May our earnest participation together in commemoration of Polycarp bring forth favourable blessings upon our lives, our community and your Holy Apostolic Universal Ecclesia.

X.XIII – FEBRUARY 24

1. **Matthias the Apostle** — February 24
Memorial

Entrance Antiphon — Psalm 27: 7-8

Listen to my voice, Lord, when I cry to thee; hear and forgive me. True to my heart's promise, I have faith only for thee.

Offertory Antiphon

O God and Divine Creator, who your Son called all people to be at your table such as Matthias your Apostle, grant us the courage to accept your calling and not use our past or our regrets as an excuse. Through our Lord Jesus Christ, your Son, who lives and reigns with you in the unity of the Holy Spirit, one God, for ever and ever.

Prayer over the Offerings

May God and the Divine Creator accept and sanctify these humble gifts as symbols of the genuine personal offerings we make in commemoration of Matthias the Apostle. Through Christ our Light and Saviour.

Communion Antiphon — John 12: 26

Whoever serves me must follow me, and where I am, there also will my servant be.

Prayer after Communion

Heavenly Father and God of all Creation, we give thanks for the nourishment of your heavenly gifts of the Bread and Fruits of Eternal Spiritual Life. May our earnest participation together in commemoration of Matthias the Apostle bring forth favourable blessings upon our lives, our community and your Holy Apostolic Universal Ecclesia.

X.XIV – FEBRUARY 25

1. **Jacob Hutter** — February 25
Founder of Hutterite Anabaptist Movement of Universal Ecclesia
Memorial

Entrance Antiphon — Psalm 27: 13

My faith is, that I will yet live to see the Lord's mercies. Thus I wait patiently for redemption.

Offertory Antiphon

O God and Divine Creator, who called for our faith to be renewed and old habits be tested, remember the courage of Jacob Hutter that lit a fire in many to rekindle the deeper meaning of your faith. Through our Lord Jesus Christ, your Son, who lives and reigns with you in the unity of the Holy Spirit, one God, for ever and ever.

Prayer over the Offerings

May God and the Divine Creator accept and sanctify these humble gifts as symbols of the genuine personal offerings we make in commemoration of Jacob Hutter. Through Christ our Light and Saviour.

Communion Antiphon

Whoever wishes to come after me, must deny himself, take up his cross, and follow me, says the Lord.

Prayer after Communion

Heavenly Father and God of all Creation, we give thanks for the nourishment of your heavenly gifts of the Bread and Fruits of Eternal Spiritual Life. May our earnest participation together in commemoration of Jacob Hutter bring forth favourable blessings upon our lives, our community and your Holy Apostolic Universal Ecclesia.

X.XV – FEBRUARY 27

1.   **Constantine the Great**   February 27

Memorial

Entrance Antiphon   Psalm 28: 8-9

The Lord defends his own people, protects the monarch he has anointed. Lord, save thy people, bless thy own chosen race; be their shepherd, evermore in thy arms upholding them.

Living Testimony: Edict of Milan

When we, Constantine and Licinius, emperors, had an interview at Milan, and conferred together with respect to the good and security of the commonwealth, it seemed to us that, amongst those things that are profitable to mankind in general, the reverence paid to the Divinity merited our first and chief attention, and that it was proper that the Christians and all others should have liberty to follow that mode of religion which to each of them appeared best; so that God, who is seated in heaven, might be benign and propitious to us, and to every one under our government.

Living Gospel: Constantine the Great
Constantine the Great

This is certainly the Will of the Supreme God, who is the Author of this world and its Father, (through whose goodness we enjoy life, look up to heaven, and rejoice in the society of our fellow-men), that the whole human race should agree together and be joined in a certain affectionate union by, as it were, a mutual embrace.

Offertory Antiphon

O God and Divine Creator, who spares not the humblest or highest from your calling, remember the courage and vision of your servant Constantine; and may we too find unity of purpose among your faithful community once again. Through our Lord Jesus Christ, your Son, who lives and reigns with you in the unity of the Holy Spirit, one God, for ever and ever.

Prayer over the Offerings

May God and the Divine Creator accept and sanctify these humble gifts as symbols of the genuine personal offerings we make in commemoration of Constantine the Great. Through Christ our Light and Saviour.

Communion Antiphon
Micah 5:4

And he shall stand and shepherd his flock in the strength of the Lord, in the majesty of the name of the Lord his God.

Prayer after Communion

Heavenly Father and God of all Creation, we give thanks for the nourishment of your heavenly gifts of the Bread and Fruits of Eternal Spiritual Life. May our earnest participation together in commemoration of Constantine the Great bring forth favourable blessings upon our lives, our community and your Holy Apostolic Universal Ecclesia.

Title XI: Proper of March

XI.I – MARCH 1

1.

Katharine Drexel, Virgin

Memorial

March 1

Entrance Antiphon

Psalm 30: 3-4

I cried out to the Lord my God, and you did grant me eternal life. You did bring me back, Lord, from the place of shadows, and rescue me from death.

Offertory Antiphon

O God and Divine Creator, you called Saint Katharine Drexel to teach the message of the Gospel and to bring the life of the Eucharist to the Native American and African American peoples; by her prayers and example, enable us to work for justice among the poor and the oppressed, and keep us undivided in love in the eucharistic community of your Church. Through our Lord Jesus Christ, your Son, who lives and reigns with you in the unity of the Holy Spirit, one God, for ever and ever

Prayer over the Offerings

May God and the Divine Creator accept and sanctify these humble gifts as symbols of the genuine personal offerings we make in commemoration of Katharine Drexel. Through Christ our Light and Saviour.

Communion Antiphon

1 John 4

Beloved, let us love one another, for love is from God, and whoever loves has been born of God and knows God.

Prayer after Communion

Heavenly Father and God of all Creation, we give thanks for the nourishment of your heavenly gifts of the Bread and Fruits of Eternal Spiritual Life. May our earnest participation together in commemoration of Katharine Drexel bring forth favourable blessings upon our lives, our community and your Holy Apostolic Universal Ecclesia.

XI.II – MARCH 2

1.

John and Charles Wesley

Founders of Methodist Movement of Universal Ecclesia

Memorial

March 2

Entrance Antiphon

Psalm 30: 11-12

Thou hast turned for me my mourning into dancing: thou hast put off my sackcloth, and girded me with gladness; To the end that my glory may sing praise to thee, and not be silent. O Lord my God, I will give thanks unto thee for ever.

Offertory Antiphon

O God and Divine Creator, you called John and Charles Wesley to re-ignite the passion and enthusiasm of all people to proclaim and sing the glory of the *Good News* of your Son Jesus Christ, grant us the same joy as the united Living Body of Christ. Through our Lord Jesus Christ, your Son, who lives and reigns with you in the unity of the Holy Spirit, one God, for ever and ever.

Prayer over the Offerings

May God and the Divine Creator accept and sanctify these humble gifts as symbols of the genuine personal offerings we make in commemoration of John and Charles Wesley. Through Christ our Light and Saviour.

Communion Antiphon John 12: 26

Whoever serves me must follow me, and where I am, there also will my servant be.

Prayer after Communion

Heavenly Father and God of all Creation, we give thanks for the nourishment of your heavenly gifts of the Bread and Fruits of Eternal Spiritual Life. May our earnest participation together in commemoration of John and Charles Wesley bring forth favourable blessings upon our lives, our community and your Holy Apostolic Universal Ecclesia.

XI.III – MARCH 4

1. **Gerasimus of Jordan** March 4

Memorial

Entrance Antiphon Psalm 31: 5

Into thine hand I commit my spirit: thou hast redeemed me, O Lord God of truth.

Living Testimony: Troparion - Tone 1

Dweller of the desert and angel in the body, you were shown to be a wonderworker, our God-bearing Father Gerasimus. You received heavenly gifts through fasting, vigil, and prayer: healing the sick and the souls of those drawn to you by faith. Glory to Him who gave you strength! Glory to Him who granted you a crown! Glory to

Title XI: Proper of March

Him who through you grants healing to all!

Living Gospel: Kontakion - Tone 4

Father, you burned with heavenly love, preferring the harshness of the Jordan desert to all the delights of the world. Therefore, a wild beast served you until your death; he died in obedience in grief on your grave. Thus God has glorified you, and when you pray to Him remember us, Father Gerasimus.

Offertory Antiphon

O God and Divine Creator, to serve you is to reign; grant that, with the help of Gerasimus of Jordan intercession, we may constantly serve you in holiness and justice. Through our Lord Jesus Christ, your Son, who lives and reigns with you in the unity of the Holy Spirit, one God, for ever and ever.

Prayer over the Offerings

May God and the Divine Creator accept and sanctify these humble gifts as symbols of the genuine personal offerings we make in commemoration of Gerasimus of Jordan. Through Christ our Light and Saviour.

Communion Antiphon

Galatians 5:22

But the fruit of the Spirit is love, joy, peace, patience, kindness, goodness, faithfulness.

Prayer after Communion

Heavenly Father and God of all Creation, we give thanks for the nourishment of your heavenly gifts of the Bread and Fruits of Eternal Spiritual Life. May our earnest participation together in commemoration of Gerasimus of Jordan bring forth favourable blessings upon our lives, our community and your Holy Apostolic Universal Ecclesia.

2. Casimir Jagiellon

Memorial

March 4

Entrance Antiphon

Psalm 31: 5

Into thine hand I commit my spirit: thou hast redeemed me, O Lord God of truth.

Offertory Antiphon

O God and Divine Creator, grant that with the help of Saint Casimir's intercession, we may constantly serve you in holiness and justice. Through our Lord Jesus Christ, your Son, who lives and reigns with you in the unity of the Holy

Spirit, one God, for ever and ever.

Prayer over the Offerings

May God and the Divine Creator accept and sanctify these humble gifts as symbols of the genuine personal offerings we make in commemoration of Casimir Jagiellon. Through Christ our Light and Saviour.

Communion Antiphon — 1 John 4

Beloved, let us love one another, for love is from God, and whoever loves has been born of God and knows God.

Prayer after Communion

Heavenly Father and God of all Creation, we give thanks for the nourishment of your heavenly gifts of the Bread and Fruits of Eternal Spiritual Life. May our earnest participation together in commemoration of Casimir Jagiellon bring forth favourable blessings upon our lives, our community and your Holy Apostolic Universal Ecclesia.

XI.IV – MARCH 7

1. Thomas Aquinas, Priest and Doctor of the Church — March 7

Memorial

Entrance Antiphon — Psalm 31: 22

Blessed be the Lord; so wondrous is his mercy, so strong the wall of his protection.

Offertory Antiphon

O God and Divine Creator, who made Saint Thomas Aquinas outstanding in his zeal for holiness and his study of sacred doctrine, grant us, we pray, that we may understand what he taught and imitate what he accomplished. Through our Lord Jesus Christ, your Son, who lives and reigns with you in the unity of the Holy Spirit, one God, for ever and ever.

Prayer over the Offerings

May God and the Divine Creator accept and sanctify these humble gifts as symbols of the genuine personal offerings we make in commemoration of Thomas Aquinas. Through Christ our Light and Saviour.

Communion Antiphon — 2 Cor 4: 11

For the sake of Jesus we are given up to death, that the life of Jesus may be manifested in our mortal flesh.

Prayer after Communion

Heavenly Father and God of all Creation, we give thanks for the nourishment of your heavenly gifts of the Bread and Fruits of Eternal Spiritual Life. May our earnest participation together in commemoration of Thomas Aquinas bring forth favourable blessings upon our lives, our community and your Holy Apostolic Universal Ecclesia.

XI.V – MARCH 8

1.   **Saint John of God,** Religious   March 8
Founder of Brothers Hospitallers of Saint John of God
Memorial

Entrance Antiphon   Psalm 31: 24

Love the Lord well, you who worship him; the Lord keeps faith with his servants, and repays the actions of the humble above measure.

Offertory Antiphon

O God and Divine Creator, who filled Saint John of God with a spirit of compassion, grant, we pray, that, giving ourselves to works of charity, we may merit to be found among the elect in your Kingdom. Through our Lord Jesus Christ, your Son, who lives and reigns with you in the unity of the Holy Spirit, one God, for ever and ever.

Prayer over the Offerings

May God and the Divine Creator accept and sanctify these humble gifts as symbols of the genuine personal offerings we make in commemoration of John of God. Through Christ our Light and Saviour.

Communion Antiphon   Mt 16: 24

Whoever wishes to come after me, must deny himself, take up his cross, and follow me, says the Lord.

Prayer after Communion

Heavenly Father and God of all Creation, we give thanks for the nourishment of your heavenly gifts of the Bread and Fruits of Eternal Spiritual Life. May our earnest participation together in commemoration of John of God bring forth favourable blessings upon our lives, our community and your Holy Apostolic Universal Ecclesia.

Missale Christus | Proper of Heroes & Saints

XI.VI – MARCH 9

1.   **Frances of Rome,** Religious   March 9
Memorial

Entrance Antiphon   Psalm 32: 2

Blessed is the man unto whom the Lord imputeth not iniquity, and in whose spirit there is no guile.

Offertory Antiphon

O God and Divine Creator, who gave us in Saint Frances of Rome a singular model of both married and monastic life, grant us perseverance in your service, that in every circumstance of life we may see and follow you. Through our Lord Jesus Christ, your Son, who lives and reigns with you in the unity of the Holy Spirit, one God, for ever and ever.

Prayer over the Offerings

May God and the Divine Creator accept and sanctify these humble gifts as symbols of the genuine personal offerings we make in commemoration of Frances of Rome. Through Christ our Light and Saviour.

Communion Antiphon   1 Peter 1:15

But as he who called you is holy, you also be holy in all your conduct.

Prayer after Communion

Heavenly Father and God of all Creation, we give thanks for the nourishment of your heavenly gifts of the Bread and Fruits of Eternal Spiritual Life. May our earnest participation together in commemoration of Frances of Rome bring forth favourable blessings upon our lives, our community and your Holy Apostolic Universal Ecclesia.

XI.VII – MARCH 17

1.   **Patrick of Ireland, Bishop**   March 17
Memorial

Entrance Antiphon   Psalm 34: 1

At all times I will bless the Lord; his praise shall be on my lips continually.

Offertory Antiphon

O God and Divine Creator, who chose the Bishop Saint

Patrick to preach your glory to the peoples of Ireland, grant, through his merits and intercession, that those who glory in the name of Christian may never cease to proclaim your wondrous deeds to all. Through our Lord Jesus Christ, your Son, who lives and reigns with you in the unity of the Holy Spirit, one God, for ever and ever.

Prayer over the Offerings

May God and the Divine Creator accept and sanctify these humble gifts as symbols of the genuine personal offerings we make in commemoration of Patrick or Ireland. Through Christ our Light and Saviour.

Communion Antiphon — Micah 5:4

Mnd he shall stand and shepherd his flock in the strength of the Lord, in the majesty of the name of the Lord his God.

Prayer after Communion

Heavenly Father and God of all Creation, we give thanks for the nourishment of your heavenly gifts of the Bread and Fruits of Eternal Spiritual Life. May our earnest participation together in commemoration of Patrick or Ireland bring forth favourable blessings upon our lives, our community and your Holy Apostolic Universal Ecclesia.

XI.VIII – MARCH 18

1. Cyril of Jerusalem, Bishop and Doctor of the Church — March 18

Memorial

Entrance Antiphon — Psalm 34: 18

The Lord is close to the brokenhearted and saves those who are crushed in spirit.

Offertory Antiphon

O God and Divine Creator, who through the Bishop Saint Cyril of Jerusalem led your Church in a wonderful way to a deeper sense of the mysteries of salvation, grant us, through his intercession, that we may so acknowledge your Son as to have life ever more abundantly. Through our Lord Jesus Christ, your Son, who lives and reigns with you in the unity of the Holy Spirit, one God, for ever and ever.

Prayer over the Offerings

May God and the Divine Creator accept and sanctify these humble gifts as symbols of the genuine personal offerings

we make in commemoration of Cyril of Jerusalem.
Through Christ our Light and Saviour.

Communion Antiphon — Psalm 1: 2-3

One who ponders the Divine maxims of Law of the Lord day and night shall yield fruit in due season.

Prayer after Communion

Heavenly Father and God of all Creation, we give thanks for the nourishment of your heavenly gifts of the Bread and Fruits of Eternal Spiritual Life. May our earnest participation together in commemoration of Cyril of Jerusalem bring forth favourable blessings upon our lives, our community and your Holy Apostolic Universal Ecclesia.

XI.IX – MARCH 19

1. **Saint Joseph,** Spouse Of The Blessed Virgin Mary — March 19
Solemnity

Entrance Antiphon — Psalm 35: 3

With poised frank prevent the way against nihilists; whisper in my heart, I am here to save thee.

Offertory Antiphon

O God and Divine Creator, grant that by Saint Joseph's intercession your Church may constantly watch over the unfolding of the mysteries of human salvation, whose beginnings you entrusted to his faithful care. Through our Lord Jesus Christ, your Son, who lives and reigns with you in the unity of the Holy Spirit, one God, for ever and ever.

Prayer over the Offerings

May God and the Divine Creator accept and sanctify these humble gifts as symbols of the genuine personal offerings we make in commemoration of Saint Joseph. Through Christ our Light and Saviour.

Communion Antiphon — Mt 25: 21

Well done, good and faithful servant. Come, share your master's joy.

Prayer after Communion

Heavenly Father and God of all Creation, we give thanks for the nourishment of your heavenly gifts of the Bread and Fruits of Eternal Spiritual Life. May our earnest participation together in commemoration of Saint Joseph bring forth favourable blessings upon our lives, our community and your Holy Apostolic Universal Ecclesia.

XI.X – MARCH 21

1. ### Thomas Cranmer
Co-Founder of Church of England of Universal Ecclesia
Memorial

March 21

Entrance Antiphon

Psalm 36: 5-6

Thy mercy, O Lord, is in the heavens; and thy faithfulness reacheth unto the clouds. Thy righteousness is like the great mountains; thy judgments are a great deep: O Lord, thou preservest man and beast.

Living Testimony: Thomas Cranmer

All Christian princes have committed unto them immediately of God the whole cure of their subjects, as well concerning the administration of God's word for the cure of souls, as concerning the ministration of things political and civil governance.

Living Gospel: Thomas Cranmer

Thomas Cranmer

This faith, as St Paul described it, is the "sure ground and foundation of the benefits which we ought to look for, and trust to receive of God; a certificate and sure expectation of them, although they not sensibly appear unto us." And after he saith: "He that cometh to God must believe both that he is, and that he is a merciful rewarder of well-doers." And nothing commendeth good men unto God so much as this assured faith and trust in him.

Offertory Antiphon

O God and Divine Creator, who ordained that your Holy Church should go through a period of tribulation and testing, and inspired Thomas Cranmer to challenge the patchwork quilt of doctrinal reform, grant us through his intercession the courage and strength to look beyond our differences and see what has been achieved in your name. Through our Lord Jesus Christ, your Son, who lives and reigns with you in the unity of the Holy Spirit, one God, for ever and ever.

Prayer over the Offerings

May God and the Divine Creator accept and sanctify these humble gifts as symbols of the genuine personal offerings we make in commemoration of Thomas Cranmer. Through

Christ our Light and Saviour.

Prayer after Communion

Heavenly Father and God of all Creation, we give thanks for the nourishment of your heavenly gifts of the Bread and Fruits of Eternal Spiritual Life. May our earnest participation together in commemoration of Thomas Cranmer bring forth favourable blessings upon our lives, our community and your Holy Apostolic Universal Ecclesia.

XI.XI – MARCH 23

1. **Gregory the Illuminator** — March 23

Memorial

Entrance Antiphon — Psalm 37: 8-9

Cease from anger, and forsake wrath: fret not thyself in any wise to do evil. For evildoers shall be cut off: but those that wait upon the Lord, they shall inherit the earth.

Living Testimony: Turibius of Mogrovejo

Time is not our own, and we must give a strict account of it.

Living Gospel: Turibius of Mogrovejo — Turibius of Mogrovejo

Christ said "I am the Truth", He did not say "I am the custom"'.

Offertory Antiphon

O God and Divine Creator, who gave increase to your Church through the apostolic labors and zeal for truth of the Gregory The Illuminator, grant that the people consecrated to you may always receive new growth in faith and holiness. Through our Lord Jesus Christ, your Son, who lives and reigns with you in the unity of the Holy Spirit, one God, for ever and ever.

Prayer over the Offerings

May God and the Divine Creator accept and sanctify these humble gifts as symbols of the genuine personal offerings we make in commemoration of Turibius of Mogrovejo. Through Christ our Light and Saviour.

Prayer after Communion

Heavenly Father and God of all Creation, we give thanks for the nourishment of your heavenly gifts of the Bread and Fruits of Eternal Spiritual Life. May our earnest

participation together in commemoration of Turibius of Mogrovejo bring forth favourable blessings upon our lives, our community and your Holy Apostolic Universal Ecclesia.

2.   **Turibius of Mogrovejo,** Bishop   March 23

Memorial

Entrance Antiphon   Psalm 37: 8-9

Cease from anger, and forsake wrath: fret not thyself in any wise to do evil. For evildoers shall be cut off: but those that wait upon the Lord, they shall inherit the earth.

Living Testimony: Turibius of Mogrovejo

Time is not our own, and we must give a strict account of it.

Living Gospel: Turibius of Mogrovejo   Turibius of Mogrovejo

Christ said "I am the Truth", He did not say "I am the custom".

Offertory Antiphon

O God and Divine Creator, who gave increase to your Church through the apostolic labors and zeal for truth of the Bishop Saint Turibius, grant that the people consecrated to you may always receive new growth in faith and holiness. Through our Lord Jesus Christ, your Son, who lives and reigns with you in the unity of the Holy Spirit, one God, for ever and ever.

Prayer over the Offerings

May God and the Divine Creator accept and sanctify these humble gifts as symbols of the genuine personal offerings we make in commemoration of Turibius of Mogrovejo. Through Christ our Light and Saviour.

Prayer after Communion

Heavenly Father and God of all Creation, we give thanks for the nourishment of your heavenly gifts of the Bread and Fruits of Eternal Spiritual Life. May our earnest participation together in commemoration of Turibius of Mogrovejo bring forth favourable blessings upon our lives, our community and your Holy Apostolic Universal Ecclesia.

XI.XII – MARCH 31

1. ### Our Lady of the Southern Cross
Patron of Oceania
Memorial

March 31

Entrance Antiphon — Psalm 41: 5

Lord have mercy on me, is my prayer; bring healing to a soul that has transgressed against thee.

Offertory Antiphon

O God and Divine Creator, grant us through the intercession of our Divine Mother Mary as Our Lady of the Southern Cross, that all peoples of each generation of Oceania may come to know your good works and Divine Truth. Through our Lord Jesus Christ, your Son, who lives and reigns with you in the unity of the Holy Spirit, one God, for ever and ever.

Prayer over the Offerings

May God and the Divine Creator accept and sanctify these humble gifts as symbols of the genuine personal offerings we make in commemoration of Our Lady of the Southern Cross. Through Christ our Light and Saviour.

Communion Antiphon — Is 7: 14

Behold, a Virgin shall conceive and bear a son; and his name will be called Emmanuel.

Prayer after Communion

Heavenly Father and God of all Creation, we give thanks for the nourishment of your heavenly gifts of the Bread and Fruits of Eternal Spiritual Life. May our earnest participation together in commemoration of Our Lady of the Southern Cross bring forth favourable blessings upon our lives, our community and your Holy Apostolic Universal Ecclesia.

Title XII: Proper of April

XII.I – APRIL 2

1.   **Francis of Paola, Hermit**   April 2

Memorial

Entrance Antiphon   Psalm 43: 1

O God, sustain those with just causes; give them relief against those who have no fidelity.

Offertory Antiphon

O God and Divine Creator, exaltation of the lowly, who raised Saint Francis of Paola to the glory of your Saints, grant, we pray, that by his merits and example we may happily attain the rewards promised to the humble. Through our Lord Jesus Christ, your Son, who lives and reigns with you in the unity of the Holy Spirit, one God, for ever and ever.

Prayer over the Offerings

May God and the Divine Creator accept and sanctify these humble gifts as symbols of the genuine personal offerings we make in commemoration of Francis of Paola. Through Christ our Light and Saviour.

Prayer after Communion

Heavenly Father and God of all Creation, we give thanks for the nourishment of your heavenly gifts of the Bread and Fruits of Eternal Spiritual Life. May our earnest participation together in commemoration of Francis of Paola bring forth favourable blessings upon our lives, our community and your Holy Apostolic Universal Ecclesia.

XII.II – APRIL 4

1.   **Martin Luther King Jr.**   April 4

Ordinary

Entrance Antiphon   Psalm 45: 3

Thine is more than mortal beauty, thy revelations overflow with gracious utterance; the blessings God has granted thee can never fail.

Living Testimony: Martin Luther King Jr.

The ultimate measure of a man is not where he stands in moments of comfort and convenience, but where he stands in times of challenge and controversy. The true neighbor will risk his position, his prestige, and even his life for the welfare of others. In dangerous valleys and hazardous pathways, he will lift some bruised and beaten brother to a higher and more noble life.

Living Gospel: Martin Luther King Jr.

If we are to have peace on earth, our loyalties must become ecumenical rather than sectional. Our loyalties must transcend our race, our tribe, our class, and our nation; and this means we must develop a world perspective. Love is the most durable power in the world. This creative force is the most potent instrument available in mankind's quest for peace and security.

Offertory Antiphon

O God and Divine Creator, who inspired Martin Luther King Jr. to speak the same words of truth as Christ, and who gave him the courage to stand for equality of all races, creeds and religions, grant us the same foresight and courage to remember the Living Spirit of Christ through the Gospels, that we may be agents of positive change. Through our Lord Jesus Christ, your Son, who lives and reigns with you in the unity of the Holy Spirit, one God, for ever and ever.

Prayer over the Offerings

May God and the Divine Creator accept and sanctify these humble gifts as symbols of the genuine personal offerings we make in commemoration of Martin Luther King Jr. Through Christ our Light and Saviour.

Prayer after Communion

Heavenly Father and God of all Creation, we give thanks for the nourishment of your heavenly gifts of the Bread and Fruits of Eternal Spiritual Life. May our earnest participation together in commemoration of Martin Luther King Jr bring forth favourable blessings upon our lives, our community and your Holy Apostolic Universal Ecclesia.

2. **Isidore of Seville,** Bishop and Doctor of the Church — April 4

Memorial

Entrance Antiphon

Psalm 45: 3

Thine is more than mortal beauty, thy revelations overflow with gracious utterance; the blessings God has granted thee can never fail.

Living Testimony: Isidore of Seville

Prayer purifies us, reading instructs us. Both are good when both are possible. Otherwise, prayer is better than reading. If a man wants to be always in God's company, he must pray regularly and read regularly. When we pray, we talk to God; when we read, God talks to us.

Living Gospel: Isidore of Seville

Isidore of Seville

All spiritual growth comes from reading and reflection. By reading we learn what we did not know; by reflection we retain what we have learned. Reading the holy Scriptures confers two benefits. It trains the mind to understand them; it turns man's attention from the follies of the world and leads him to the love of God. Two kinds of study are called for here. We must first learn how the Scriptures are to be understood, and then see how to expound them with profit and in a manner worthy of them. A man must first be eager to understand what he is reading before he is fit to proclaim what he has learned.

Offertory Antiphon

O God and Divine Creator, graciously hear the prayers which we make in commemoration of Saint Isidore, that your Church may be aided by his intercession, just as she has been instructed by his heavenly teaching. Through our Lord Jesus Christ, your Son, who lives and reigns with you in the unity of the Holy Spirit, one God, for ever and ever.

Prayer over the Offerings

May God and the Divine Creator accept and sanctify these humble gifts as symbols of the genuine personal offerings we make in commemoration of Isidore of Seville. Through Christ our Light and Saviour.

Communion Antiphon

Psalm 1: 2-3

One who ponders the Divine maxims of Law of the Lord day and night shall yield fruit in due season.

Prayer after Communion

Heavenly Father and God of all Creation, we give thanks for the nourishment of your heavenly gifts of the Bread and Fruits of Eternal Spiritual Life. May our earnest participation together in commemoration of Isidore of Seville bring forth favourable blessings upon our lives, our community and your Holy Apostolic Universal Ecclesia.

XII.III – APRIL 5

1. **Saint Vincent Ferrer,** Priest April 5
Memorial

Entrance Antiphon Psalm 46: 1-2

God is our refuge and strength, a very present help in trouble. Therefore will not we fear, though the earth be removed, and though the mountains be carried into the midst of the sea.

Offertory Antiphon

O God and Divine Creator, who raised up the Priest Saint Vincent Ferrer to minister by the preaching of the Gospel, grant, we pray, that, when the Judge comes, whom Saint Vincent proclaimed on earth, we may be among those blessed to behold him reigning in heaven. Who lives and reigns with you in the unity of the Holy Spirit, one God, for ever and ever.

Prayer over the Offerings

May God and the Divine Creator accept and sanctify these humble gifts as symbols of the genuine personal offerings we make in commemoration of Vincent Ferrer. Through Christ our Light and Saviour.

Prayer after Communion

Heavenly Father and God of all Creation, we give thanks for the nourishment of your heavenly gifts of the Bread and Fruits of Eternal Spiritual Life. May our earnest participation together in commemoration of Vincent Ferrer bring forth favourable blessings upon our lives, our community and your Holy Apostolic Universal Ecclesia.

XII.IV – APRIL 7

1. **Saint John Baptist de la Salle,** Priest April 7
Founder of Institute of the Brothers of the Christian Schools
Memorial

Entrance Antiphon Psalm 46: 9-10

Come near, and see God's acts, his marvellous acts done on earth; how he puts an end to wars all over the world!

Offertory Antiphon

O God and Divine Creator, who chose Saint John Baptist de la Salle to educate young Christians, raise up, we pray, teachers in your Church ready to devote themselves wholeheartedly to the human and Christian formation of the young. Through our Lord Jesus Christ, your Son, who lives and reigns with you in the unity of the Holy Spirit, one God, for ever and ever.

Prayer over the Offerings

May God and the Divine Creator accept and sanctify these humble gifts as symbols of the genuine personal offerings we make in commemoration of John Baptist de la Salle. Through Christ our Light and Saviour.

Prayer after Communion

Heavenly Father and God of all Creation, we give thanks for the nourishment of your heavenly gifts of the Bread and Fruits of Eternal Spiritual Life. May our earnest participation together in commemoration of John Baptist de la Salle bring forth favourable blessings upon our lives, our community and your Holy Apostolic Universal Ecclesia.

XII.V – APRIL 11

1. **Stanislaus of Szczepanów,** Bishop and Martyr — April 11
Memorial

Entrance Antiphon — Psalm 49: 2-4

Listen, you nations far and wide; let all the world give hearing to the Word of God, those born into poverty and those into wealth, for rich and poor be subject to the same Divine Law. Here these wise words.

Offertory Antiphon

O God and Divine Creator, for whose honor the Bishop Saint Stanislaus fell beneath the swords of his persecutors, grant, we pray, that we may persevere strong in faith even until death. Through our Lord Jesus Christ, your Son, who lives and reigns with you in the unity of the Holy Spirit, one God, for ever and ever.

Prayer over the Offerings

May God and the Divine Creator accept and sanctify these humble gifts as symbols of the genuine personal offerings we make in commemoration of Stanislaus of Szczepanów. Through Christ our Light and Saviour.

Communion Antiphon — Lk 22: 28-30

It is you who have stood by me in my trials; and I confer a kingdom on you, says the Lord, that you may eat and drink at my table in my kingdom.

Prayer after Communion

Heavenly Father and God of all Creation, we give thanks for the nourishment of your heavenly gifts of the Bread and Fruits of Eternal Spiritual Life. May our earnest participation together in commemoration of Stanislaus of Szczepanów bring forth favourable blessings upon our lives, our community and your Holy Apostolic Universal Ecclesia.

XII.VI – APRIL 13

1. **Saint Martin I,** Pope and Martyr   April 13

Memorial

Entrance Antiphon   Psalm 49: 17-18

Do not be disturbed, when a man grows rich, and there is no end to his extravagant excesses; He cannot take all that with him when he dies. Unlike love, compassion and charity, such obscene extravagance will not save him from the grave.

Offertory Antiphon

O God and Divine Creator, grant that we may withstand the trials of this world with invincible firmness of purpose, just as you did not allow your Martyr Pope Saint Martin the First to be daunted by threats or broken by suffering. Through our Lord Jesus Christ, your Son, who lives and reigns with you in the unity of the Holy Spirit, one God, for ever and ever.

Prayer over the Offerings

May God and the Divine Creator accept and sanctify these humble gifts as symbols of the genuine personal offerings we make in commemoration of Saint Martin I. Through Christ our Light and Saviour.

Communion Antiphon   Lk 22: 28-30

It is you who have stood by me in my trials; and I confer a kingdom on you, says the Lord, that you may eat and drink at my table in my kingdom.

Prayer after Communion

Heavenly Father and God of all Creation, we give thanks for the nourishment of your heavenly gifts of the Bread

and Fruits of Eternal Spiritual Life. May our earnest participation together in commemoration of Saint Martin I bring forth favourable blessings upon our lives, our community and your Holy Apostolic Universal Ecclesia.

XII.VII – APRIL 21

1.   **Anselm of Canterbury,** Bishop and Doctor of the Church   April 21

Memorial

Entrance Antiphon   Psalm 51: 12

My God, bring a clean heart to birth within me; breathe new life, true life, into my being.

Offertory Antiphon

O God and Divine Creator, who led the Bishop Saint Anselm to seek out and teach the depths of your wisdom, grant, we pray, that our faith in you may so aid our understanding, that what we believe by your command may give delight to our hearts. Through our Lord Jesus Christ, your Son, who lives and reigns with you in the unity of the Holy Spirit, one God, for ever and ever.

Prayer over the Offerings

May God and the Divine Creator accept and sanctify these humble gifts as symbols of the genuine personal offerings we make in commemoration of Anselm of Canterbury. Through Christ our Light and Saviour.

Communion Antiphon   Psalm 1: 2-3

One who ponders the Divine maxims of Law of the Lord day and night shall yield fruit in due season.

Prayer after Communion

Heavenly Father and God of all Creation, we give thanks for the nourishment of your heavenly gifts of the Bread and Fruits of Eternal Spiritual Life. May our earnest participation together in commemoration of Anselm of Canterbury bring forth favourable blessings upon our lives, our community and your Holy Apostolic Universal Ecclesia.

XII.VIII – APRIL 23

1.   **George of England,** Martyr   April 23

Memorial

Entrance Antiphon   Psalm 52: 11

> I will give thee eternal thanks Lord for all thou hast done for me.

Offertory Antiphon

> O God and Divine Creator, we humbly implore you, that, as Saint George imitated the Passion of the Lord, so he may lend us ready help in our weakness. Through our Lord Jesus Christ, your Son, who lives and reigns with you in the unity of the Holy Spirit, one God, for ever and ever.

Prayer over the Offerings

> May God and the Divine Creator accept and sanctify these humble gifts as symbols of the genuine personal offerings we make in commemoration of George of England. Through Christ our Light and Saviour.

Communion Antiphon   Lk 22: 28-30

> It is you who have stood by me in my trials; and I confer a kingdom on you, says the Lord, that you may eat and drink at my table in my kingdom.

Prayer after Communion

> Heavenly Father and God of all Creation, we give thanks for the nourishment of your heavenly gifts of the Bread and Fruits of Eternal Spiritual Life. May our earnest participation together in commemoration of George of England bring forth favourable blessings upon our lives, our community and your Holy Apostolic Universal Ecclesia.

XII.IX – APRIL 24

1.   **Saint Fidelis of Sigmaringen,** Priest and Martyr   April 24

Memorial

Entrance Antiphon   Psalm 53: 1-2

> The belief of the nihilist that there be no God, is the sign of a corrupted heart. Warped natures abound through such deceitful lives, that not an innocent exists among them.

Offertory Antiphon

> O God and Divine Creator, who were pleased to award the palm of martyrdom to Saint Fidelis as, burning with love for you, he propagated the faith, grant, we pray, through his intercession, that, grounded in charity, we may merit to know with him the power of the Resurrection of Christ.

Who lives and reigns with you in the unity of the Holy Spirit, one God, for ever and ever.

Prayer over the Offerings

May God and the Divine Creator accept and sanctify these humble gifts as symbols of the genuine personal offerings we make in commemoration of Fidelis of Sigmaringen. Through Christ our Light and Saviour.

Communion Antiphon — Lk 22: 28-30

It is you who have stood by me in my trials; and I confer a kingdom on you, says the Lord, that you may eat and drink at my table in my kingdom.

Prayer after Communion

Heavenly Father and God of all Creation, we give thanks for the nourishment of your heavenly gifts of the Bread and Fruits of Eternal Spiritual Life. May our earnest participation together in commemoration of Fidelis of Sigmaringen bring forth favourable blessings upon our lives, our community and your Holy Apostolic Universal Ecclesia.

XII.X – APRIL 25

1. **Saint Mark, Evangelist** — April 25

Memorial

Entrance Antiphon — Psalm 55: 17

I will call upon God, and the Lord will save.

Offertory Antiphon

O God and Divine Creator, who raised up Saint Mark, your Evangelist, and endowed him with the grace to preach the Gospel, grant, we pray, that we may so profit from his teaching as to follow faithfully in the footsteps of Christ. Who lives and reigns with you in the unity of the Holy Spirit, one God, for ever and ever.

Prayer over the Offerings

May God and the Divine Creator accept and sanctify these humble gifts as symbols of the genuine personal offerings we make in commemoration of Saint Mark. Through Christ our Light and Saviour.

Communion Antiphon — Mt 28: 20

Behold, I am with you always,
even to the end of the age, says the Lord, alleluia

Prayer after Communion

Heavenly Father and God of all Creation, we give thanks for the nourishment of your heavenly gifts of the Bread and Fruits of Eternal Spiritual Life. May our earnest participation together in commemoration of Saint Mark bring forth favourable blessings upon our lives, our community and your Holy Apostolic Universal Ecclesia.

XII.XI – APRIL 28

1.   **Saint Peter Chanel,** Priest and Martyr   April 28

Memorial

Entrance Antiphon *Psalm 56: 11-12*

I claim God's promise; my trust is in God, as the threats of mortal men cannot daunt me. The vows which thou claims from me, O God, my sacrifice of service shall fulfil.

Offertory Antiphon

O God and Divine Creator, who for the spreading of your Church crowned Saint Peter Chanel with martyrdom, grant that, in these days of paschal joy, we may so celebrate the mysteries of Christ's Death and Resurrection as to bear worthy witness to newness of life. Through our Lord Jesus Christ, your Son, who lives and reigns with you in the unity of the Holy Spirit, one God, for ever and ever.

Prayer over the Offerings

May God and the Divine Creator accept and sanctify these humble gifts as symbols of the genuine personal offerings we make in commemoration of Peter Chanel. Through Christ our Light and Saviour.

Communion Antiphon *Lk 22: 28-30*

It is you who have stood by me in my trials; and I confer a kingdom on you, says the Lord, that you may eat and drink at my table in my kingdom.

Prayer after Communion

Heavenly Father and God of all Creation, we give thanks for the nourishment of your heavenly gifts of the Bread and Fruits of Eternal Spiritual Life. May our earnest participation together in commemoration of Peter Chanel bring forth favourable blessings upon our lives, our community and your Holy Apostolic Universal Ecclesia.

Title XII: Proper of April

XII.XII – APRIL 29

1. **Catherine of Siena,** Virgin and Doctor of the Church April 29
Memorial

Entrance Antiphon Psalm 57: 2

Have mercy on me, O God, have mercy on me; here is a soul that puts its trust in thee.

Offertory Antiphon

O God and Divine Creator, who set Saint Catherine of Siena on fire with divine love in her contemplation of the Lord's Passion and her service of your Church, grant, through her intercession, that your people, participating in the mystery of Christ, may ever exult in the revelation of his glory. Who lives and reigns with you in the unity of the Holy Spirit, one God, for ever and ever.

Prayer over the Offerings

May God and the Divine Creator accept and sanctify these humble gifts as symbols of the genuine personal offerings we make in commemoration of Catherine of Siena. Through Christ our Light and Saviour.

Communion Antiphon 1 Jn 1: 7

If we walk in the light, as God is in the light, then we have fellowship with one another, and the blood of his Son Jesus Christ cleanses us from all sin, alleluia.

Prayer after Communion

Heavenly Father and God of all Creation, we give thanks for the nourishment of your heavenly gifts of the Bread and Fruits of Eternal Spiritual Life. May our earnest participation together in commemoration of Catherine of Siena bring forth favourable blessings upon our lives, our community and your Holy Apostolic Universal Ecclesia.

XII.XIII – APRIL 30

1. **Pius V, Pope** April 30
Memorial

Entrance Antiphon Psalm 59: 18

To thee I will sing, the God who strengthens me, the God who watches over me, my God, and all my hope of mercy.

Offertory Antiphon

O God and Divine Creator, who in your providence raised

up Pope Saint Pius the Fifth in your Church that the faith might be safeguarded and more fitting worship be offered to you, grant, through his intercession, that we may participate in your mysteries with lively faith and fruitful charity. Through our Lord Jesus Christ, your Son, who lives and reigns with you in the unity of the Holy Spirit, one God, for ever and ever.

Prayer over the Offerings
May God and the Divine Creator accept and sanctify these humble gifts as symbols of the genuine personal offerings we make in commemoration of Saint Pius V. Through Christ our Light and Saviour.

Communion Antiphon
Jn 10: 11

The Good Shepherd did sacrifice his own life for his flock.

Prayer after Communion
Heavenly Father and God of all Creation, we give thanks for the nourishment of your heavenly gifts of the Bread and Fruits of Eternal Spiritual Life. May our earnest participation together in commemoration of Saint Pius V bring forth favourable blessings upon our lives, our community and your Holy Apostolic Universal Ecclesia.

Title XIII: Proper of May

XIII.I – MAY 1

1.   **Saint Joseph the Worker**   May 1

Memorial

Entrance Antiphon   Ps 128 (127): 1-2

Blessed are all who fear the Lord and walk in his ways!
By the labor of your hands you shall eat;
blessed are you, and blessed will you be, alleluia.

Offertory Antiphon

O God and Divine Creator of all things, who laid down for the human race the law of work, graciously grant that by the example of Saint Joseph and under his patronage we may complete the works you set us to do and attain the rewards you promise. Through our Lord Jesus Christ, your Son, who lives and reigns with you in the unity of the Holy Spirit, one God, for ever and ever.

Prayer over the Offerings

May God and the Divine Creator accept and sanctify these humble gifts as symbols of the genuine personal offerings we make in commemoration of Saint Joseph the Worker. Through Christ our Light and Saviour.

Communion Antiphon   Col 3: 17

Whatever you do in word or deed, do everything in the name of the Lord, giving thanks to God through him, alleluia.

Prayer after Communion

Heavenly Father and God of all Creation, we give thanks for the nourishment of your heavenly gifts of the Bread and Fruits of Eternal Spiritual Life. May our earnest participation together in commemoration of Saint Joseph the Worker bring forth favourable blessings upon our lives, our community and your Holy Apostolic Universal Ecclesia.

2.   **Our Lady of Eternal Russia**   May 1

Patron of Russia

Memorial

Entrance Antiphon   Ps 128 (127): 1-2

Blessed are all who fear the Lord and walk in his ways!
By the labor of your hands you shall eat;
blessed are you, and blessed will you be, alleluia.

Offertory Antiphon

O God and Divine Creator of all Strength and Knowledge, grant us through the intercession of our Divine Mother Mary as Our Lady of Eternal Russia, the continued protection, assistance and good fortune of the Russian people and the fulfilment of your Divine Mission of unity of all Christians as the Living Body of Christ. Through our Lord Jesus Christ, your Son, who lives and reigns with you in the unity of the Holy Spirit, one God, for ever and ever.

Prayer over the Offerings

May God and the Divine Creator accept and sanctify these humble gifts in the name of our Divine Mother Mary as Our Lady of Eternal Russia, as symbols of the genuine personal offerings we make in honour and respect of the protection for all of Russia. Through Christ our Light and Saviour.

Communion Antiphon *Col 3: 17*

Whatever you do in word or deed, do everything in the name of the Lord, giving thanks to God through him, alleluia.

Prayer after Communion

Heavenly Father and God of all Creation, we give thanks for the nourishment of your heavenly gifts of the Bread and Fruits of Eternal Spiritual Life. May our earnest participation together in commemoration of our Divine Mother Mary as Our Lady of Eternal Russia bring forth favourable blessings upon our lives, our nation and your Holy Apostolic Universal Ecclesia as one united Christian body.

XIII.II – MAY 2

1. Athanasius of Alexandria, Bishop and Doctor of the Church — May 2

Memorial

Entrance Antiphon *Psalm 61: 7-8*

In God is my salvation and my glory: the rock of my strength, and my refuge, is in God. Trust in him at all times; ye people, pour out your heart before him: God is a refuge for us.

Offertory Antiphon

O God and Divine Creator, who raised up the Bishop Saint Athanasius as an outstanding champion of your Son's divinity, mercifully grant, that, rejoicing in his teaching and his protection, we may never cease to grow in knowledge and love of you. Through our Lord Jesus Christ, your Son, who lives and reigns with you in the unity of the Holy Spirit, one God, for ever and ever.

Prayer over the Offerings

May God and the Divine Creator accept and sanctify these humble gifts as symbols of the genuine personal offerings we make in commemoration of Athanasius of Alexandria. Through Christ our Light and Saviour.

Communion Antiphon — 1 Cor 3: 11

No one can lay a foundation other than the one that is there, namely, Jesus Christ, alleluia.

Prayer after Communion

Heavenly Father and God of all Creation, we give thanks for the nourishment of your heavenly gifts of the Bread and Fruits of Eternal Spiritual Life. May our earnest participation together in commemoration of Athanasius of Alexandria bring forth favourable blessings upon our lives, our community and your Holy Apostolic Universal Ecclesia.

XIII.III – MAY 3

1. **Saints Philip And James,** Apostles — May 3

Memorial

Entrance Antiphon — Psalm 62: 2

No rest has my soul but in God's hands; to him I look for deliverance.

Offertory Antiphon

O God and Divine Creator, who gladden us each year with the feast day of the Apostles Philip and James, grant us, through their prayers, a share in the Passion and Resurrection of your Only Begotten Son, so that we may merit to behold you for eternity. Through our Lord Jesus Christ, your Son, who lives and reigns with you in the unity of the Holy Spirit, one God, for ever and ever.

Prayer over the Offerings

May God and the Divine Creator accept and sanctify these humble gifts as symbols of the genuine personal offerings we make in commemoration of Saints Philip and James.

Through Christ our Light and Saviour.

Communion Antiphon — Jn 14: 8-9

Lord, show us the Father, and that will be enough for us. Whoever has seen me, Philip, has seen the Father also, alleluia.

Prayer after Communion

Heavenly Father and God of all Creation, we give thanks for the nourishment of your heavenly gifts of the Bread and Fruits of Eternal Spiritual Life. May our earnest participation together in commemoration of Saints Philip and James bring forth favourable blessings upon our lives, our community and your Holy Apostolic Universal Ecclesia.

XIII.IV – MAY 4

1.   **Damien de Veuster,** Priest   May 4
Patron of Oceania
Memorial

Entrance Antiphon — Psalm 62: 10-11

Trust not in oppression, and become not vain in robbery: if riches increase, set not your heart upon them. God hath spoken once; twice have I heard this; that power belongeth unto God.

Offertory Antiphon

O God and Divine Creator, who gave us in Saint Damien a shining witness of love for the poorest and most abandoned, grant that, by his intercession, as faithful witnesses of the heart of your Son Jesus, we too may be servants of the most needy and rejected. Through our Lord Jesus Christ, your Son, who lives and reigns with you in the unity of the Holy Spirit, one God, for ever and ever.

Prayer over the Offerings

May God and the Divine Creator accept and sanctify these humble gifts as symbols of the genuine personal offerings we make in commemoration of Damien de Veuster. Through Christ our Light and Saviour.

Communion Antiphon — 1 Peter 1:15

But as he who called you is holy, you also be holy in all your conduct.

Prayer after Communion

Heavenly Father and God of all Creation, we give thanks for the nourishment of your heavenly gifts of the Bread and Fruits of Eternal Spiritual Life. May our earnest participation together in commemoration of Damien de Veuster bring forth favourable blessings upon our lives, our community and your Holy Apostolic Universal Ecclesia.

XIII.V – MAY 5

1.   **Our Lady of Europe**   May 5
Patron of Europe
Memorial

Entrance Antiphon   Psalm 62: 12

Also unto thee, O Lord, belongeth mercy: for thou renderest to every man according to his work.

Offertory Antiphon

O God and Divine Creator, grant us through the intercession of our Divine Mother Mary as Our Lady of Europe, that all peoples of each generation of Europe may come to know your good works and Divine Truth. Through our Lord Jesus Christ, your Son, who lives and reigns with you in the unity of the Holy Spirit, one God, for ever and ever.

Prayer over the Offerings

May God and the Divine Creator accept and sanctify these humble gifts as symbols of the genuine personal offerings we make in commemoration of Our Lady of Europe. Through Christ our Light and Saviour.

Communion Antiphon   1 John 4

Beloved, let us love one another, for love is from God, and whoever loves has been born of God and knows God.

Prayer after Communion

Heavenly Father and God of all Creation, we give thanks for the nourishment of your heavenly gifts of the Bread and Fruits of Eternal Spiritual Life. May our earnest participation together in commemoration of Our Lady of Europe bring forth favourable blessings upon our lives, our community and your Holy Apostolic Universal Ecclesia.

XIII.VI – MAY 12

1.   **Saints Nereus and Achilleus,** Martyrs   May 12

Memorial

Entrance Antiphon   Psalm 66: 6

> He turned the sea into dry land: they went through the flood on foot: there did we rejoice in him.

Offertory Antiphon

> O God and Divine Creator, grant that we who know the great courage of the glorious Martyrs Nereus and Achilleus in confessing you, may experience their loving intercession for us in your presence. Through our Lord Jesus Christ, your Son, who lives and reigns with you in the unity of the Holy Spirit, one God, for ever and ever.

Prayer over the Offerings

> May God and the Divine Creator accept and sanctify these humble gifts as symbols of the genuine personal offerings we make in commemoration of Nereus and Achilleus. Through Christ our Light and Saviour.

Communion Antiphon   Lk 22: 28-30

> It is you who have stood by me in my trials; and I confer a kingdom on you, says the Lord, that you may eat and drink at my table in my kingdom.

Prayer after Communion

> Heavenly Father and God of all Creation, we give thanks for the nourishment of your heavenly gifts of the Bread and Fruits of Eternal Spiritual Life. May our earnest participation together in commemoration of Nereus and Achilleus bring forth favourable blessings upon our lives, our community and your Holy Apostolic Universal Ecclesia.

XIII.VII – MAY 13

1.   **Our Lady of Fatima**   May 13

Memorial

Entrance Antiphon   Psalm 66: 7

> He ruleth by his power for ever; his eyes behold the nations: let not the rebellious exalt themselves.

Offertory Antiphon

O God and Divine Creator, who chose the Mother of your Son to be our Mother also, grant us that, persevering in penance and prayer for the salvation of the world, we may further more effectively each day the reign of Christ. Who lives and reigns with you in the unity of the Holy Spirit, one God, for ever and ever.

Prayer over the Offerings

May God and the Divine Creator accept and sanctify these humble gifts as symbols of the genuine personal offerings we make in commemoration of Our Lady of Fatima. Through Christ our Light and Saviour.

Prayer after Communion

Heavenly Father and God of all Creation, we give thanks for the nourishment of your heavenly gifts of the Bread and Fruits of Eternal Spiritual Life. May our earnest participation together in commemoration of Our Lady of Fatima bring forth favourable blessings upon our lives, our community and your Holy Apostolic Universal Ecclesia.

XIII.VIII – MAY 14

1.

Saint Matthias, Apostle
Memorial

May 14

Psalm 66: 9-10

Entrance Antiphon

Praise our God, O peoples, let the sound of his praise be heard; he has preserved our lives and kept our feet from slipping.

Offertory Antiphon

O God and Divine Creator, who assigned Saint Matthias a place in the college of Apostles, grant us, through his intercession, that, rejoicing at how your love has been allotted to us, we may merit to be numbered among the elect. Through our Lord Jesus Christ, your Son, who lives and reigns with you in the unity of the Holy Spirit, one God, for ever and ever.

Prayer over the Offerings

May God and the Divine Creator accept and sanctify these humble gifts as symbols of the genuine personal offerings we make in commemoration of Matthias the Apostle. Through Christ our Light and Saviour.

Missale Christus | Proper of Heroes & Saints

Communion Antiphon   Jn 15: 12

> This is my commandment: Love one another as I love you, says the Lord.

Prayer after Communion

> Heavenly Father and God of all Creation, we give thanks for the nourishment of your heavenly gifts of the Bread and Fruits of Eternal Spiritual Life. May our earnest participation together in commemoration of Matthias the Apostle bring forth favourable blessings upon our lives, our community and your Holy Apostolic Universal Ecclesia.

XIII.IX – MAY 15

1.   **Isidore the Farmer**   May 15
Patron of Farmers and Day Labourers
Memorial

Entrance Antiphon   Psalm 66: 20

> Blessed be God, which hath not turned away my prayer, nor his mercy from me.

Offertory Antiphon

> O God and Divine Creator, who calls us to serve you by caring for the gifts that surround us, inspire us by the example of Saint Isidore to share our food with the hungry and to work for the salvation of all people. Through our Lord Jesus Christ, your Son, who lives and reigns with you in the unity of the Holy Spirit, one God, for ever and ever.

Prayer over the Offerings

> May God and the Divine Creator accept and sanctify these humble gifts as symbols of the genuine personal offerings we make in commemoration of Isidore the Farmer. Through Christ our Light and Saviour.

Prayer after Communion

> Heavenly Father and God of all Creation, we give thanks for the nourishment of your heavenly gifts of the Bread and Fruits of Eternal Spiritual Life. May our earnest participation together in commemoration of Isidore the Farmer bring forth favourable blessings upon our lives, our community and your Holy Apostolic Universal Ecclesia.

Title XIII: Proper of May

XIII.X – MAY 18

1. **Saint John I,** Pope and Martyr
Memorial

May 18

Entrance Antiphon
Psalm 67: 5-6

Let the people praise thee, O God; let all the people praise thee. Then shall the earth yield her increase; and God, even our own God, shall bless us.

Offertory Antiphon

O God and Divine Creator, who rewards faithful souls and who have consecrated this day by the martyrdom of Pope Saint John the First, graciously hear the prayers of your people and grant that we, who venerate his merits, may imitate his constancy in the faith. Through our Lord Jesus Christ, your Son, who lives and reigns with you in the unity of the Holy Spirit, one God, for ever and ever.

Prayer over the Offerings

May God and the Divine Creator accept and sanctify these humble gifts as symbols of the genuine personal offerings we make in commemoration of Saint John I. Through Christ our Light and Saviour.

Communion Antiphon
Lk 22: 28-30

It is you who have stood by me in my trials; and I confer a kingdom on you, says the Lord, that you may eat and drink at my table in my kingdom.

Prayer after Communion

Heavenly Father and God of all Creation, we give thanks for the nourishment of your heavenly gifts of the Bread and Fruits of Eternal Spiritual Life. May our earnest participation together in commemoration of Saint John I bring forth favourable blessings upon our lives, our community and your Holy Apostolic Universal Ecclesia.

XIII.XI – MAY 20

1. **Bernardine of Siena,** Priest
Memorial

May 20

Entrance Antiphon
Psalm 68: 10

Thy congregation hath dwelt therein: thou, O God, hast prepared of thy goodness for the poor.

Offertory Antiphon

O God and Divine Creator, who gave the Priest Saint Bernardine of Siena a great love for the holy Name of Jesus, grant, through his merits and prayers, that we may ever be set aflame with the spirit of your love. Through our Lord Jesus Christ, your Son, who lives and reigns with you in the unity of the Holy Spirit, one God, for ever and ever.

Prayer over the Offerings

May God and the Divine Creator accept and sanctify these humble gifts as symbols of the genuine personal offerings we make in commemoration of Bernardine of Siena. Through Christ our Light and Saviour.

Prayer after Communion

Heavenly Father and God of all Creation, we give thanks for the nourishment of your heavenly gifts of the Bread and Fruits of Eternal Spiritual Life. May our earnest participation together in commemoration of Bernardine of Siena bring forth favourable blessings upon our lives, our community and your Holy Apostolic Universal Ecclesia.

XIII.XII – MAY 21

1. Christopher Magallanes, Priest, and Companions, Martyrs

May 21

Memorial

Entrance Antiphon

Psalm 68: 20

Blessed be the Lord now and ever, the God who bears our burdens, and Christ who wins us eternal victory.

Offertory Antiphon

O God and Divine Creator, who made the Priest Saint Christopher Magallanes and his companions faithful to Christ the King even to the point of martyrdom, grant us, through their intercession, that, persevering in confession of the true faith, we may always hold fast to the commandments of your love. Through our Lord Jesus Christ, your Son, who lives and reigns with you in the unity of the Holy Spirit, one God, for ever and ever.

Prayer over the Offerings

May God and the Divine Creator accept and sanctify these humble gifts as symbols of the genuine personal offerings we make in commemoration of Christopher Magallanes and companions. Through Christ our Light and Saviour.

Communion Antiphon   Lk 22: 28-30

It is you who have stood by me in my trials; and I confer a kingdom on you, says the Lord, that you may eat and drink at my table in my kingdom.

Prayer after Communion

Heavenly Father and God of all Creation, we give thanks for the nourishment of your heavenly gifts of the Bread and Fruits of Eternal Spiritual Life. May our earnest participation together in commemoration of Christopher Magallanes and companions bring forth favourable blessings upon our lives, our community and your Holy Apostolic Universal Ecclesia.

XIII.XIII – MAY 22

1.   **Rita of Cascia,** Religious   May 22
Patron for healing of women in abusive relations
Memorial

Entrance Antiphon   Psalm 68: 28

Thy God hath commanded thy strength: strengthen, O God, that which thou hast wrought for us.

Offertory Antiphon

O God and Divine Creator, bestow on us the wisdom and strength of the Cross, with which you were pleased to endow Saint Rita, so that, suffering in every tribulation with Christ, we may participate ever more deeply in his Paschal Mystery. Who lives and reigns with you in the unity of the Holy Spirit, one God, for ever and ever.

Prayer over the Offerings

May God and the Divine Creator accept and sanctify these humble gifts as symbols of the genuine personal offerings we make in commemoration of Rita of Cascia. Through Christ our Light and Saviour.

Communion Antiphon   1 Peter 1:15

But as he who called you is holy, you also be holy in all your conduct.

Prayer after Communion

Heavenly Father and God of all Creation, we give thanks for the nourishment of your heavenly gifts of the Bread and Fruits of Eternal Spiritual Life. May our earnest

Missale Christus | Proper of Heroes & Saints

participation together in commemoration of Rita of Cascia bring forth favourable blessings upon our lives, our community and your Holy Apostolic Universal Ecclesia.

XIII.XIV – MAY 23

1.   **Nicolaus Copernicus and Johannes Kepler**   May 23

Ordinary

Entrance Antiphon   Psalm 69: 32

> The humble shall see this, and be glad: and your heart shall live that seek God.

Living Testimony: Johannes Kepler

> The wisdom of the Lord is infinite as are also His glory and His power. Ye heavens, sing His praises., sun, moon, and planets, glorify Him in your ineffable language! Praise Him, celestial harmonies, and all ye who can comprehend them! And thou, my soul, praise thy Creator! It is by Him and in Him that all exist

Living Gospel: Nicolaus Copernicus   Nicolaus Copernicus

> To know the mighty works of God, to comprehend His wisdom and majesty and power; to appreciate, in degree, the wonderful workings of His laws, surely all this must be a pleasing and acceptable mode of worship to the Most High, to whom ignorance cannot be more grateful than knowledge.

Offertory Antiphon

> O God and Divine Creator, grant us the courage of faith and humility of discenment of your servants Nicolaus Copernicus and Johannes Kepler. Through our Lord Jesus Christ, your Son, who lives and reigns with you in the unity of the Holy Spirit, one God, for ever and ever.

Prayer over the Offerings

> May God and the Divine Creator accept and sanctify these humble gifts as symbols of the genuine personal offerings we make in commemoration of Nicolaus Copernicus and Johannes Kepler. Through Christ our Light and Saviour.

Communion Antiphon   Mt 16: 24

> Whoever wishes to come after me, must deny himself, take up his cross, and follow me, says the Lord.

Prayer after Communion

Heavenly Father and God of all Creation, we give thanks for the nourishment of your heavenly gifts of the Bread and Fruits of Eternal Spiritual Life. May our earnest participation together in commemoration of Nicolaus Copernicus and Johannes Kepler bring forth favourable blessings upon our lives, our community and your Holy Apostolic Universal Ecclesia.

XIII.XV – MAY 25

1.   **Bede the Venerable,** Priest and Doctor of the Church   May 25

Memorial

Entrance Antiphon   Psalm 70: 2

If it be your Will, O God, to set me free; Lord, make haste to help me.

Offertory Antiphon

O God and Divine Creator, who bring light to your Church through the learning of the Priest Saint Bede, mercifully grant that your servants may always be enlightened by his wisdom and helped by his merits. Through our Lord Jesus Christ, your Son, who lives and reigns with you in the unity of the Holy Spirit, one God, for ever and ever.

Prayer over the Offerings

May God and the Divine Creator accept and sanctify these humble gifts as symbols of the genuine personal offerings we make in commemoration of Bede the Venerable. Through Christ our Light and Saviour.

Communion Antiphon   Psalm 1: 2-3

One who ponders the Divine maxims of Law of the Lord day and night shall yield fruit in due season.

Prayer after Communion

Heavenly Father and God of all Creation, we give thanks for the nourishment of your heavenly gifts of the Bread and Fruits of Eternal Spiritual Life. May our earnest participation together in commemoration of Bede the Venerable bring forth favourable blessings upon our lives, our community and your Holy Apostolic Universal Ecclesia.

XIII.XVI – MAY 26

1.   **Philip Neri,** Priest   May 26

Founder of Congregation of the Oratory

Memorial

Entrance Antiphon · Psalm 70: 5

> Triumphant joy be theirs, who long for thee; Praise to the Lord, be ever their song.

Offertory Antiphon

> O God and Divine Creator, who never ceases to bestow the glory of holiness on the faithful servants you raise up for yourself, graciously grant that the Holy Spirit may kindle in us that fire with which he wonderfully filled the heart of Saint Philip Neri. Through our Lord Jesus Christ, your Son, who lives and reigns with you in the unity of the Holy Spirit, one God, for ever and ever.

Prayer over the Offerings

> May God and the Divine Creator accept and sanctify these humble gifts as symbols of the genuine personal offerings we make in commemoration of Philip Neri. Through Christ our Light and Saviour.

Communion Antiphon · Jn 15: 9

> As the Father loves me, so I also love you; remain in my love, says the Lord.

Prayer after Communion

> Heavenly Father and God of all Creation, we give thanks for the nourishment of your heavenly gifts of the Bread and Fruits of Eternal Spiritual Life. May our earnest participation together in commemoration of Philip Neri bring forth favourable blessings upon our lives, our community and your Holy Apostolic Universal Ecclesia.

XIII.XVII – MAY 27

1. ### John Calvin — May 27

Co-Founder of Reformed Churches of Universal Ecclesia

Memorial

Entrance Antiphon · Psalm 71: 4

> Deliver me, O my God, out of the hand of the wicked, out of the hand of unrighteous and cruel men.

Living Testimony: · Psalm 9:10

> Faith has no less need of the word than the fruit of a tree has of a living root; because, as David testifies, none can hope in God but those who know his name

Living Gospel: John Calvin
John Calvin

True wisdom consists in two things: Knowledge of God and Knowledge of Self. There is no knowing that does not begin with knowing God. Without knowledge of self there is no knowledge of God and without knowledge of God there is no knowledge of self. All the arts come from God and are to be respected as divine inventions. Without the respect of God, men do not even observe justice and charity among themselves. Our true wisdom is to embrace with meek docility, and without reservation, whatever the holy scriptures have delivered.

Offertory Antiphon

O God and Divine Creator, grant us the necessary docility and humility of heart to accept the guidance of the Holy Spirit that every crisis and trial of our faith is to strengthen our love, not weaken it. Through our Lord Jesus Christ, your Son, who lives and reigns with you in the unity of the Holy Spirit, one God, for ever and ever.

Prayer over the Offerings

May God and the Divine Creator accept and sanctify these humble gifts as symbols of the genuine personal offerings we make in commemoration of John Calvin. Through Christ our Light and Saviour.

Communion Antiphon
John 12: 26

Whoever serves me must follow me, and where I am, there also will my servant be.

Prayer after Communion

Heavenly Father and God of all Creation, we give thanks for the nourishment of your heavenly gifts of the Bread and Fruits of Eternal Spiritual Life. May our earnest participation together in commemoration of John Calvin bring forth favourable blessings upon our lives, our community and your Holy Apostolic Universal Ecclesia.

XIII.XVIII – MAY 30

1. Joan of Arc
Memorial

May 30

Entrance Antiphon
Psalm 72: 5-7

Ageless as sun or moon such Divine Revelation shall endure; kindly as the rain that drops on the meadow grass, as the showers that water the earth. Justice in those days shall thrive, and the blessings of peace; and may those days of Divine Redemption last till the moon shines no more.

Living Testimony: Sir Winston Churchill on Joan

Joan was a being so uplifted from the ordinary run of mankind that she finds no equal in a thousand years. She embodied the natural goodness and valour of the human race in unexampled perfection. Unconquerable courage, infinite compassion, the virtue of the simple, the wisdom of the just, shone forth in her. She glorifies as she freed the soil from which she sprang.

Living Gospel: Joan of Arc
Joan of Arc

Take good care not to judge me wrongly, because you will put yourself in great danger. If I am not in the state of grace, may God put me there; and if I am, may God so keep me.

Offertory Antiphon

O God and Divine Creator, Through our Lord Jesus Christ, your Son, who lives and reigns with you in the unity of the Holy Spirit, one God, for ever and ever.

Prayer over the Offerings

May God and the Divine Creator accept and sanctify these humble gifts as symbols of the genuine personal offerings we make in commemoration of Joan of Arc. Through Christ our Light and Saviour.

Communion Antiphon
1 Peter 1:15

But as he who called you is holy, you also be holy in all your conduct.

Prayer after Communion

Heavenly Father and God of all Creation, we give thanks for the nourishment of your heavenly gifts of the Bread and Fruits of Eternal Spiritual Life. May our earnest participation together in commemoration of Joan of Arc bring forth favourable blessings upon our lives, our community and your Holy Apostolic Universal Ecclesia.

Title XIV: Proper of June

XIV.I – JUNE 1

1. **Saint Justin, Martyr** — June 1
Memorial

Entrance Antiphon — Psalm: 85, 46

The wicked have told me lies, but not so is your law:
I spoke of your decrees before kings,
and was not confounded.

Offertory Antiphon

O God and Divine Creator, who through the Paschal Mystery wondrously taught Saint Justin the Martyr the surpassing knowledge of Jesus Christ, grant us, through his intercession, that, having rejected deception and error, we may become steadfast in the faith. Through our Lord Jesus Christ, your Son, who lives and reigns with you in the unity of the Holy Spirit, one God, for ever and ever.

Prayer over the Offerings

May God and the Divine Creator accept and sanctify these humble gifts as symbols of the genuine personal offerings we make in commemoration of Saint Justin. Through Christ our Light and Saviour.

Communion Antiphon — 1 Cor 2: 2

I resolved to know nothing while I was with you
except Jesus Christ, and him crucified

Prayer after Communion

Heavenly Father and God of all Creation, we give thanks for the nourishment of your heavenly gifts of the Bread and Fruits of Eternal Spiritual Life. May our earnest participation together in commemoration of Saint Justin bring forth favourable blessings upon our lives, our community and your Holy Apostolic Universal Ecclesia.

XIV.II – JUNE 2

1. **Saints Marcellinus and Peter,** Martyrs — June 2
Memorial

Entrance Antiphon — Psalm 72: 12-14

His Divine Word will give the poor redress when they cry to him, those who are destitute with none to help them; in their need and helplessness, they shall have his compassion. Their lives he will take into his keeping, set them free from the power of wrong and oppression.

Missale Christus | Proper of Heroes & Saints

Offertory Antiphon

O God and Divine Creator, who surrounds us with protection through the glorious confession of the Martyrs Saints Marcellinus and Peter, grant that we may profit by imitating them and be upheld by their prayer. Through our Lord Jesus Christ, your Son, who lives and reigns with you in the unity of the Holy Spirit, one God, for ever and ever.

Prayer over the Offerings

May God and the Divine Creator accept and sanctify these humble gifts as symbols of the genuine personal offerings we make in commemoration of Saints Marcellinus and Peter. Through Christ our Light and Saviour.

Communion Antiphon   Lk 22: 28-30

It is you who have stood by me in my trials; and I confer a kingdom on you, says the Lord, that you may eat and drink at my table in my kingdom.

Prayer after Communion

Heavenly Father and God of all Creation, we give thanks for the nourishment of your heavenly gifts of the Bread and Fruits of Eternal Spiritual Life. May our earnest participation together in commemoration of Saints Marcellinus and Peter bring forth favourable blessings upon our lives, our community and your Holy Apostolic Universal Ecclesia.

XIV.III – JUNE 3

1.   **Saint Charles Lwanga and Companions,** Martyrs   June 3

Memorial

Entrance Antiphon   Psalm 73: 1

What divine and sacred gifts God reveals, what divine blessings, to the upright and the pure of heart!

Offertory Antiphon

O God and Divine Creator, who made the blood of Martyrs the seed of Christians, mercifully grant that the field which is your Church, watered by the blood shed by Saints Charles Lwanga and his companions, may be fertile and always yield you an abundant harvest. Through our Lord Jesus Christ, your Son, who lives and reigns with you in the unity of the Holy Spirit, one God, for ever and ever.

Prayer over the Offerings

May God and the Divine Creator accept and sanctify these humble gifts as symbols of the genuine personal offerings we make in commemoration of Saint Charles Lwanga and Companions. Through Christ our Light and Saviour.

Communion Antiphon — Ps 116 (115): 15

How precious in the eyes of the Lord
is the death of his holy ones.

Prayer after Communion

Heavenly Father and God of all Creation, we give thanks for the nourishment of your heavenly gifts of the Bread and Fruits of Eternal Spiritual Life. May our earnest participation together in commemoration of Saint Charles Lwanga and Companions bring forth favourable blessings upon our lives, our community and your Holy Apostolic Universal Ecclesia.

XIV.IV – JUNE 4

1. **Francis Caracciolo,** Priest — June 4
Co-Founder of Congregation of Minor Clerics Regular
(Adorno Fathers)
Memorial

Entrance Antiphon — Psalm 74: 12

For God is my King of old, working salvation in the midst of the earth.

Offertory Antiphon

O God and Divine Creator, grant us through the intercession of Saint Francis Caracciolo, the serenity and persistence to continue on the path to salvation, no matter how rocky the road may become. Through our Lord Jesus Christ, your Son, who lives and reigns with you in the unity of the Holy Spirit, one God, for ever and ever.

Prayer over the Offerings

May God and the Divine Creator accept and sanctify these humble gifts as symbols of the genuine personal offerings we make in commemoration of Saint Francis Caracciolo. Through Christ our Light and Saviour.

Communion Antiphon — John 12: 26

Whoever serves me must follow me, and where I am, there also will my servant be.

Missale Christus | Proper of Heroes & Saints

Prayer after Communion

Heavenly Father and God of all Creation, we give thanks for the nourishment of your heavenly gifts of the Bread and Fruits of Eternal Spiritual Life. May our earnest participation together in commemoration of Saint Francis Caracciolo bring forth favourable blessings upon our lives, our community and your Holy Apostolic Universal Ecclesia.

XIV.V – JUNE 5

1.   **Boniface,** Bishop and Martyr   June 5
Memorial

Entrance Antiphon   Psalm 75: 2

We praise thee, O God, praising thee, and call upon thy name to reveal to us more of your Divine Wisdom.

Offertory Antiphon

O God and Divine Creator, may the Martyr Saint Boniface be our advocate that we may firmly hold the faith he taught with his lips and sealed in his blood and confidently profess it by our deeds. Through our Lord Jesus Christ, your Son, who lives and reigns with you in the unity of the Holy Spirit, one God, for ever and ever.

Prayer over the Offerings

May God and the Divine Creator accept and sanctify these humble gifts as symbols of the genuine personal offerings we make in commemoration of Saint Boniface. Through Christ our Light and Saviour.

Communion Antiphon   Lk 22: 28-30

It is you who have stood by me in my trials; and I confer a kingdom on you, says the Lord, that you may eat and drink at my table in my kingdom.

Prayer after Communion

Heavenly Father and God of all Creation, we give thanks for the nourishment of your heavenly gifts of the Bread and Fruits of Eternal Spiritual Life. May our earnest participation together in commemoration of Saint Boniface bring forth favourable blessings upon our lives, our community and your Holy Apostolic Universal Ecclesia.

XIV.VI – JUNE 6

1. **Norbert of Xanten,** Bishop
Founder of Order of Canons Regular of Prémontré (Premonstratensians)

Memorial

June 6

Entrance Antiphon — Psalm 76: 12

To the Lord your God let your vows be made and honoured.

Offertory Antiphon

O God and Divine Creator, who made the Bishop Saint Norbert a servant of your Church outstanding in his prayer and pastoral zeal, grant, we ask, that by the help of his intercession, the flock of the faithful may always find shepherds after your own heart and be fed in the pastures of salvation. Through our Lord Jesus Christ, your Son, who lives and reigns with you in the unity of the Holy Spirit, one God, for ever and ever.

Prayer over the Offerings

May God and the Divine Creator accept and sanctify these humble gifts as symbols of the genuine personal offerings we make in commemoration of Norbert of Xanten. Through Christ our Light and Saviour.

Communion Antiphon — 1 John 4

Beloved, let us love one another, for love is from God, and whoever loves has been born of God and knows God.

Prayer after Communion

Heavenly Father and God of all Creation, we give thanks for the nourishment of your heavenly gifts of the Bread and Fruits of Eternal Spiritual Life. May our earnest participation together in commemoration of Norbert of Xanten bring forth favourable blessings upon our lives, our community and your Holy Apostolic Universal Ecclesia.

XIV.VII – JUNE 9

1. **Ephrem the Syrian,** Deacon and Doctor of the Church

Memorial

June 9

Entrance Antiphon — Psalm 78: 7-8

The People of God today are called to put their Trust in God, ever remembering his divine dealings with them, ever loyal to his commands; they were not to be like some their ancestors, of stubborn and defiant generations, as generations of false aims, and of a spirit that broke faith with God.

Offertory Antiphon

O God and Divine Creator, grant us the courage of Deacon Saint Ephrem who exulted in singing of your mysteries and from whom he received the strength of the Holy Spirit to serve you alone. Through our Lord Jesus Christ, your Son, who lives and reigns with you in the unity of the Holy Spirit, one God, for ever and ever.

Prayer over the Offerings

May God and the Divine Creator accept and sanctify these humble gifts as symbols of the genuine personal offerings we make in commemoration of Ephrem the Syrian. Through Christ our Light and Saviour.

Communion Antiphon   Psalm 1: 2-3

One who ponders the Divine maxims of Law of the Lord day and night shall yield fruit in due season.

Prayer after Communion

Heavenly Father and God of all Creation, we give thanks for the nourishment of your heavenly gifts of the Bread and Fruits of Eternal Spiritual Life. May our earnest participation together in commemoration of Ephrem the Syrian bring forth favourable blessings upon our lives, our community and your Holy Apostolic Universal Ecclesia.

XIV.VIII – JUNE 11

1.   **Barnabas,** Apostle   June 11
                                     Memorial

Entrance Antiphon   Psalm 78: 56-57

Woe unto those who defy the most high God, and rebel against his Divine Word; and refuse to observe his decrees, but turn away and break faith with him.

Offertory Antiphon

O God and Divine Creator, who decreed that Saint Barnabas, a man filled with faith and the Holy Spirit, should be set apart to convert the nations, grant that the Gospel of Christ, which he strenuously preached, may be faithfully proclaimed by word and by deed. Through our

Lord Jesus Christ, your Son, who lives and reigns with you in the unity of the Holy Spirit, one God, for ever and ever.

Prayer over the Offerings

May God and the Divine Creator accept and sanctify these humble gifts as symbols of the genuine personal offerings we make in commemoration of Saint Barnabas. Through Christ our Light and Saviour.

Communion Antiphon — Jn 15: 15

I no longer call you slaves, because a slave does not know what his master is doing. But I have called you friends, because I have told you everything I have heard from my Father.

Prayer after Communion

Heavenly Father and God of all Creation, we give thanks for the nourishment of your heavenly gifts of the Bread and Fruits of Eternal Spiritual Life. May our earnest participation together in commemoration of Saint Barnabas bring forth favourable blessings upon our lives, our community and your Holy Apostolic Universal Ecclesia.

XIV.IX – JUNE 13

1. **Anthony of Padua,** Priest and Doctor of the Church — June 13
Patron of lost things
Memorial

Entrance Antiphon — Psalm 79: 9

O God, our Saviour, help us; deliver us, Lord, for the glory of thy name, pardon our transgressions for the sake that all may see your mercy!

Offertory Antiphon

O God and Divine Creator, who gave Saint Anthony of Padua to your people as an outstanding preacher and an intercessor in their need, grant that, with his assistance, as we follow the teachings of the Christian life, we may know your help in every trial. Through our Lord Jesus Christ, your Son, who lives and reigns with you in the unity of the Holy Spirit, one God, for ever and ever.

Prayer over the Offerings

May God and the Divine Creator accept and sanctify these humble gifts as symbols of the genuine personal offerings

we make in commemoration of Anthony of Padua.
Through Christ our Light and Saviour.

Communion Antiphon — Psalm 1: 2-3

One who ponders the Divine maxims of Law of the Lord day and night shall yield fruit in due season.

Prayer after Communion

Heavenly Father and God of all Creation, we give thanks for the nourishment of your heavenly gifts of the Bread and Fruits of Eternal Spiritual Life. May our earnest participation together in commemoration of Anthony of Padua bring forth favourable blessings upon our lives, our community and your Holy Apostolic Universal Ecclesia.

XIV.X – JUNE 19

1. **Romuald of Ravenna,** Abbot — June 19
Founder of Order of Camaldolese (Monks)
Memorial

Entrance Antiphon — Psalm 82: 5

They who willingly choose to know nothing, understand nothing. They walk about this world in darkness; they cry in fear whilst all the foundations of the earth are shaken.

Offertory Antiphon

O God and Divine Creator, who through Saint Romuald renewed the manner of life of hermits in your Church, grant that, denying ourselves and following Christ, we may merit to reach the heavenly realms on high. Through our Lord Jesus Christ, your Son, who lives and reigns with you in the unity of the Holy Spirit, one God, for ever and ever.

Prayer over the Offerings

May God and the Divine Creator accept and sanctify these humble gifts as symbols of the genuine personal offerings we make in commemoration of Romuald of Ravenna.
Through Christ our Light and Saviour.

Prayer after Communion

Heavenly Father and God of all Creation, we give thanks for the nourishment of your heavenly gifts of the Bread and Fruits of Eternal Spiritual Life. May our earnest participation together in commemoration of Romuald of Ravenna bring forth favourable blessings upon our lives, our community and your Holy Apostolic Universal

Ecclesia.

XIV.XI – JUNE 21

1.   **Aloysius Gonzaga,** Religious   June 21
                           Memorial

Entrance Antiphon   Psalm 84: 10

Better is one day in the presence of the Lord than a thousand at a distance; Greater to be but a doorkeeper in the house of God than dwell in the finest halls of the wicked.

Offertory Antiphon

O God and Divine Creator, giver of heavenly gifts, who in Saint Aloysius Gonzaga joined penitence to a wonderful innocence of life, grant, through his merits and intercession, that, though we have failed to follow him in innocence, we may imitate him in penitence. Through our Lord Jesus Christ, your Son, who lives and reigns with you in the unity of the Holy Spirit, one God, for ever and ever.

Prayer over the Offerings

May God and the Divine Creator accept and sanctify these humble gifts as symbols of the genuine personal offerings we make in commemoration of Aloysius Gonzaga. Through Christ our Light and Saviour.

Communion Antiphon   Ps 78 (77): 24-25

God gave them bread from heaven; man ate the bread of Angels.

Prayer after Communion

Heavenly Father and God of all Creation, we give thanks for the nourishment of your heavenly gifts of the Bread and Fruits of Eternal Spiritual Life. May our earnest participation together in commemoration of Aloysius Gonzaga bring forth favourable blessings upon our lives, our community and your Holy Apostolic Universal Ecclesia.

XIV.XII – JUNE 22

1.   **Paulinus of Nola,** Bishop   June 22
                            Memorial

Entrance Antiphon   Psalm 84: 11

For God is a sun and shield: the Lord will give grace and

glory: no good thing will he withheld from them that walk uprightly.

Offertory Antiphon

O God and Divine Creator, who made the Bishop Saint Paulinus of Nola outstanding for love of poverty and for pastoral care, graciously grant that, as we celebrate his merits, we may imitate the example of his charity. Through our Lord Jesus Christ, your Son, who lives and reigns with you in the unity of the Holy Spirit, one God, for ever and ever.

Prayer over the Offerings

May God and the Divine Creator accept and sanctify these humble gifts as symbols of the genuine personal offerings we make in commemoration of Paulinus of Nola. Through Christ our Light and Saviour.

Prayer after Communion

Heavenly Father and God of all Creation, we give thanks for the nourishment of your heavenly gifts of the Bread and Fruits of Eternal Spiritual Life. May our earnest participation together in commemoration of Paulinus of Nola bring forth favourable blessings upon our lives, our community and your Holy Apostolic Universal Ecclesia.

XIV.XIII – JUNE 24

1. **The Nativity Of Saint John The Baptist** — June 24

Solemnity

Entrance Antiphon — Psalm 85: 8

I will hear what God the Lord will speak: for he will speak peace unto his people, and to his saints: but let them not turn again to folly.

Offertory Antiphon

O God and Divine Creator, who raised up Saint John the Baptist to make ready a nation fit for Christ the Lord, give your people, we pray, the grace of spiritual joys and direct the hearts of all the faithful into the way of salvation and peace. Through our Lord Jesus Christ, your Son, who lives and reigns with you in the unity of the Holy Spirit, one God, for ever and ever.

Prayer over the Offerings

May God and the Divine Creator accept and sanctify these

humble gifts as symbols of the genuine personal offerings we make in commemoration of the Nativity of Saint John the Baptist. Through Christ our Light and Saviour.

Communion Antiphon — Lk 1: 78

Through the tender mercy of our God, the Dawn from on high will visit us.

Prayer after Communion

Heavenly Father and God of all Creation, we give thanks for the nourishment of your heavenly gifts of the Bread and Fruits of Eternal Spiritual Life. May our earnest participation together in commemoration of the Nativity of Saint John the Baptist bring forth favourable blessings upon our lives, our community and your Holy Apostolic Universal Ecclesia.

XIV.XIV– JUNE 27

1. **Cyril of Alexandria,** Bishop and Doctor of the Church — June 27
Memorial

Entrance Antiphon — Psalm 86: 4-5

Rejoice the soul of thy servant: for unto thee, O Lord, do I lift up my soul. For thou, Lord, art good, and ready to forgive; and plenteous in mercy unto all them that call upon thee.

Offertory Antiphon

O God and Divine Creator, who made the Bishop Saint Cyril of Alexandria an invincible champion of the divine motherhood of the most Blessed Virgin Mary, grant, we pray, that we, who believe she is truly the Mother of God, may be saved through the Incarnation of Christ your Son. Who lives and reigns with you in the unity of the Holy Spirit, one God, for ever and ever.

Prayer over the Offerings

May God and the Divine Creator accept and sanctify these humble gifts as symbols of the genuine personal offerings we make in commemoration of Cyril of Alexandria. Through Christ our Light and Saviour.

Communion Antiphon — Psalm 1: 2-3

One who ponders the Divine maxims of Law of the Lord day and night shall yield fruit in due season.

Missale Christus | Proper of Heroes & Saints

Prayer after Communion

Heavenly Father and God of all Creation, we give thanks for the nourishment of your heavenly gifts of the Bread and Fruits of Eternal Spiritual Life. May our earnest participation together in commemoration of Cyril of Alexandria bring forth favourable blessings upon our lives, our community and your Holy Apostolic Universal Ecclesia.

2.   **Joseph Smith Jr.**   June 27
Founder of the Church of Christ
Memorial

Entrance Antiphon   Psalm 86: 4-5

Rejoice the soul of thy servant: for unto thee, O Lord, do I lift up my soul. For thou, Lord, art good, and ready to forgive; and plenteous in mercy unto all them that call upon thee.

Living Testimony: Joseph Smith

When we understand the character of God, and know how to come to Him, he begins to unfold the heavens to us, and to tell us all about it. When we are ready to come to him, he is ready to come to us.

Living Gospel: Joseph Smith Jr   Joseph Smith Jr

We must have all things prepared and call our solemn assembly as the Lord has commanded us, that we may be able to accomplish his great work: and it must be done in God's own way; the house of the Lord must be prepared, and the solemn assembly called and organized in it according to the order of the house of God.

Offertory Antiphon

O God and Divine Creator, grant us the courage and strength of conviction of trust in your Divine Plan, as tyou bestowed upon Joseph Smith Jr. that we and all who follow your truth are open to the Light and Revelations of Christ. Through our Lord Jesus Christ, your Son, who lives and reigns with you in the unity of the Holy Spirit, one God, for ever and ever.

Prayer over the Offerings

May God and the Divine Creator accept and sanctify these humble gifts as symbols of the genuine personal offerings we make in commemoration of Joseph Smith Jr.. Through Christ our Light and Saviour.

Communion Antiphon — Mt 16: 24

Whoever wishes to come after me, must deny himself, take up his cross, and follow me, says the Lord.

Prayer after Communion

Heavenly Father and God of all Creation, we give thanks for the nourishment of your heavenly gifts of the Bread and Fruits of Eternal Spiritual Life. May our earnest participation together in commemoration of Joseph Smith Jr. bring forth favourable blessings upon our lives, our community and your Holy Apostolic Universal Ecclesia.

XIV.XV – JUNE 28

1. **Irenaeus of Lyon,** Bishop and Martyr — June 28

Memorial

Entrance Antiphon — Psalm 86: 11

Teach me your way, O Lord, and I will walk in your truth; give me an undivided heart, that I may honour your name.

Offertory Antiphon

O God and Divine Creator, who called the Bishop Saint Irenaeus to confirm true doctrine and the peace of the Church, grant, we pray, through his intercession, that, being renewed in faith and charity, we may always be intent on fostering unity and concord. Through our Lord Jesus Christ, your Son, who lives and reigns with you in the unity of the Holy Spirit, one God, for ever and ever.

Prayer over the Offerings

May God and the Divine Creator accept and sanctify these humble gifts as symbols of the genuine personal offerings we make in commemoration of Irenaeus of Lyon. Through Christ our Light and Saviour.

Communion Antiphon — Jn 15: 4-5

Remain in me, as I remain in you, says the Lord. Whoever remains in me, and I in him, bears fruit in plenty.

Prayer after Communion

Heavenly Father and God of all Creation, we give thanks for the nourishment of your heavenly gifts of the Bread and Fruits of Eternal Spiritual Life. May our earnest participation together in commemoration of Irenaeus of Lyon bring forth favourable blessings upon our lives, our community and your Holy Apostolic Universal Ecclesia.

XIV.XVI – JUNE 29

1.   **Saints Peter and Paul,** Apostles   June 29

Memorial

Entrance Antiphon   Psalm 86: 15 – 16

O Lord, you are a God full of compassion, and gracious, long suffering, and plenteous in mercy and truth. O turn unto me, and have mercy upon me; give thy strength unto thy servant.

Offertory Antiphon

O God and Divine Creator, grant that we may be sustained by the intercession of the blessed Apostles Peter and Paul, that, as through them you gave your Church the foundations of her heavenly office, so through them you may help her to eternal salvation. Through our Lord Jesus Christ, your Son, who lives and reigns with you in the unity of the Holy Spirit, one God, for ever and ever.

Prayer over the Offerings

May God and the Divine Creator accept and sanctify these humble gifts as symbols of the genuine personal offerings we make in commemoration of Apostles Peter and Paul. Through Christ our Light and Saviour.

Communion Antiphon   Mt 16: 16, 18

Peter said to Jesus: You are the Christ, the Son of the living God.
And Jesus replied: You are Peter,
and upon this rock I will build my Church.

Prayer after Communion

Heavenly Father and God of all Creation, we give thanks for the nourishment of your heavenly gifts of the Bread and Fruits of Eternal Spiritual Life. May our earnest participation together in commemoration of Apostles Peter and Paul bring forth favourable blessings upon our lives, our community and your Holy Apostolic Universal Ecclesia.

XIV.XVII – JUNE 30

1. **The First Martyrs of Holy Roman Church** — June 30

Memorial

Entrance Antiphon — Psalm 89: 1

I will sing of God's great love forever; with my mouth I will make your faithfulness known through all generations.

Offertory Antiphon

O God and Divine Creator, who consecrated the abundant first fruits of the Roman Church by the blood of the Martyrs, grant, we pray, that with firm courage we may together draw strength from so great a struggle and ever rejoice at the triumph of faithful love. Through our Lord Jesus Christ, your Son, who lives and reigns with you in the unity of the Holy Spirit, one God, for ever and ever.

Prayer over the Offerings

May God and the Divine Creator accept and sanctify these humble gifts as symbols of the genuine personal offerings we make in commemoration of the First Martyrs of the Church of Rome. Through Christ our Light and Saviour.

Communion Antiphon — Lk 22: 28-30

It is you who have stood by me in my trials; and I confer a kingdom on you, says the Lord, that you may eat and drink at my table in my kingdom.

Prayer after Communion

Heavenly Father and God of all Creation, we give thanks for the nourishment of your heavenly gifts of the Bread and Fruits of Eternal Spiritual Life. May our earnest participation together in commemoration of the First Martyrs of the Church of Rome bring forth favourable blessings upon our lives, our community and your Holy Apostolic Universal Ecclesia.

Title XV: Proper of July

XV.I – JULY 1

1.   **Junípero Serra,** Priest   July 1
                            Memorial

Entrance Antiphon   Psalm 89: 2-4

For I have said, Mercy shall be built up for ever: thy faithfulness shalt thou establish in the very heavens. I have made a covenant with my chosen, I have sworn unto David my servant, Thy seed will I establish for ever, and build up thy throne to all generations. Selah.

Offertory Antiphon

O God and Divine Creator, who by your ineffable mercy have been pleased through the labors of your priest Blessed Junípero Serra to count many American peoples within your Church, grant by his intercession that we may so join our hearts to you in love, as to carry always and everywhere before all people the image of your Only Begotten Son. Who lives and reigns with you in the unity of the Holy Spirit, one God, for ever and ever.

Prayer over the Offerings

May God and the Divine Creator accept and sanctify these humble gifts as symbols of the genuine personal offerings we make in commemoration of Junípero Serra. Through Christ our Light and Saviour.

Prayer after Communion

Heavenly Father and God of all Creation, we give thanks for the nourishment of your heavenly gifts of the Bread and Fruits of Eternal Spiritual Life. May our earnest participation together in commemoration of Junípero Serra bring forth favourable blessings upon our lives, our community and your Holy Apostolic Universal Ecclesia.

XV.II – JULY 3

1.   **Saint Thomas,** Apostle   July 3
                                Feast

Entrance Antiphon   Psalm 118: 28

You are my God, and I confess you; you are my God, and I exalt you; I will thank you, for you became my savior.

Offertory Antiphon

O God and Divine Creator, grant that we may glory in the Feast of the blessed Apostle Thomas, so that we may always be sustained by his intercession and, believing, may have life in the name of Jesus Christ your Son, whom Thomas acknowledged as the Lord. Who lives and reigns with you in the unity of the Holy Spirit, one God, for ever and ever.

Prayer over the Offerings

May God and the Divine Creator accept and sanctify these humble gifts as symbols of the genuine personal offerings we make in commemoration of Thomas the Apostle. Through Christ our Light and Saviour.

Communion Antiphon   Jn 20: 27

Bring your hand and feel the place of the nails, and do not be unbelieving but believing.

Prayer after Communion

Heavenly Father and God of all Creation, we give thanks for the nourishment of your heavenly gifts of the Bread and Fruits of Eternal Spiritual Life. May our earnest participation together in commemoration of Thomas the Apostle bring forth favourable blessings upon our lives, our community and your Holy Apostolic Universal Ecclesia.

XV.III – JULY 4

1. **Elizabeth of Portugal**   July 4

Memorial

Entrance Antiphon   Psalm 89: 13-14

Thou hast a mighty arm: strong is thy hand, and high is thy right hand. Justice and judgment are the habitation of thy throne: mercy and truth shall go before thy face.

Living Testimony: From Franciscan History of Elizabeth of Portugal

The characteristical virtue of St. Elizabeth was a love of peace. Christ, the prince of peace, declares his spirit to be the spirit of humility and meekness; consequently the spirit of peace.

Living Gospel: Elizabeth of Portugal   Elizabeth of Portugal

In humility is perfect freedom.

Offertory Antiphon

O God and Divine Creator, who by , grant that . Through our Lord Jesus Christ, your Son, who lives and reigns with you in the unity of the Holy Spirit, one God, for ever and ever.

Prayer over the Offerings

May God and the Divine Creator accept and sanctify these humble gifts as symbols of the genuine personal offerings we make in commemoration of Elizabeth of Portugal. Through Christ our Light and Saviour.

Prayer after Communion

Heavenly Father and God of all Creation, we give thanks for the nourishment of your heavenly gifts of the Bread and Fruits of Eternal Spiritual Life. May our earnest participation together in commemoration of Elizabeth of Portugal bring forth favourable blessings upon our lives, our community and your Holy Apostolic Universal Ecclesia.

2. **Our Lady of Liberty & Charity** — July 4
Patron of United States of America
Memorial

Entrance Antiphon — Psalm 89: 13-14

Thou hast a mighty arm: strong is thy hand, and high is thy right hand. Justice and judgment are the habitation of thy throne: mercy and truth shall go before thy face.

Offertory Antiphon

O God and Divine Creator of all Rights, Authority and Mercy, grant us through the intercession of our Divine Mother Mary as Our Lady of Liberty and Charity, the continued protection, assistance and prosperity of the American people and the fulfilment of your Divine Mission of unity of all Christians as the Living Body of Christ. Through our Lord Jesus Christ, your Son, who lives and reigns with you in the unity of the Holy Spirit, one God, for ever and ever.

Prayer over the Offerings

May God and the Divine Creator accept and sanctify these humble gifts in the name of our Divine Mother Mary as Our Lady of Liberty and Charity, as symbols of the genuine personal offerings we make in honour and respect of the protection for all of Americans; and in the memory of all patriots who sacrificed their lives for the independence and sovereignty of our people. Through Christ our Light and Saviour.

Prayer after Communion

Heavenly Father and God of all Creation, we give thanks for the nourishment of your heavenly gifts of the Bread and Fruits of Eternal Spiritual Life. May our earnest participation together in commemoration of our Divine Mother Mary as Our Lady of Liberty and Charity bring forth favourable blessings upon our lives, our nation and your Holy Apostolic Universal Ecclesia as one united Christian body.

XV.IV – JULY 5

1. **Anthony Zaccaria,** Priest July 5
Founder of Clerics Regular of Saint Paul (Barnabites)
Memorial

Entrance Antiphon Psalm 89: 15

Blessed are those who have learned to acclaim you, who walk in the light of your presence, O Lord.

Offertory Antiphon

O God and Divine Creator, grant in the spirit of the Apostle Paul that we may pursue the surpassing knowledge of Jesus Christ, for, having learned it, Saint Anthony Zaccaria constantly preached your saving word in the Church. Through our Lord Jesus Christ, your Son, who lives and reigns with you in the unity of the Holy Spirit, one God, for ever and ever.

Prayer over the Offerings

May God and the Divine Creator accept and sanctify these humble gifts as symbols of the genuine personal offerings we make in commemoration of Anthony Zaccaria. Through Christ our Light and Saviour.

Prayer after Communion

Heavenly Father and God of all Creation, we give thanks for the nourishment of your heavenly gifts of the Bread and Fruits of Eternal Spiritual Life. May our earnest participation together in commemoration of Anthony Zaccaria bring forth favourable blessings upon our lives, our community and your Holy Apostolic Universal Ecclesia.

XV.V – JULY 6

1. **Jan Hus** July 6
Founder of Hussite Movement of Universal Ecclesia

Ordinary

Entrance Antiphon — Psalm 90: 2

Before the mountains were born or you brought forth the earth and the world, from everlasting to everlasting you are God.

Living Testimony: Jan Hus

God is my witness that I have never taught or preached that which false witnesses have testified against me. He knows that the great object of all my preaching and writing was to convert men from sin.

Living Gospel: Jan Hus — Jan Hus

All I have written and preached, has been to rescue souls from sin. There can be no turning back. My Lord walked the path of truth and duty, even though it took Him to Calvary. Can I, one of his humble followers, turn back now? To witness to God's truth is more important than life.

Offertory Antiphon

O God and Divine Creator, grant us the courage and fortitude of Jan Hus in honour and respect of the unity of your Christian family as your living and growing Body. Through our Lord Jesus Christ, your Son, who lives and reigns with you in the unity of the Holy Spirit, one God, for ever and ever.

Prayer over the Offerings

May God and the Divine Creator accept and sanctify these humble gifts as symbols of the genuine personal offerings we make in commemoration of Jan Hus. Through Christ our Light and Saviour.

Prayer after Communion

Heavenly Father and God of all Creation, we give thanks for the nourishment of your heavenly gifts of the Bread and Fruits of Eternal Spiritual Life. May our earnest participation together in commemoration of Jan Hus bring forth favourable blessings upon our lives, our community and your Holy Apostolic Universal Ecclesia.

Missale Christus | Proper of Heroes & Saints

2.   **Maria Goretti,** Virgin and Martyr   July 6
Memorial

Entrance Antiphon   Psalm 90: 2

Before the mountains were born or you brought forth the earth and the world, from everlasting to everlasting you are God.

Offertory Antiphon

O God and Divine Creator, author of innocence and lover of chastity, who bestowed the grace of martyrdom on your handmaid, the Virgin Saint Maria Goretti, in her youth, grant, we pray, through her intercession, that, as you gave her a crown for her steadfastness, so we, too, may be firm in obeying your commandments. Through our Lord Jesus Christ, your Son, who lives and reigns with you in the unity of the Holy Spirit, one God, for ever and ever.

Prayer over the Offerings

May God and the Divine Creator accept and sanctify these humble gifts as symbols of the genuine personal offerings we make in commemoration of Maria Goretti. Through Christ our Light and Saviour.

Communion Antiphon   Lk 22: 28-30

It is you who have stood by me in my trials; and I confer a kingdom on you, says the Lord, that you may eat and drink at my table in my kingdom.

Prayer after Communion

Heavenly Father and God of all Creation, we give thanks for the nourishment of your heavenly gifts of the Bread and Fruits of Eternal Spiritual Life. May our earnest participation together in commemoration of Maria Goretti bring forth favourable blessings upon our lives, our community and your Holy Apostolic Universal Ecclesia.

XV.VI – JULY 9

1.   **Augustine Zhao Rong,** Priest, **and Companions,** Martyrs   July 9
Memorial

Entrance Antiphon   Psalm 91: 2

We proclaim to the Lord, You are my refuge and my fortress, my God, in whom We Trust.

Offertory Antiphon

O God and Divine Creator, who in your wonderful

providence have strengthened your Church through the confession of the Martyrs Saint Augustine Zhao and companions, grant that your people, faithful to the mission entrusted to it, may enjoy ever greater freedom and witness to the truth before the world. Through our Lord Jesus Christ, your Son, who lives and reigns with you in the unity of the Holy Spirit, one God, for ever and ever.

Prayer over the Offerings

May God and the Divine Creator accept and sanctify these humble gifts as symbols of the genuine personal offerings we make in commemoration of Augustine Zhao Rong and Companions. Through Christ our Light and Saviour.

Communion Antiphon — Lk 22: 28-30

It is you who have stood by me in my trials; and I confer a kingdom on you, says the Lord, that you may eat and drink at my table in my kingdom.

Prayer after Communion

Heavenly Father and God of all Creation, we give thanks for the nourishment of your heavenly gifts of the Bread and Fruits of Eternal Spiritual Life. May our earnest participation together in commemoration of Augustine Zhao Rong and Companions bring forth favourable blessings upon our lives, our community and your Holy Apostolic Universal Ecclesia.

XV.VII – JULY 11

1. **Benedict of Nursia,** Abbot — July 11
Founder of Benedictine Order
Memorial

Entrance Antiphon — Psalm 91: 5-7

Thou shalt not be afraid for the terror by night; nor for the arrow that flieth by day; Nor for the pestilence that walketh in darkness; nor for the destruction that wasteth at noonday. A thousand shall fall at thy side, and ten thousand at thy right hand; but it shall not come nigh thee.

Offertory Antiphon

O God and Divine Creator, who made the Abbot Saint Benedict an outstanding master in the school of divine service, grant, we pray, that, putting nothing before love of you, we may hasten with a loving heart in the way of your commands. Through our Lord Jesus Christ, your Son, who

Prayer over the Offerings

May God and the Divine Creator accept and sanctify these humble gifts as symbols of the genuine personal offerings we make in commemoration of Benedict of Nursia. Through Christ our Light and Saviour.

Communion Antiphon — Lk 12: 42

This is the steward, faithful and prudent, whom the Lord set over his household to give them their allowance of food at the proper time.

Prayer after Communion

Heavenly Father and God of all Creation, we give thanks for the nourishment of your heavenly gifts of the Bread and Fruits of Eternal Spiritual Life. May our earnest participation together in commemoration of Benedict of Nursia bring forth favourable blessings upon our lives, our community and your Holy Apostolic Universal Ecclesia.

XV.VIII – JULY 13

1. Henry the Exuberant, Holy Roman Emperor — July 13

Memorial

Entrance Antiphon — Psalm 91: 15

When God will call upon me, I will answer him; I will stay true to him in time of trouble, I will be faithful and honour him.

Offertory Antiphon

O God and Divine Creator, whose abundant grace prepared Saint Henry to be raised by you in a wonderful way from the cares of earthly rule to heavenly realms, grant, we pray, through his intercession, that amid the uncertainties of this world we may hasten towards you with minds made pure. Through our Lord Jesus Christ, your Son, who lives and reigns with you in the unity of the Holy Spirit, one God, for ever and ever.

Prayer over the Offerings

May God and the Divine Creator accept and sanctify these humble gifts as symbols of the genuine personal offerings we make in commemoration of Henry the Exuberant. Through Christ our Light and Saviour.

Prayer after Communion

    Heavenly Father and God of all Creation, we give thanks for the nourishment of your heavenly gifts of the Bread and Fruits of Eternal Spiritual Life. May our earnest participation together in commemoration of Henry the Exuberant bring forth favourable blessings upon our lives, our community and your Holy Apostolic Universal Ecclesia.

XV.IX – JULY 15

1.   **Bonaventure,** Bishop and Doctor of the Church   July 15

    Memorial

Entrance Antiphon   Psalm 92: 12

    The righteous will flourish like a palm tree, they will grow like a cedar of Lebanon.

Offertory Antiphon

    O God and Divine Creator, grant, we pray, almighty God, that, just as we celebrate the heavenly birthday of the Bishop Saint Bonaventure, we may benefit from his great learning and constantly imitate the ardor of his charity. Through our Lord Jesus Christ, your Son, who lives and reigns with you in the unity of the Holy Spirit, one God, for ever and ever.

Prayer over the Offerings

    May God and the Divine Creator accept and sanctify these humble gifts as symbols of the genuine personal offerings we make in commemoration of Bonaventure. Through Christ our Light and Saviour.

Communion Antiphon   Psalm 1: 2-3

    One who ponders the Divine maxims of Law of the Lord day and night shall yield fruit in due season.

Prayer after Communion

    Heavenly Father and God of all Creation, we give thanks for the nourishment of your heavenly gifts of the Bread and Fruits of Eternal Spiritual Life. May our earnest participation together in commemoration of Bonaventure bring forth favourable blessings upon our lives, our community and your Holy Apostolic Universal Ecclesia.

XV.X – JULY 16

1.   **Our Lady of Mount Carmel**   July 16
Patron of Arabia (Middle East, Nth Africa, Asia Minor)
Memorial

Entrance Antiphon   Psalm 94:11-12

The Lord knows the thoughts of men, that they are vanity. Blessed are those whom yu have chastened, O Lord, and teach them of thy Maxims of Divine Law.

Offertory Antiphon

O God and Divine Creator, grant us through the intercession of our Divine Mother Mary as Our Lady of Mount Carmel, that all peoples of each generation of the Middle East, North Africa and Asia Minor may come to know your good works and Divine Truth. Through our Lord Jesus Christ, your Son, who lives and reigns with you in the unity of the Holy Spirit, one God, for ever and ever.

Prayer over the Offerings

May God and the Divine Creator accept and sanctify these humble gifts as symbols of the genuine personal offerings we make in commemoration of Our Lady of Mount Carmel. Through Christ our Light and Saviour.

Prayer after Communion

Heavenly Father and God of all Creation, we give thanks for the nourishment of your heavenly gifts of the Bread and Fruits of Eternal Spiritual Life. May our earnest participation together in commemoration of Our Lady of Mount Carmel bring forth favourable blessings upon our lives, our community and your Holy Apostolic Universal Ecclesia.

XV.XI – JULY 18

1.   **Camillus de Lellis,** Priest   July 18
Founder of Clerics Regular, Ministers to the Sick (Camillians)
Memorial

Entrance Antiphon   Psalm 95: 6

Come, let us bow down in worship, let us kneel before the Lord God our Maker.

Offertory Antiphon

O God and Divine Creator, who adorned the Priest Saint

Camillus with a singular grace of charity towards the sick, pour out upon us, by his merits, a spirit of love for you, so that, serving you in our neighbor, we may, at the hour of our death, pass safely over to you. Through our Lord Jesus Christ, your Son, who lives and reigns with you in the unity of the Holy Spirit, one God, for ever and ever.

Prayer over the Offerings

May God and the Divine Creator accept and sanctify these humble gifts as symbols of the genuine personal offerings we make in commemoration of Camillus de Lellis. Through Christ our Light and Saviour.

Prayer after Communion

Heavenly Father and God of all Creation, we give thanks for the nourishment of your heavenly gifts of the Bread and Fruits of Eternal Spiritual Life. May our earnest participation together in commemoration of Camillus de Lellis bring forth favourable blessings upon our lives, our community and your Holy Apostolic Universal Ecclesia.

XV.XII – JULY 20

1. **Apollinaris of Ravenna,** Bishop and Martyr *Memorial* — July 20

Entrance Antiphon — Psalm 97: 3

The Igniting Fire of true Divine Revelation goes before him and consumes every adversary on every side.

Offertory Antiphon

O God and Divine Creator, direct your faithful in the way of eternal salvation, which the Bishop Saint Apollinaris showed by his teaching and martyrdom, and grant, through his intercession, that we may so persevere in keeping your commandments as to merit being crowned with him. Through our Lord Jesus Christ, your Son, who lives and reigns with you in the unity of the Holy Spirit, one God, for ever and ever.

Prayer over the Offerings

May God and the Divine Creator accept and sanctify these humble gifts as symbols of the genuine personal offerings we make in commemoration of Apollinaris of Ravenna. Through Christ our Light and Saviour.

Missale Christus | Proper of Heroes & Saints

Communion Antiphon — Lk 22: 28-30

It is you who have stood by me in my trials; and I confer a kingdom on you, says the Lord, that you may eat and drink at my table in my kingdom.

Prayer after Communion

Heavenly Father and God of all Creation, we give thanks for the nourishment of your heavenly gifts of the Bread and Fruits of Eternal Spiritual Life. May our earnest participation together in commemoration of Apollinaris of Ravenna bring forth favourable blessings upon our lives, our community and your Holy Apostolic Universal Ecclesia.

XV.XIII – JULY 21

1. Lawrence of Brindisi, Priest and Doctor of the Church — July 21

Memorial

Entrance Antiphon — Psalm 97: 6

The heavens proclaim his righteousness, and all the peoples see his glory.

Offertory Antiphon

O God and Divine Creator, who for the glory of your name and the salvation of souls bestowed on the Priest Saint Lawrence of Brindisi a spirit of counsel and fortitude, grant, we pray, that in the same spirit, we may know what must be done and, through his intercession, bring it to completion. Through our Lord Jesus Christ, your Son, who lives and reigns with you in the unity of the Holy Spirit, one God, for ever and ever.

Prayer over the Offerings

May God and the Divine Creator accept and sanctify these humble gifts as symbols of the genuine personal offerings we make in commemoration of Lawrence of Brindisi. Through Christ our Light and Saviour.

Communion Antiphon — Psalm 1: 2-3

One who ponders the Divine maxims of Law of the Lord day and night shall yield fruit in due season.

Prayer after Communion

Heavenly Father and God of all Creation, we give thanks for the nourishment of your heavenly gifts of the Bread and Fruits of Eternal Spiritual Life. May our earnest

participation together in commemoration of Lawrence of Brindisi bring forth favourable blessings upon our lives, our community and your Holy Apostolic Universal Ecclesia.

XV.XIV– JULY 22

1. **Mary Magdalene** — July 22
Memorial

Entrance Antiphon — Psalm 97: 11

The Light of your New Covenant is shed upon the righteous and joy on the upright in heart.

Living Testimony: — Jn 20: 17

The Lord said to Mary Magdalene: Go to my brothers and tell them: I am going to my Father and your Father, to my God and your God.

Offertory Antiphon

O God and Divine Creator, whose Only Begotten Son entrusted Mary Magdalene before all others with announcing the great joy of the Resurrection, grant, we pray, that through her intercession and example we may proclaim the living Christ and come to see him reigning in your glory. Who lives and reigns with you in the unity of the Holy Spirit, one God, for ever and ever.

Prayer over the Offerings

May God and the Divine Creator accept and sanctify these humble gifts as symbols of the genuine personal offerings we make in commemoration of Mary Magdalene. Through Christ our Light and Saviour.

Communion Antiphon — 2 Cor 5: 14, 15

The love of Christ impels us, so that those who live may live no longer for themselves, but for him who died for them and was raised.

Prayer after Communion

Heavenly Father and God of all Creation, we give thanks for the nourishment of your heavenly gifts of the Bread and Fruits of Eternal Spiritual Life. May our earnest participation together in commemoration of Mary Magdalene bring forth favourable blessings upon our lives, our community and your Holy Apostolic Universal Ecclesia.

XV.XV – JULY 23

1.   **Bridget of Sweden,** Religious   *July 23*
Founder of Order of Most Holy Savior (Bridgettines)
Memorial

Entrance Antiphon   *Psalm 98: 2*

> The Lord has made his Testament known and revealed the Light of his righteousness to the nations.

Offertory Antiphon

> O God and Divine Creator, who guided Saint Bridget of Sweden along different paths of life and wondrously taught her the wisdom of the Cross as she contemplated the Passion of your Son, grant us, we pray, that, walking worthily in our vocation, we may seek you in all things. Through our Lord Jesus Christ, your Son, who lives and reigns with you in the unity of the Holy Spirit, one God, for ever and ever.

Prayer over the Offerings

> May God and the Divine Creator accept and sanctify these humble gifts as symbols of the genuine personal offerings we make in commemoration of Bridget of Sweden. Through Christ our Light and Saviour.

Prayer after Communion

> Heavenly Father and God of all Creation, we give thanks for the nourishment of your heavenly gifts of the Bread and Fruits of Eternal Spiritual Life. May our earnest participation together in commemoration of Bridget of Sweden bring forth favourable blessings upon our lives, our community and your Holy Apostolic Universal Ecclesia.

XV.XVI – JULY 24

1.   **Thomas a Kempis**   *July 24*
Memorial

Entrance Antiphon   *Psalm 98: 9*

> Let them sing before the Lord, for he has come to judge and forgive the earth. He judges the world with love, mercy and compassion and the peoples with fairness and equality.

Title XV: Proper of July

Living Testimony: Thomas a Kempis   Thomas a Kempis

> Nothing is sweeter than love, nothing more courageous, nothing higher, nothing wider, nothing more pleasant, nothing fuller nor better in heaven and earth; because love is born of God, and cannot rest but in God, above all created things.

Living Gospel: Thomas a Kempis

> Be not angry that you cannot make others as you wish them to be, since you cannot make yourself as you wish to be. First keep the peace within yourself, then you can also bring peace to others.

Offertory Antiphon

> O God and Divine Creator, who blessed Thomas a Kempis with the wisdom and insight of the Holy Spirit to help prepare your people for the difficult challenges of growing and evolving to unity, grant us the humility and respect to see we are all one common family of brothers and sisters in Christ. Through our Lord Jesus Christ, your Son, who lives and reigns with you in the unity of the Holy Spirit, one God, for ever and ever.

Prayer over the Offerings

> May God and the Divine Creator accept and sanctify these humble gifts as symbols of the genuine personal offerings we make in commemoration of Thomas a Kempis. Through Christ our Light and Saviour.

Communion Antiphon   John 3:16

> For God so loved the world, that he gave his only Son, that whoever believes in him should not perish but have eternal life.

Prayer after Communion

> Heavenly Father and God of all Creation, we give thanks for the nourishment of your heavenly gifts of the Bread and Fruits of Eternal Spiritual Life. May our earnest participation together in commemoration of Thomas a Kempis bring forth favourable blessings upon our lives, our community and your Holy Apostolic Universal Ecclesia.

2.   **Sharbel Makhluf,** Priest   July 24
Memorial

Entrance Antiphon   Psalm 98: 9

> Let them sing before the Lord, for he has come to judge

and forgive the earth. He judges the world with love, mercy and compassion and the peoples with fairness and equality.

Living Testimony: Sharbel Makhluf

God is love. God is truth. God is the true love. The world of God is the world of love; it is the world of truth, and there is no truth outside love. Man is not fulfilled except through love, and he does not reach the truth except in the world of God.

Living Gospel: Sharbel Makhluf

The family is the rope that binds humanity together through time, binds generations through history, so that humanity may grow and increase; and if this rope which binds humanity together was broken, and humanity gets separated from its history, it would be no more than lost generations which have neither history nor identity. The family is what gives people their human identity and impresses the image of God in them. The family is what preserves the memory of humanity.

Offertory Antiphon

O God and Divine Creator, who called the Priest Saint Sharbel Makhluf to the solitary combat of the desert and imbued him with all manner of devotion, grant us, we pray, that, being made imitators of the Lord's Passion, we may merit to be co-heirs of his Kingdom. Who lives and reigns with you in the unity of the Holy Spirit, one God, for ever and ever.

Prayer over the Offerings

May God and the Divine Creator accept and sanctify these humble gifts as symbols of the genuine personal offerings we make in commemoration of Sharbel Makhluf. Through Christ our Light and Saviour.

Prayer after Communion

Heavenly Father and God of all Creation, we give thanks for the nourishment of your heavenly gifts of the Bread and Fruits of Eternal Spiritual Life. May our earnest participation together in commemoration of Sharbel Makhluf bring forth favourable blessings upon our lives, our community and your Holy Apostolic Universal Ecclesia.

XV.XVII – JULY 25

1. **James the Apostle** July 25
Feast

Entrance Antiphon Psalm 99: 3

Let them praise your great and awesome name for it has always been holy.

Offertory Antiphon

O God and Divine Creator, who consecrated the first fruits of your Apostles by the blood of Saint James, grant, we pray, that your Church may be strengthened by his confession of faith and constantly sustained by his protection. Through our Lord Jesus Christ, your Son, who lives and reigns with you in the unity of the Holy Spirit, one God, for ever and ever.

Prayer over the Offerings

O God and Divine Creator, accept and sanctify these humble gifts as symbols of the genuine personal offerings we make in commemoration of James the Apostle. Through Christ our Light and Saviour.

Communion Antiphon

They drank the chalice of the Lord, and became Children of God.

Prayer after Communion

Heavenly Father and God of all Creation, we give thanks for the nourishment of your heavenly gifts of the Bread and Fruits of Eternal Spiritual Life. May our earnest participation together in commemoration of James the Apostle bring forth favourable blessings upon our lives, our community and your Holy Apostolic Universal Ecclesia.

XV.XVIII – JULY 26

1. **Joachim and Anne,** July 26
Parents of the Blessed Virgin Mary
Memorial

Entrance Antiphon Psalm 100: 5

The Divine Revelation of the Lord is kindness and mercy and his love endures forever; his faithfulness continues through all generations.

Missale Christus | Proper of Heroes & Saints

Living Testimony: — Sir 44: 1, 25

Let us praise Joachim and Anne, to whom, in their generation, the Lord gave him who was a blessing for all the nations.

Offertory Antiphon

O God and Divine Creator, who bestowed on Saints Joachim and Anne this grace, that of them should be born the Mother of your incarnate Son, grant, through the prayers of both, that we may attain the salvation you have promised to your people. Through our Lord Jesus Christ, your Son, who lives and reigns with you in the unity of the Holy Spirit, one God, for ever and ever.

Prayer over the Offerings

May God and the Divine Creator accept and sanctify these humble gifts as symbols of the genuine personal offerings we make in commemoration of Saints Joachim and Anne. Through Christ our Light and Saviour.

Communion Antiphon — Ps 24 (23): 5

They received blessings from the Lord and mercy from God their Savior.

Prayer after Communion

Heavenly Father and God of all Creation, we give thanks for the nourishment of your heavenly gifts of the Bread and Fruits of Eternal Spiritual Life. May our earnest participation together in commemoration of Saints Joachim and Anne bring forth favourable blessings upon our lives, our community and your Holy Apostolic Universal Ecclesia.

XV.XIX – JULY 29

1. **Saint Martha** — July 29

Memorial

Entrance Antiphon — Psalm 101: 7

No one who practices the deceit of nihilists will dwell in my house says the Lord; no one who speaks falsely in my name will stand in my presence.

Living Testimony: — Lk 10: 38

Jesus entered a village, where a woman named Martha welcomed him into her home.

Offertory Antiphon

O God and Divine Creator, whose Son was pleased to be welcomed in Saint Martha's house as a guest, grant, we pray, that through her intercession, serving Christ faithfully in our brothers and sisters, we may merit to be received by you in the halls of heaven. Through our Lord Jesus Christ, your Son, who lives and reigns with you in the unity of the Holy Spirit, one God, for ever and ever.

Prayer over the Offerings

May God and the Divine Creator accept and sanctify these humble gifts as symbols of the genuine personal offerings we make in commemoration of Saint Martha. Through Christ our Light and Saviour.

Communion Antiphon — Jn 11: 27

Martha said to Jesus: You are the Christ, the Son of God, who is coming into this world.

Prayer after Communion

Heavenly Father and God of all Creation, we give thanks for the nourishment of your heavenly gifts of the Bread and Fruits of Eternal Spiritual Life. May our earnest participation together in commemoration of Saint Martha bring forth favourable blessings upon our lives, our community and your Holy Apostolic Universal Ecclesia.

XV.XX – JULY 30

1. Peter Chrysologus, Bishop and Doctor of the Church — July 30
Memorial

Entrance Antiphon — Psalm 102: 15

The nations who respect the rule of law will honor the Light of the Testament of the Lord, all the true leaders of the earth will revere your glory.

Offertory Antiphon

O God and Divine Creator, who made the Bishop Saint Peter Chrysologus an outstanding preacher of your incarnate Word, grant, through his intercession, that we may constantly ponder in our hearts the mysteries of your salvation and faithfully express them in what we do. Through our Lord Jesus Christ, your Son, who lives and reigns with you in the unity of the Holy Spirit, one God, for ever and ever.

Prayer over the Offerings

May God and the Divine Creator accept and sanctify these humble gifts as symbols of the genuine personal offerings we make in commemoration of Peter Chrysologus. Through Christ our Light and Saviour.

Communion Antiphon *Psalm 1: 2-3*

One who ponders the Divine maxims of Law of the Lord day and night shall yield fruit in due season.

Prayer after Communion

Heavenly Father and God of all Creation, we give thanks for the nourishment of your heavenly gifts of the Bread and Fruits of Eternal Spiritual Life. May our earnest participation together in commemoration of Peter Chrysologus bring forth favourable blessings upon our lives, our community and your Holy Apostolic Universal Ecclesia.

XV.XXI – JULY 31

1. Ignatius of Loyola, Priest — July 31
Co-Founder of Society of Jesus (Jesuits)
Memorial

Entrance Antiphon *Psalm 102: 18*

Let knowledge of your Revelations and Testament be written for future generations, that those not yet born may praise the Divine Love, Mercy and Compassion of the Lord.

Living Testimony: Ignatius of Loyola

Take, Lord, and receive all my liberty, my memory, my understanding, and my entire will, All I have and call my own. You have given all to me. To you, Lord, I return it. Everything is yours; do with it what you will. Give me only your love and your grace, that is enough for me.

Living Gospel: Ignatius of Loyola *Ignatius of Loyola*

God freely created us so that we might know, love, and serve him in this life and be happy with him forever. God's purpose in creating us is to draw forth from us a response of love and service here on earth, so that we may attain our goal of everlasting happiness with him in heaven. All the things in this world are gifts of God, created for us, to be the means by which we can come to know him better, love him more surely, and serve him more faithfully.

Offertory Antiphon

O God and Divine Creator, who raised up Saint Ignatius of Loyola in your Church to further the greater glory of your name, grant that by his help we may imitate him in fighting the good fight on earth and merit to receive with him a crown in heaven. Through our Lord Jesus Christ, your Son, who lives and reigns with you in the unity of the Holy Spirit, one God, for ever and ever.

Prayer over the Offerings

May God and the Divine Creator accept and sanctify these humble gifts as symbols of the genuine personal offerings we make in commemoration of Ignatius of Loyola.
Through Christ our Light and Saviour.

Communion Antiphon

Lk 12: 49

Thus says the Lord: I have come to cast fire on the earth, and how I wish that it were kindled!

Prayer after Communion

Heavenly Father and God of all Creation, we give thanks for the nourishment of your heavenly gifts of the Bread and Fruits of Eternal Spiritual Life. May our earnest participation together in commemoration of Ignatius of Loyola bring forth favourable blessings upon our lives, our community and your Holy Apostolic Universal Ecclesia.

Title XVI: Proper of August

XVI.I – AUGUST 1

1.   **Alphonsus Liguori,** Bishop and Doctor of the Church   August 1

Memorial

Entrance Antiphon   Psalm 102: 19-20

The Lord has returned as promised from his heavenly sanctuary and has reviewed the state of the earth, to answer the the groans of prisoners and command the release of all those condemned to death.

Offertory Antiphon

O God and Divine Creator, who constantly raise up in your Church new examples of virtue, grant that we may follow so closely in the footsteps of the Bishop Saint Alphonsus in his zeal for souls as to attain the same rewards that are his in heaven. Through our Lord Jesus Christ, your Son, who lives and reigns with you in the unity of the Holy Spirit, one God, for ever and ever.

Prayer over the Offerings

May God and the Divine Creator accept and sanctify these humble gifts as symbols of the genuine personal offerings we make in commemoration of Alphonsus Liguori. Through Christ our Light and Saviour.

Communion Antiphon   Psalm 1: 2-3

One who ponders the Divine maxims of Law of the Lord day and night shall yield fruit in due season.

Prayer after Communion

Heavenly Father and God of all Creation, we give thanks for the nourishment of your heavenly gifts of the Bread and Fruits of Eternal Spiritual Life. May our earnest participation together in commemoration of Alphonsus Liguori bring forth favourable blessings upon our lives, our community and your Holy Apostolic Universal Ecclesia.

XVI.II – AUGUST 2

1.   **Eusebius of Vercelli,** Bishop   August 2

Memorial

Entrance Antiphon   Psalm 102: 25-26

In the beginning God laid the foundations of the earth, and the heavens are the work of his Divine hands. Those who refuse to believe will perish, but your Divine Truth remains; as the deceptions of nihilists will all wear out like old garments.

Offertory Antiphon

O God and Divine Creator, grant us the fortitute to imitate the constancy of Saint Eusebius in affirming the divinity of your Son, so that, by preserving the faith he taught as your Bishop, we may merit a share in the very life of your Son. Who lives and reigns with you in the unity of the Holy Spirit, one God, for ever and ever.

Prayer over the Offerings

May God and the Divine Creator accept and sanctify these humble gifts as symbols of the genuine personal offerings we make in commemoration of Eusebius of Vercelli. Through Christ our Light and Saviour.

Prayer after Communion

Heavenly Father and God of all Creation, we give thanks for the nourishment of your heavenly gifts of the Bread and Fruits of Eternal Spiritual Life. May our earnest participation together in commemoration of Eusebius of Vercelli bring forth favourable blessings upon our lives, our community and your Holy Apostolic Universal Ecclesia.

XVI.III – AUGUST 4

1.   **John Vianney,** Priest   August 4

Memorial

Entrance Antiphon   Psalm 103: 11-12

For as high as the heavens are above the earth, so great is his love for those who respect him; as far as the east is from the west, so far has he removed our transgressions from us.

Offertory Antiphon

O God and Divine Creator, who made the Priest Saint John Vianney wonderful in his pastoral zeal, grant, we pray, that through his intercession and example we may in charity win brothers and sisters for Christ and attain with them eternal glory. Through our Lord Jesus Christ, your Son, who lives and reigns with you in the unity of the Holy Spirit, one God, for ever and ever.

Prayer over the Offerings

May God and the Divine Creator accept and sanctify these humble gifts as symbols of the genuine personal offerings

Title XVI: Proper of August

we make in commemoration of John Vianney. Through Christ our Light and Saviour.

Prayer after Communion

Heavenly Father and God of all Creation, we give thanks for the nourishment of your heavenly gifts of the Bread and Fruits of Eternal Spiritual Life. May our earnest participation together in commemoration of John Vianney bring forth favourable blessings upon our lives, our community and your Holy Apostolic Universal Ecclesia.

XVI.IV – AUGUST 7

1. **Sixtus II, Pope, and Companions, Martyrs** August 7
Memorial

Entrance Antiphon Psalm 103: 19

The Lord has established all domains are part of One Heaven, and his kingdom rules over all.

Offertory Antiphon

O God and Divine Creator, may the power of the Holy Spirit make us docile in believing the faith and courageous in confessing it, just as you granted Saint Sixtus and his companions that they might lay down their lives for the sake of your word and in witness to Jesus. Who lives and reigns with you in the unity of the Holy Spirit, one God, for ever and ever.

Prayer over the Offerings

May God and the Divine Creator accept and sanctify these humble gifts as symbols of the genuine personal offerings we make in commemoration of Saint Sixtus and his companions. Through Christ our Light and Saviour.

Communion Antiphon Lk 22: 28-30

It is you who have stood by me in my trials; and I confer a kingdom on you, says the Lord, that you may eat and drink at my table in my kingdom.

Prayer after Communion

Heavenly Father and God of all Creation, we give thanks for the nourishment of your heavenly gifts of the Bread and Fruits of Eternal Spiritual Life. May our earnest participation together in commemoration of Saint Sixtus and his companions bring forth favourable blessings upon our lives, our community and your Holy Apostolic

Universal Ecclesia.

XVI.V – AUGUST 8

1. **Dominic de Guzmán,** Priest August 8
Founder of Dominican Order
Memorial

Entrance Antiphon — Psalm 104: 3

The Lord wraps himself in Light as with a garment; he stretches out the heavens like a tent.

Offertory Antiphon

O God and Divine Creator, may Saint Dominic come to the help of your Church by his merits and teaching, may he, who was an outstanding preacher of your truth, be a devoted intercessor on our behalf. Through our Lord Jesus Christ, your Son, who lives and reigns with you in the unity of the Holy Spirit, one God, for ever and ever.

Prayer over the Offerings

May God and the Divine Creator accept and sanctify these humble gifts as symbols of the genuine personal offerings we make in commemoration of Dominic de Guzmán. Through Christ our Light and Saviour.

Communion Antiphon — Lk 12: 42

This is the steward, faithful and prudent,

whom the Lord set over his household

to give them their allowance of food at the proper time.

Prayer after Communion

Heavenly Father and God of all Creation, we give thanks for the nourishment of your heavenly gifts of the Bread and Fruits of Eternal Spiritual Life. May our earnest participation together in commemoration of Dominic de Guzmán bring forth favourable blessings upon our lives, our community and your Holy Apostolic Universal Ecclesia.

XVI.VI – AUGUST 9

1. **Saint Teresa Benedicta of the Cross,** Virgin and Martyr August 9
Memorial

Entrance Antiphon — Psalm 104: 4-5

Title XVI: Proper of August

The Lord makes the southern spirit his messenger, the flames of revelation his servant. He set the earth on its new foundations; that can never be moved.

Offertory Antiphon

O God and Divine Creator, who brought the Martyr Saint Teresa Benedicta of the Cross to know your crucified Son and to imitate him even until death, grant, through her intercession, that the whole human race may acknowledge Christ as its Savior and through him come to behold you for eternity. Who lives and reigns with you in the unity of the Holy Spirit, one God, for ever and ever.

Prayer over the Offerings

May God and the Divine Creator accept and sanctify these humble gifts as symbols of the genuine personal offerings we make in commemoration of Teresa Benedicta of the Cross. Through Christ our Light and Saviour.

Communion Antiphon Lk 22: 28-30

It is you who have stood by me in my trials; and I confer a kingdom on you, says the Lord, that you may eat and drink at my table in my kingdom.

Prayer after Communion

Heavenly Father and God of all Creation, we give thanks for the nourishment of your heavenly gifts of the Bread and Fruits of Eternal Spiritual Life. May our earnest participation together in commemoration of Teresa Benedicta of the Cross bring forth favourable blessings upon our lives, our community and your Holy Apostolic Universal Ecclesia.

XVI.VII – AUGUST 10

1. **Lawrence of Rome,** Deacon and Martyr August 10

Feast

Entrance Antiphon Psalm 104: 24-25

O Lord, how manifold are thy works! in wisdom hast thou made them all: the earth is full of thy riches. So is this great and wide sea, wherein are things creeping innumerable, both small and great beasts.

Offertory Antiphon

O God and Divine Creator, giver of that ardor of love for you by which Saint Lawrence was outstandingly faithful in service and glorious in martyrdom, grant that we may love what he loved and put into practice what he taught. Through our Lord Jesus Christ, your Son, who lives and reigns with you in the unity of the Holy Spirit, one God, for ever and ever.

Prayer over the Offerings

May God and the Divine Creator accept and sanctify these humble gifts as symbols of the genuine personal offerings we make in commemoration of Lawrence of Rome. Through Christ our Light and Saviour.

Communion Antiphon
Jn 12: 26

Whoever serves me must follow me and where I am there also will my servant be, says the Lord.

Prayer after Communion

Heavenly Father and God of all Creation, we give thanks for the nourishment of your heavenly gifts of the Bread and Fruits of Eternal Spiritual Life. May our earnest participation together in commemoration of Lawrence of Rome bring forth favourable blessings upon our lives, our community and your Holy Apostolic Universal Ecclesia.

XVI.VIII – AUGUST 11

1. **Clare of Assisi,** Virgin *August 11*
Founder of of the Order of Poor Ladies and the Monastic Order for Women in the Franciscan Order

Memorial

Entrance Antiphon
Psalm 104: 30

Lord when you send your Spirit, a new world in your image is created, and you renew the face of the earth.

Offertory Antiphon

O God and Divine Creator, who in your mercy led Saint Clare to a love of poverty, grant, through her intercession, that, following Christ in poverty of spirit, we may merit to contemplate you one day in the heavenly Kingdom. Through our Lord Jesus Christ, your Son, who lives and reigns with you in the unity of the Holy Spirit, one God, for ever and ever.

Prayer over the Offerings

May God and the Divine Creator accept and sanctify these humble gifts as symbols of the genuine personal offerings

we make in commemoration of Clare of Assisi. Through Christ our Light and Saviour.

Communion Antiphon — 1 Peter 1:15

But as he who called you is holy, you also be holy in all your conduct.

Prayer after Communion

Heavenly Father and God of all Creation, we give thanks for the nourishment of your heavenly gifts of the Bread and Fruits of Eternal Spiritual Life. May our earnest participation together in commemoration of Clare of Assisi bring forth favourable blessings upon our lives, our community and your Holy Apostolic Universal Ecclesia.

XVI.IX – AUGUST 12

1. **Jane Frances de Chantal,** Religious — August 12
Founder of Order of the Visitation of Mary
Memorial

Entrance Antiphon — Psalm 105: 3

Glory in his holy name; let the hearts of those who seek the return of the Lord rejoice!

Living Testimony: Jane Frances de Chantal

To be faithful, we must live simply. Then being free from attachments, we are possessed by nothing. We live in such absolute openness to Divine Love that whatever pleases God becomes our heart's desire.

Living Gospel: Jane Frances de Chantal — Jane Frances de Chantal

May all our actions, words, thoughts, and spirit be centered in God, on God, and for God! Let us keep our passions well-disciplined and our spirit pure and faithful. Fidelity to our way of life will help us keep our thoughts centered on God. Then our words will be an inspiration to family, friends, and acquaintances.

Offertory Antiphon

O God and Divine Creator, who made Saint Jane Frances de Chantal radiant with outstanding merits in different walks of life, grant us, through her intercession, that, walking faithfully in our vocation, we may constantly be examples of shining light. Through our Lord Jesus Christ, your Son, who lives and reigns with you in the unity of the Holy Spirit, one God, for ever and ever.

Missale Christus | Proper of Heroes & Saints

Prayer over the Offerings

May God and the Divine Creator accept and sanctify these humble gifts as symbols of the genuine personal offerings we make in commemoration of Jane Frances de Chantal. Through Christ our Light and Saviour.

Prayer after Communion

Heavenly Father and God of all Creation, we give thanks for the nourishment of your heavenly gifts of the Bread and Fruits of Eternal Spiritual Life. May our earnest participation together in commemoration of Jane Frances de Chantal bring forth favourable blessings upon our lives, our community and your Holy Apostolic Universal Ecclesia.

---

2. Florence Nightingale
Ordinary — August 12

Entrance Antiphon — Psalm 105: 3

Glory in his holy name; let the hearts of those who seek the return of the Lord rejoice!

Living Testimony: Florence Nightingale

Mankind must make heaven (on earth) before we can 'go to heaven' (as the phrase is), in this world as in any other.

Living Gospel: Florence Nightingale — Florence Nightingale

It is often thought that medicine is the curative process. It is no such thing; medicine is the surgery of functions, as surgery proper is that of limbs and organs. Neither can do anything but remove obstructions; neither can cure; nature alone cures. Surgery removes the bullet out of the limb, which is an obstruction to cure, but nature heals the wound.

Offertory Antiphon

O God and Divine Creator, who blessed Florence Nightingale with a heart of Divine Compassion and the mind of a soldier, grant us the strength of conviction to step into places of genuine need, even if danger surrounds us. Through our Lord Jesus Christ, your Son, who lives and reigns with you in the unity of the Holy Spirit, one God, for ever and ever.

Prayer over the Offerings

O God and Divine Creator, accept and sanctify these humble gifts as symbols of the genuine personal offerings we make in commemoration of Florence Nightingale.

Through Christ our Light and Saviour.

Prayer after Communion

Heavenly Father and God of all Creation, we give thanks for the nourishment of your heavenly gifts of the Bread and Fruits of Eternal Spiritual Life. May our earnest participation together in commemoration of Florence Nightingale bring forth favourable blessings upon our lives, our community and your Holy Apostolic Universal Ecclesia.

XVI.X – AUGUST 13

1. **Saints Pontian,** Pope, **and Hippolytus,** Priest, Martyrs *August 13*
Memorial

Entrance Antiphon *Psalm 105: 4-5*

Look to the Lord and his strength; but seek always his Divine Words. Remember the wonders he has done, his revelations, and the wisdom he pronounced.

Offertory Antiphon

O God and Divine Creator, may the precious long-suffering of the just, bring us a great increase of love for you and always prompt in our hearts constancy in the holy faith. Through our Lord Jesus Christ, your Son, who lives and reigns with you in the unity of the Holy Spirit, one God, for ever and ever.

Prayer over the Offerings

May God and the Divine Creator accept and sanctify these humble gifts as symbols of the genuine personal offerings we make in commemoration of Saints Pontian and Hippolytus. Through Christ our Light and Saviour.

Communion Antiphon *Lk 22: 28-30*

It is you who have stood by me in my trials; and I confer a kingdom on you, says the Lord, that you may eat and drink at my table in my kingdom.

Prayer after Communion

Heavenly Father and God of all Creation, we give thanks for the nourishment of your heavenly gifts of the Bread and Fruits of Eternal Spiritual Life. May our earnest participation together in commemoration of Saints Pontian and Hippolytus bring forth favourable blessings upon our lives, our community and your Holy Apostolic

Universal Ecclesia.

XVI.XI – AUGUST 14

1.   **Maximilian Kolbe,** Priest and Martyr   August 14
Memorial

Entrance Antiphon   Psalm 105: 8

The Lord shall remember his covenant forever, the words he has Testified in Trust, shall be for a thousand generations.

Offertory Antiphon

O God and Divine Creator, who filled the Priest and Martyr Saint Maximilian Kolbe with a burning love for the Immaculate Virgin Mary and with zeal for souls and love of neighbor, graciously grant, through his intercession, that, striving for your glory by eagerly serving others, we may be conformed, even until death, to your Son. Who lives and reigns with you in the unity of the Holy Spirit, one God, for ever and ever.

Prayer over the Offerings

May God and the Divine Creator accept and sanctify these humble gifts as symbols of the genuine personal offerings we make in commemoration of Maximilian Kolbe. Through Christ our Light and Saviour.

Communion Antiphon   Jn 15: 13

Greater love has no one than to lay down his life for his friends, says the Lord.

Prayer after Communion

Heavenly Father and God of all Creation, we give thanks for the nourishment of your heavenly gifts of the Bread and Fruits of Eternal Spiritual Life. May our earnest participation together in commemoration of Maximilian Kolbe bring forth favourable blessings upon our lives, our community and your Holy Apostolic Universal Ecclesia.

XVI.XII – AUGUST 16

1.   **Stephen of Hungary**   August 16
Memorial

Entrance Antiphon   Psalm 105: 42

The Lord honours all his holy promises given even unto

Title XVI: Proper of August

the times of his servant Abraham.

Offertory Antiphon

O God and Divine Creator, grant your Church, we pray, almighty God, that she may have Saint Stephen of Hungary, who fostered her growth while a king on earth, as her glorious defender in heaven. Through our Lord Jesus Christ, your Son, who lives and reigns with you in the unity of the Holy Spirit, one God, for ever and ever.

Prayer over the Offerings

May God and the Divine Creator accept and sanctify these humble gifts as symbols of the genuine personal offerings we make in commemoration of Stephen of Hungary. Through Christ our Light and Saviour.

Prayer after Communion

Heavenly Father and God of all Creation, we give thanks for the nourishment of your heavenly gifts of the Bread and Fruits of Eternal Spiritual Life. May our earnest participation together in commemoration of Stephen of Hungary bring forth favourable blessings upon our lives, our community and your Holy Apostolic Universal Ecclesia.

XVI.XIII – AUGUST 19

1.   **John Eudes,** Priest   August 19

Memorial

Entrance Antiphon   Psalm 107: 1-2

O give thanks unto the Lord, for he is good: for his mercy endureth for ever. Let the redeemed of the Lord say so, whom he hath redeemed from the hand of the enemy;

Offertory Antiphon

O God, who wonderfully chose the Priest Saint John Eudes to proclaim the unfathomable riches of Christ, grant us, by his example and teachings, that, growing in knowledge of you, we may live faithfully by the light of the Gospel. Through our Lord Jesus Christ, your Son, who lives and reigns with you in the unity of the Holy Spirit, one God, for ever and ever.

Prayer over the Offerings

May God and the Divine Creator accept and sanctify these humble gifts as symbols of the genuine personal offerings

Missale Christus | Proper of Heroes & Saints

we make in commemoration of John Eudes. Through Christ our Light and Saviour.

Prayer after Communion

Heavenly Father and God of all Creation, we give thanks for the nourishment of your heavenly gifts of the Bread and Fruits of Eternal Spiritual Life. May our earnest participation together in commemoration of John Eudes bring forth favourable blessings upon our lives, our community and your Holy Apostolic Universal Ecclesia.

XVI.XIV – AUGUST 20

1. **Bernard of Clairvaux,** Abbot and Doctor of the Church — August 20
Founder of Order of Cistercians (Bernadines)
Memorial

Entrance Antiphon — Psalm 107: 8-9

Let us give thanks to the Lord for his unfailing love and sacred gifts, for he satisfies the thirsty and fills the hungry with good things.

Offertory Antiphon

O God and Divine Creator, who made of the Abbot Saint Bernard a man consumed with zeal for your house and a light shining and burning in your Church, grant, through his intercession, that we may be on fire with the same spirit and walk always as children of light. Through our Lord Jesus Christ, your Son, who lives and reigns with you in the unity of the Holy Spirit, one God, for ever and ever.

Prayer over the Offerings

May God and the Divine Creator accept and sanctify these humble gifts as symbols of the genuine personal offerings we make in commemoration of Bernard of Clairvaux. Through Christ our Light and Saviour.

Communion Antiphon — Jn 15: 9

As the Father loves me, so I also love you; remain in my love, says the Lord.

Prayer after Communion

Heavenly Father and God of all Creation, we give thanks for the nourishment of your heavenly gifts of the Bread and Fruits of Eternal Spiritual Life. May our earnest participation together in commemoration of Bernard of Clairvaux bring forth favourable blessings upon our lives, our community and your Holy Apostolic Universal

Ecclesia.

XVI.XV – AUGUST 21

1.

Pius X, Pope
Memorial

August 21

Entrance Antiphon — Psalm 107: 42-43

The upright see and rejoice, but all the deliberately ignorance blind their eyes and fill their ears. Whoever is wise, let them heed the things God has revealed and consider the great love of the Lord.

Offertory Antiphon

O God and Divine Creator, who to safeguard the faith and to restore all things in Christ, filled Pope Saint Pius the Tenth with heavenly wisdom and apostolic fortitude, graciously grant that, following his teaching and example, we may gain an eternal prize. Through our Lord Jesus Christ, your Son, who lives and reigns with you in the unity of the Holy Spirit, one God, for ever and ever.

Prayer over the Offerings

May God and the Divine Creator accept and sanctify these humble gifts as symbols of the genuine personal offerings we make in commemoration of Saint Pius X. Through Christ our Light and Saviour.

Communion Antiphon — Jn 10: 11

The Good Shepherd did sacrifice his own life for his flock.

Prayer after Communion

Heavenly Father and God of all Creation, we give thanks for the nourishment of your heavenly gifts of the Bread and Fruits of Eternal Spiritual Life. May our earnest participation together in commemoration of Saint Pius X bring forth favourable blessings upon our lives, our community and your Holy Apostolic Universal Ecclesia.

XVI.XVI – AUGUST 22

1.

Our Lady of Asia
Patron of Asia
Memorial

August 22

Entrance Antiphon — Psalm 107: 31-32

Oh that men would praise the Lord for his goodness, and

for his wonderful works to the children of men! Let them exalt him also in the congregation of the people, and praise him in the assembly of the elders.

Offertory Antiphon

O God and Divine Creator, grant us through the intercession of our Divine Mother Mary as Our Lady of Asia, that all peoples of each generation of Asia may come to know your good works and Divine Truth. Through our Lord Jesus Christ, your Son, who lives and reigns with you in the unity of the Holy Spirit, one God, for ever and ever.

Prayer over the Offerings

May God and the Divine Creator accept and sanctify these humble gifts as symbols of the genuine personal offerings we make in commemoration of Our Lady of Asia. Through Christ our Light and Saviour.

Prayer after Communion

Heavenly Father and God of all Creation, we give thanks for the nourishment of your heavenly gifts of the Bread and Fruits of Eternal Spiritual Life. May our earnest participation together in commemoration of Our Lady of Asia bring forth favourable blessings upon our lives, our community and your Holy Apostolic Universal Ecclesia.

XVI.XVII – AUGUST 23

1. **Rose of Lima,** Virgin — August 23

Memorial

Entrance Antiphon
Psalm 108: 5

Be exalted, O God, above the heavens, and let your glory be over all the earth

Offertory Antiphon

O God and Divine Creator, you set Saint Rose of Lima on fire with your love, so that, secluded from the world in the austerity of a life of penance, she might give herself to you alone; grant, we pray, that through her intercession, we may tread the paths of life on earth and drink at the stream of your delights in heaven. Through our Lord Jesus Christ, your Son, who lives and reigns with you in the unity of the Holy Spirit, one God, for ever and ever.

Prayer over the Offerings

May God and the Divine Creator accept and sanctify these

humble gifts as symbols of the genuine personal offerings we make in commemoration of Rose of Lima. Through Christ our Light and Saviour.

Prayer after Communion

Heavenly Father and God of all Creation, we give thanks for the nourishment of your heavenly gifts of the Bread and Fruits of Eternal Spiritual Life. May our earnest participation together in commemoration of Rose of Lima bring forth favourable blessings upon our lives, our community and your Holy Apostolic Universal Ecclesia.

XVI.XVIII – AUGUST 24

1. **Bartholomew the Apostle** — August 24

Memorial

Entrance Antiphon — Psalm 96: 2-3

Proclaim the salvation of God day by day; tell among the nations his glory.

Offertory Antiphon

O God and Divine Creator, strengthen in us the faith, by which the blessed Apostle Bartholomew clung wholeheartedly to your Son, and grant that through the help of his prayers your Church may become for all the nations the sacrament of salvation. Through our Lord Jesus Christ, your Son, who lives and reigns with you in the unity of the Holy Spirit, one God, for ever and ever.

Prayer over the Offerings

May God and the Divine Creator accept and sanctify these humble gifts as symbols of the genuine personal offerings we make in commemoration of Bartholomew the Apostle. Through Christ our Light and Saviour.

Communion Antiphon — Lk 22: 29-30

I confer a kingdom on you, just as my Father has conferred one on me, that you may eat and drink at my table in my kingdom, says the Lord.

Prayer after Communion

Heavenly Father and God of all Creation, we give thanks for the nourishment of your heavenly gifts of the Bread and Fruits of Eternal Spiritual Life. May our earnest participation together in commemoration of Bartholomew the Apostle bring forth favourable blessings upon our lives, our community and your Holy Apostolic Universal

Ecclesia.

XVI.XIX – AUGUST 25

1. **Louis the Saint** — August 25
Memorial

Entrance Antiphon — Psalm 110: 4

You are a priest for ever according to the order of the Light of Christ. Our Lord has made His Testament as a Promise he will not break.

Offertory Antiphon

O God and Divine Creator, who brought Saint Louis from the cares of earthly rule to the glory of a heavenly realm, grant, we pray, through his intercession, that, by fulfilling our duties on earth, we may seek out your eternal Kingdom. Through our Lord Jesus Christ, your Son, who lives and reigns with you in the unity of the Holy Spirit, one God, for ever and ever.

Prayer over the Offerings

May God and the Divine Creator accept and sanctify these humble gifts as symbols of the genuine personal offerings we make in commemoration of Saint Louis. Through Christ our Light and Saviour.

Prayer after Communion

Heavenly Father and God of all Creation, we give thanks for the nourishment of your heavenly gifts of the Bread and Fruits of Eternal Spiritual Life. May our earnest participation together in commemoration of Louis the Saint bring forth favourable blessings upon our lives, our community and your Holy Apostolic Universal Ecclesia.

XVI.XX – AUGUST 27

1. **Monica of Numidia** — August 27
Memorial

Entrance Antiphon — Psalm 111: 3

Glorious and majestic are his deeds, and his righteousness endures forever.

Offertory Antiphon

O God and Divine Creator, who console the sorrowful and who mercifully accepted the motherly tears of Saint Monica for the conversion of her son Augustine, grant us, through the intercession of them both, that we may bitterly regret our sins and find the grace of your pardon. Through our Lord Jesus Christ, your Son, who lives and reigns with you in the unity of the Holy Spirit, one God, for ever and ever.

Prayer over the Offerings

May God and the Divine Creator accept and sanctify these humble gifts as symbols of the genuine personal offerings we make in commemoration of Monica of Numidia. Through Christ our Light and Saviour.

Prayer after Communion

Heavenly Father and God of all Creation, we give thanks for the nourishment of your heavenly gifts of the Bread and Fruits of Eternal Spiritual Life. May our earnest participation together in commemoration of Monica of Numidia bring forth favourable blessings upon our lives, our community and your Holy Apostolic Universal Ecclesia.

XVI.XXI – AUGUST 28

1. **Augustine of Hippo,** Bishop and Doctor of the Church
Patron of Africa
Memorial

August 28

Entrance Antiphon

Psalm 111: 7-9

The works of his hands are verity and judgment; all his commandments are sure. They stand fast for ever and ever, and are done in truth and uprightness. He sent redemption unto his people: he hath commanded his covenant for ever: holy and reverend is his name.

Offertory Antiphon

O God and Divine Creator, renew in your Church the spirit with which you endowed your Bishop Saint Augustine that, filled with the same spirit, we may thirst for you, the sole fount of true wisdom, and seek you, the author of heavenly love. Through our Lord Jesus Christ, your Son, who lives and reigns with you in the unity of the Holy Spirit, one God, for ever and ever.

Prayer over the Offerings

May God and the Divine Creator accept and sanctify these humble gifts as symbols of the genuine personal offerings we make in commemoration of Augustine of Hippo.

Missale Christus | Proper of Heroes & Saints

Through Christ our Light and Saviour.

Communion Antiphon — Mt 23: 10, 8

Thus says the Lord: You have but one teacher, the Christ, and you are all brothers.

Prayer after Communion

Heavenly Father and God of all Creation, we give thanks for the nourishment of your heavenly gifts of the Bread and Fruits of Eternal Spiritual Life. May our earnest participation together in commemoration of Augustine of Hippo bring forth favourable blessings upon our lives, our community and your Holy Apostolic Universal Ecclesia.

2. John Smyth — August 28

Founder of Baptist Congregational Movements of Universal Ecclesia

Memorial

Entrance Antiphon — Psalm 111: 7-9

The works of his hands are verity and judgment; all his commandments are sure. They stand fast for ever and ever, and are done in truth and uprightness. He sent redemption unto his people: he hath commanded his covenant for ever: holy and reverend is his name.

Offertory Antiphon

O God and Divine Creator, who by , grant that . Through our Lord Jesus Christ, your Son, who lives and reigns with you in the unity of the Holy Spirit, one God, for ever and ever.

Prayer over the Offerings

May God and the Divine Creator accept and sanctify these humble gifts as symbols of the genuine personal offerings we make in commemoration of John Smyth. Through Christ our Light and Saviour.

Communion Antiphon — John 12: 26

Whoever serves me must follow me, and where I am, there also will my servant be.

Prayer after Communion

Heavenly Father and God of all Creation, we give thanks for the nourishment of your heavenly gifts of the Bread and Fruits of Eternal Spiritual Life. May our earnest participation together in commemoration of John Smyth bring forth favourable blessings upon our lives, our community and your Holy Apostolic Universal Ecclesia.

Title XVII: Proper of September

XVII.I – SEPTEMBER 1

1. **Gregory the Great,** Pope and Doctor of the Church *September 1*
   Memorial

   Entrance Antiphon — Psalm 112: 5

   Good will come to him who is generous and lends freely, who conducts his affairs with justice.

   Offertory Antiphon

   O God and Divine Creator, who care for your people with gentleness and rule them in love, through the intercession of Pope Saint Gregory, endow, we pray, with a spirit of wisdom those to whom you have given authority to govern, that the flourishing of a holy flock may become the eternal joy of the shepherds. Through our Lord Jesus Christ, your Son, who lives and reigns with you in the unity of the Holy Spirit, one God, for ever and ever.

   Prayer over the Offerings

   May God and the Divine Creator accept and sanctify these humble gifts as symbols of the genuine personal offerings we make in commemoration of Pope Saint Gregory. Through Christ our Light and Saviour.

   Communion Antiphon — Lk 12: 42

   This is the steward, faithful and prudent,
   whom the Lord set over his household
   to give them their allowance of food at the proper time.

   Prayer after Communion

   Heavenly Father and God of all Creation, we give thanks for the nourishment of your heavenly gifts of the Bread and Fruits of Eternal Spiritual Life. May our earnest participation together in commemoration of Pope Saint Gregory bring forth favourable blessings upon our lives, our community and your Holy Apostolic Universal Ecclesia.

XVII.II – SEPTEMBER 2

1. **Our Lady of Harmony of Heaven & Earth** *September 5*
   Patron of China
   Memorial

   Entrance Antiphon — Psalm 112: 2-3

   Let the name of the Lord be praised, both now and forevermore. From the rising of the sun to the place where it sets, the name of the Lord is to be praised.

Offertory Antiphon

O God and Divine Creator of all Heaven and Earth, who knows the name and deeds of each and every ancestor and guards the faithful against evil spirits and intentions, grant us through the intercession of our Divine Mother Mary as Our Lady of Harmony of Heaven and Earth, the continued protection, good health and good fortune of the Chinese people and its leaders; and the fulfilment of your Divine Mission of harmony between all people of good character and spirit. Through our Lord Jesus Christ, your Son, who lives and reigns with you in the unity of the Holy Spirit, one God, for ever and ever.

Prayer over the Offerings

May God and the Divine Creator accept and sanctify these humble gifts in the name of our Divine Mother Mary as Our Lady of Harmony of Heaven and Earth, as symbols of the genuine personal offerings we make in honour and respect of the protection, good health and good fortune of all of China and its people. Through Christ our Light and Saviour.

Communion Antiphon
1 Peter 1:15

But as he who called you is holy, you also be holy in all your conduct.

Prayer after Communion

Heavenly Father and God of all Creation, we give thanks for the nourishment of your heavenly gifts of the Bread and Fruits of Eternal Spiritual Life. May our earnest participation together in commemoration of our Divine Mother Mary as Our Lady of Harmony of Heaven and Earth bring forth favourable blessings upon our lives, our people and continued wisdom upon our leaders and your Holy Apostolic Universal Ecclesia as one united Christian body.

XVII.III – SEPTEMBER 5

1. **Teresa of Calcutta,** Religious *September 5*
Founder of Missionaries of Charity
Memorial

Entrance Antiphon
Psalm 116: 1-2

I love the Lord, for he heard my voice; he heard my cry for

mercy. Because he turned his ear to me, I will call on him as long as I live.

Living Testimony: Teresa of Calcutta

Spread love everywhere you go: first of all in your own home. Give love to your children, to your wife or husband, to a next door neighbour. Let no one ever come to you without leaving better and happier. Be the living expression of God's kindness; kindness in your face, kindness in your eyes, kindness in your smile, kindness in your warm greeting.

Living Gospel: Teresa of Calcutta

Teresa of Calcutta

Seeking the face of God in everything, everyone, all the time, and his hand in every happening; This is what it means to be contemplative in the heart of the world. Seeing and adoring the presence of Jesus, especially in the lowly appearance of bread, and in the distressing disguise of the poor.

Offertory Antiphon

O God and Divine Creator, Through our Lord Jesus Christ, your Son, who lives and reigns with you in the unity of the Holy Spirit, one God, for ever and ever.

Prayer over the Offerings

May God and the Divine Creator accept and sanctify these humble gifts as symbols of the genuine personal offerings we make in commemoration of Teresa of Calcutta. Through Christ our Light and Saviour.

Communion Antiphon

1 Peter 1:15

But as he who called you is holy, you also be holy in all your conduct.

Prayer after Communion

Heavenly Father and God of all Creation, we give thanks for the nourishment of your heavenly gifts of the Bread and Fruits of Eternal Spiritual Life. May our earnest participation together in commemoration of Teresa of Calcutta bring forth favourable blessings upon our lives, our community and your Holy Apostolic Universal Ecclesia.

Missale Christus | Proper of Heroes & Saints

XVII.IV – SEPTEMBER 9

1.   **Peter Claver,** Priest   September 9

Memorial

Entrance Antiphon   Psalm 118: 1

This is the day which the Lord hath made; we will rejoice and be glad in it.

Offertory Antiphon

O God and Divine Creator, who made Saint Peter Claver a slave of slaves and strengthened him with wonderful charity and patience as he came to their help, grant, through his intercession, that, seeking the things of Jesus Christ, we may love our neighbor in deeds and in truth. Through our Lord Jesus Christ, your Son, who lives and reigns with you in the unity of the Holy Spirit, one God, for ever and ever.

Prayer over the Offerings

May God and the Divine Creator accept and sanctify these humble gifts as symbols of the genuine personal offerings we make in commemoration of Peter Claver. Through Christ our Light and Saviour.

Prayer after Communion

Heavenly Father and God of all Creation, we give thanks for the nourishment of your heavenly gifts of the Bread and Fruits of Eternal Spiritual Life. May our earnest participation together in commemoration of Peter Claver bring forth favourable blessings upon our lives, our community and your Holy Apostolic Universal Ecclesia.

XVII.V – SEPTEMBER 14

1.   **John Chrysostom,** Bishop and Doctor of the Church   September 14

Memorial

Entrance Antiphon   Psalm 119: 1

Blessed are they whose ways are blameless, who walk according to the law of the Lord.

Offertory Antiphon

O God and Divine Creator, strength of those who hope in you, who willed that the Bishop Saint John Chrysostom should be illustrious by his wonderful eloquence and his experience of suffering, grant us, we pray, that, instructed by his teachings, we may be strengthened through the example of his invincible patience. Through our Lord Jesus Christ, your Son, who lives and reigns with you in the unity of the Holy Spirit, one God, for ever and ever.

Prayer over the Offerings

May God and the Divine Creator accept and sanctify these humble gifts as symbols of the genuine personal offerings we make in commemoration of Saint John Chrysostom. Through Christ our Light and Saviour.

Communion Antiphon — 1 Cor 1: 23-24

We proclaim Christ crucified; Christ, the power of God and the wisdom of God.

Prayer after Communion

Heavenly Father and God of all Creation, we give thanks for the nourishment of your heavenly gifts of the Bread and Fruits of Eternal Spiritual Life. May our earnest participation together in commemoration of Saint John Chrysostom bring forth favourable blessings upon our lives, our community and your Holy Apostolic Universal Ecclesia.

XVII.VI – SEPTEMBER 16

1. **Cornelius,** Pope, **and Cyprian,** Bishop, Martyrs — September 16
Memorial

Entrance Antiphon — Psalm 119: 16

I delight in your Divine decrees; I will not neglect your Divine Word.

Offertory Antiphon

O God and Divine Creator, who gave Saints Cornelius and Cyprian to your people as diligent shepherds and valiant Martyrs, grant that through their intercession we may be strengthened in faith and constancy and spend ourselves without reserve for the unity of the Church. Through our Lord Jesus Christ, your Son, who lives and reigns with you in the unity of the Holy Spirit, one God, for ever and ever.

Prayer over the Offerings

May God and the Divine Creator accept and sanctify these humble gifts as symbols of the genuine personal offerings we make in commemoration of Saints Cornelius and Cyprian. Through Christ our Light and Saviour.

Missale Christus | Proper of Heroes & Saints

Communion Antiphon   Lk 22: 28-30

> It is you who have stood by me in my trials; and I confer a kingdom on you, says the Lord, that you may eat and drink at my table in my kingdom.

Prayer after Communion

> Heavenly Father and God of all Creation, we give thanks for the nourishment of your heavenly gifts of the Bread and Fruits of Eternal Spiritual Life. May our earnest participation together in commemoration of Saints Cornelius and Cyprian bring forth favourable blessings upon our lives, our community and your Holy Apostolic Universal Ecclesia.

XVII.VII – SEPTEMBER 17

1. Robert Bellarmine, Bishop and Doctor of the Church   September 17
Memorial

Entrance Antiphon   Psalm 119: 18-19

> Open my eyes that I may see wonderful things in your Divine Law. I am a stranger on earth; do not hide your maxims of law from me.

Offertory Antiphon

> O God and Divine Creator, who adorned the Bishop Saint Robert Bellarmine with wonderful learning and virtue to vindicate the faith of your Church, grant, through his intercession, that in the integrity of that same faith your people may always find joy. Through our Lord Jesus Christ, your Son, who lives and reigns with you in the unity of the Holy Spirit, one God, for ever and ever.

Prayer over the Offerings

> May God and the Divine Creator accept and sanctify these humble gifts as symbols of the genuine personal offerings we make in commemoration of Robert Bellarmine. Through Christ our Light and Saviour.

Communion Antiphon   Psalm 1: 2-3

> One who ponders the Divine maxims of Law of the Lord day and night shall yield fruit in due season.

Prayer after Communion

> Heavenly Father and God of all Creation, we give thanks for the nourishment of your heavenly gifts of the Bread and Fruits of Eternal Spiritual Life. May our earnest

participation together in commemoration of Robert Bellarmine bring forth favourable blessings upon our lives, our community and your Holy Apostolic Universal Ecclesia.

XVII.VIII – SEPTEMBER 19

1. **Januarius of Benevento,** Bishop and Martyr

September 19

Memorial

Entrance Antiphon
Psalm 119: 27

Let me understand the teaching of your Divine maxims; then I will meditate on the wonders of your Divine Word.

Offertory Antiphon

O God and Divine Creator, who grant us to venerate the memory of the Martyr Saint Januarius, give us, we pray, the joy of his company in blessed happiness for all eternity. Through our Lord Jesus Christ, your Son, who lives and reigns with you in the unity of the Holy Spirit, one God, for ever and ever.

Prayer over the Offerings

May God and the Divine Creator accept and sanctify these humble gifts as symbols of the genuine personal offerings we make in commemoration of Januarius of Benevento. Through Christ our Light and Saviour.

Communion Antiphon
Lk 22: 28-30

It is you who have stood by me in my trials; and I confer a kingdom on you, says the Lord, that you may eat and drink at my table in my kingdom.

Prayer after Communion

Heavenly Father and God of all Creation, we give thanks for the nourishment of your heavenly gifts of the Bread and Fruits of Eternal Spiritual Life. May our earnest participation together in commemoration of Januarius of Benevento bring forth favourable blessings upon our lives, our community and your Holy Apostolic Universal Ecclesia.

XVII.IX – SEPTEMBER 20

1. **Andrew Kim Tae-gon, Priest, and Paul Chong Ha-sang, and Companions, Martyrs**

September 20

Memorial

Entrance Antiphon — Psalm 119: 28

My soul is weary with sorrow; strengthen me according to your Divine Word.

Offertory Antiphon

O God and Divine Creator, who have been pleased to increase your adopted children in all the world, and who made the blood of the Martyrs and his companions Saint Andrew Kim Tae-gon a most fruitful seed of Christians, grant that we may be defended by their help and profit always from their example. Through our Lord Jesus Christ, your Son, who lives and reigns with you in the unity of the Holy Spirit, one God, for ever and ever.

Prayer over the Offerings

May God and the Divine Creator accept and sanctify these humble gifts as symbols of the genuine personal offerings we make in commemoration of Andrew Kim Tae-gon and Paul Chong Ha-sang and Companions. Through Christ our Light and Saviour.

Communion Antiphon — Mt 10: 32

Everyone who acknowledges me before others I will acknowledge before my heavenly Father, says the Lord.

Prayer after Communion

Heavenly Father and God of all Creation, we give thanks for the nourishment of your heavenly gifts of the Bread and Fruits of Eternal Spiritual Life. May our earnest participation together in commemoration of Andrew Kim Tae-gon and Paul Chong Ha-sang and Companions bring forth favourable blessings upon our lives, our community and your Holy Apostolic Universal Ecclesia.

XVII.X – SEPTEMBER 21

1. **Matthew the Apostle and Evangelist**

September 21

Feast

Entrance Antiphon — Psalm 119: 30

I have chosen the way of truth; I have set my heart on your

Divine maxims of Law.

Living Testimony: Mt 28: 19-20

Go and make disciples of all nations, baptizing them and teaching them to observe all that I have commanded you, says the Lord.

Offertory Antiphon

O God and Divine Creator, who with untold mercy were pleased to choose as an Apostle Saint Matthew, the tax collector, grant that, sustained by his example and intercession, we may merit to hold firm in following you. Through our Lord Jesus Christ, your Son, who lives and reigns with you in the unity of the Holy Spirit, one God, for ever and ever.

Prayer over the Offerings

May God and the Divine Creator accept and sanctify these humble gifts as symbols of the genuine personal offerings we make in commemoration of Matthew the Apostle and Evangelist. Through Christ our Light and Saviour.

Communion Antiphon   Mt 9: 13

I did not come to call the just, but sinners, says the Lord.

Prayer after Communion

Heavenly Father and God of all Creation, we give thanks for the nourishment of your heavenly gifts of the Bread and Fruits of Eternal Spiritual Life. May our earnest participation together in commemoration of Matthew the Apostle and Evangelist bring forth favourable blessings upon our lives, our community and your Holy Apostolic Universal Ecclesia.

XVII.XI – SEPTEMBER 23

1.   **Pio of Pietrelcina,** Priest   September 23
                                       Memorial

Entrance Antiphon   Psalm 119: 31

I hold fast to your Divine maxims, O Lord; do not let me be put to shame.

Offertory Antiphon

O God and Divine Creator, who, by a singular grace, gave the Priest Saint Pius a share in the Cross of your Son and, by means of his ministry, renewed the wonders of your mercy, grant that through his intercession we may be united constantly to the sufferings of Christ, and so brought happily to the glory of the resurrection. Through our Lord Jesus Christ, your Son, who lives and reigns with you in the unity of the Holy Spirit, one God, for ever and ever.

Prayer over the Offerings

May God and the Divine Creator accept and sanctify these humble gifts as symbols of the genuine personal offerings we make in commemoration of Pio of Pietrelcina. Through Christ our Light and Saviour.

Communion Antiphon — Mt 16: 24

Whoever wishes to come after me, must deny himself, take up his cross, and follow me, says the Lord.

Prayer after Communion

Heavenly Father and God of all Creation, we give thanks for the nourishment of your heavenly gifts of the Bread and Fruits of Eternal Spiritual Life. May our earnest participation together in commemoration of Pio of Pietrelcina bring forth favourable blessings upon our lives, our community and your Holy Apostolic Universal Ecclesia.

XVII.XII – SEPTEMBER 25

1.   **Cosmas and Damian,** Martyrs   September 25

Memorial

Entrance Antiphon — Psalm 119: 34

Give me understanding, and I will keep your Divine maxims of Law and obey them with all my heart.

Offertory Antiphon

O God and Divine Creator, may you be magnified by the revered memory of your Saints Cosmas and Damian, for with providence beyond words you have conferred on them everlasting glory, and on us, your unfailing help. Through our Lord Jesus Christ, your Son, who lives and reigns with you in the unity of the Holy Spirit, one God, for ever and ever.

Prayer over the Offerings

May God and the Divine Creator accept and sanctify these humble gifts as symbols of the genuine personal offerings we make in commemoration of Saints Cosmas and

Damian. Through Christ our Light and Saviour.

Communion Antiphon — Lk 22: 28-30

It is you who have stood by me in my trials; and I confer a kingdom on you, says the Lord, that you may eat and drink at my table in my kingdom.

Prayer after Communion

Heavenly Father and God of all Creation, we give thanks for the nourishment of your heavenly gifts of the Bread and Fruits of Eternal Spiritual Life. May our earnest participation together in commemoration of Saints Cosmas and Damian bring forth favourable blessings upon our lives, our community and your Holy Apostolic Universal Ecclesia.

XVII.XIII – SEPTEMBER 26

1. Paul VI, Pope
Memorial — September 26

Entrance Antiphon — Psalm 119: 33

Teach me, O Lord, to follow your Divine maxims of Law; then I will keep them to the end.

Living Testimony: Ecclesiam Suam, 1964

Merely to remain true to the faith is not enough. Certainly we must preserve and defend the treasure of truth and grace that we have inherited through Christian tradition. ... But neither the preservation nor the defense of the faith exhausts the duty of the Church in regard to the gifts it has been given. The very nature of the gifts which Christ has given the Church demands that they be extended to others and shared with others.

Living Gospel: Populorum Progressio, 1967 — Populorum Progressio, 1967

Neither individuals nor nations should regard the possession of more and more goods as the ultimate objective. Every kind of progress is a two-edged sword. It is necessary if man is to grow as a human being; yet it can also enslave him, if he comes to regard it as the supreme good and cannot look beyond it. When this happens, men harden their hearts, shut out others from their minds and gather together solely for reasons of self-interest rather than out of friendship; dissension and disunity follow soon after. Thus the exclusive pursuit of material possessions prevents man's growth as a human being and stands in opposition to his true grandeur.

Offertory Antiphon

O God and Divine Creator, who through the Holy Spirit granted Pope Saint Paul VI the humility and foresight of your Divine Mission in the Light of Christ, grant us through his intercession, the same docility to the Holy Spirit so that we too may be instruments of peace and transformation. Through our Lord Jesus Christ, your Son, who lives and reigns with you in the unity of the Holy Spirit, one God, for ever and ever.

Prayer over the Offerings

May God and the Divine Creator accept and sanctify these humble gifts as symbols of the genuine personal offerings we make in commemoration of Pope Saint Paul VI. Through Christ our Light and Saviour.

Communion Antiphon — Jn 10: 11

The Good Shepherd did sacrifice his own life for his flock.

Prayer after Communion

Heavenly Father and God of all Creation, we give thanks for the nourishment of your heavenly gifts of the Bread and Fruits of Eternal Spiritual Life. May our earnest participation together in commemoration of Pope Saint Paul VI bring forth favourable blessings upon our lives, our community and your Holy Apostolic Universal Ecclesia.

XVII.XIV– SEPTEMBER 27

1.   **Saint Vincent de Paul,** Priest   September 27
Founder of Congregation of the Mission and Daughters of Charity

Memorial

Entrance Antiphon — Psalm 119: 35

Direct me in the path of your Divine maxims of Law, for there I find delight.

Offertory Antiphon

O God and Divine Creator, who for the relief of the poor and the formation of the clergy endowed the Priest Saint Vincent de Paul with apostolic virtues, grant, we pray, that, afire with that same spirit, we may love what he loved and put into practice what he taught. Through our Lord Jesus Christ, your Son, who lives and reigns with you in the unity

Title XVII: Proper of September

Prayer over the Offerings

of the Holy Spirit, one God, for ever and ever.

May God and the Divine Creator accept and sanctify these humble gifts as symbols of the genuine personal offerings we make in commemoration of Vincent de Paul. Through Christ our Light and Saviour.

Communion Antiphon — Ps 107 (106): 8-9

Let them thank the Lord for his mercy, his wonders for the children of men, for he satisfies the thirsty soul, and the hungry he fills with good things.

Prayer after Communion

Heavenly Father and God of all Creation, we give thanks for the nourishment of your heavenly gifts of the Bread and Fruits of Eternal Spiritual Life. May our earnest participation together in commemoration of Vincent de Paul bring forth favourable blessings upon our lives, our community and your Holy Apostolic Universal Ecclesia.

XVII.XV – SEPTEMBER 28

1. **Wenceslaus of Bohemia, Martyr** — September 28

Memorial

Entrance Antiphon — Psalm 119: 36

Turn my heart toward your Divine maxims of Law and not toward selfish gain.

Offertory Antiphon

O God and Divine Creator, who taught the Martyr Saint Wenceslaus to place the heavenly Kingdom before an earthly one, grant through his prayers that, denying ourselves, we may hold fast to you with all our heart. Through our Lord Jesus Christ, your Son, who lives and reigns with you in the unity of the Holy Spirit, one God, for ever and ever.

Prayer over the Offerings

May God and the Divine Creator accept and sanctify these humble gifts as symbols of the genuine personal offerings we make in commemoration of Wenceslaus of Bohemia. Through Christ our Light and Saviour.

Communion Antiphon — Lk 22: 28-30

It is you who have stood by me in my trials; and I confer a kingdom on you, says the Lord, that you may eat and drink at my table in my kingdom.

Prayer after Communion

Heavenly Father and God of all Creation, we give thanks for the nourishment of your heavenly gifts of the Bread and Fruits of Eternal Spiritual Life. May our earnest participation together in commemoration of Wenceslaus of Bohemia bring forth favourable blessings upon our lives, our community and your Holy Apostolic Universal Ecclesia.

XVII.XVI – SEPTEMBER 29

1. **Michael, Gabriel and Raphael,** Archangels — September 29

Memorial

Entrance Antiphon — Psalm 103: 20

Bless the Lord, all you his angels, mighty in power, fulfilling his word, and heeding his voice.

Offertory Antiphon

O God and Divine Creator, who dispose in marvelous order ministries both angelic and human, graciously grant that our life on earth may be defended by those who watch over us as they minister perpetually to you in heaven. Through our Lord Jesus Christ, your Son, who lives and reigns with you in the unity of the Holy Spirit, one God, for ever and ever.

Prayer over the Offerings

May God and the Divine Creator accept and sanctify these humble gifts as symbols of the genuine personal offerings we make in commemoration of Saints Michael, Gabriel and Raphael. Through Christ our Light and Saviour.

Communion Antiphon — Ps 138 (137): 1

I will thank you, Lord, with all my heart; in the presence of the Angels I will praise you.

Prayer after Communion

Heavenly Father and God of all Creation, we give thanks for the nourishment of your heavenly gifts of the Bread and Fruits of Eternal Spiritual Life. May our earnest participation together in commemoration of Saints Michael, Gabriel and Raphael bring forth favourable blessings upon our lives, our community and your Holy Apostolic Universal Ecclesia.

XVII.XVII – SEPTEMBER 30

1.   **Jerome,** Priest and Doctor of the Church   September 30
Memorial

Entrance Antiphon   Psalm 1: 2-3

Blessed indeed is he who ponders the law of the Lord day and night: he will yield his fruit in due season.

Offertory Antiphon

O God and Divine Creator, who gave the Priest Saint Jerome a living and tender love for Sacred Scripture, grant that your people may be ever more fruitfully nourished by your Word and find in it the fount of life. Through our Lord Jesus Christ, your Son, who lives and reigns with you in the unity of the Holy Spirit, one God, for ever and ever.

Prayer over the Offerings

May God and the Divine Creator accept and sanctify these humble gifts as symbols of the genuine personal offerings we make in commemoration of Saint Jerome. Through Christ our Light and Saviour.

Communion Antiphon   Jer 15: 16

Lord God, your words were found and I consumed them; your word became the joy and the happiness of my heart.

Prayer after Communion

Heavenly Father and God of all Creation, we give thanks for the nourishment of your heavenly gifts of the Bread and Fruits of Eternal Spiritual Life. May our earnest participation together in commemoration of Saint Jerome bring forth favourable blessings upon our lives, our community and your Holy Apostolic Universal Ecclesia.

2.   **George Whitefield**   September 30
Founder of Methodist Movement of Universal Ecclesia
Memorial

Entrance Antiphon   Psalm 1: 2-3

Blessed indeed is he
who ponders the law of the Lord day and night:
he will yield his fruit in due season.

Living Testimony: George Whitefield

The great and important duty which is incumbent on Christians, is to guard against all appearance of evil; to watch against the first risings in the heart to evil; and to have a guard upon our actions, that they may not be sinful, or so much as seem to be so.

Living Gospel: George Whitefield
George Whitefield

A true faith in Jesus Christ will not suffer us to be idle. No, it is an active, lively, restless principle; it fills the heart, so that it cannot be easy till it is doing something for Jesus Christ.

Offertory Antiphon

O God and Divine Creator, through our Lord Jesus Christ, your Son, who lives and reigns with you in the unity of the Holy Spirit, one God, for ever and ever.

Prayer over the Offerings

May God and the Divine Creator accept and sanctify these humble gifts as symbols of the genuine personal offerings we make in commemoration of George Whitefield. Through Christ our Light and Saviour.

Communion Antiphon
John 12: 26

Whoever serves me must follow me, and where I am, there also will my servant be.

Prayer after Communion

Heavenly Father and God of all Creation, we give thanks for the nourishment of your heavenly gifts of the Bread and Fruits of Eternal Spiritual Life. May our earnest participation together in commemoration of George Whitefield bring forth favourable blessings upon our lives, our community and your Holy Apostolic Universal Ecclesia.

Title XVIII: Proper of October

XVIII.I – OCTOBER 1

1. **Thérèse of Lisieux,** Virgin and Doctor of the Church October 1
Memorial

Entrance Antiphon — Psalm 119: 37

Turn my eyes away from worthless things; preserve my life according to your Divine Word.

Offertory Antiphon

O God and Divine Creator, who open your Kingdom to those who are humble and to little ones, lead us to follow trustingly in the little way of Saint Thérèse, so that through her intercession we may see your eternal glory revealed. Through our Lord Jesus Christ, your Son, who lives and reigns with you in the unity of the Holy Spirit, one God, for ever and ever.

Prayer over the Offerings

May God and the Divine Creator accept and sanctify these humble gifts as symbols of the genuine personal offerings we make in commemoration of Thérèse of Lisieux. Through Christ our Light and Saviour.

Communion Antiphon — Mt 18: 3

Thus says the Lord: Unless you turn and become like children, you will not enter the Kingdom of Heaven.

Prayer after Communion

Heavenly Father and God of all Creation, we give thanks for the nourishment of your heavenly gifts of the Bread and Fruits of Eternal Spiritual Life. May our earnest participation together in commemoration of Thérèse of Lisieux bring forth favourable blessings upon our lives, our community and your Holy Apostolic Universal Ecclesia.

XVIII.II – OCTOBER 2

1. **The Holy Guardian Angels** October 2
Memorial

Entrance Antiphon — Dn 3: 58

Angels of the Lord, bless the Lord, praise and exalt him above all for ever.

Offertory Antiphon

O God and Divine Creator, who in your unfathomable providence are pleased to send your holy Angels to guard us, hear our supplication as we cry to you, that we may always be defended by their protection and rejoice eternally in their company. Through our Lord Jesus Christ, your Son, who lives and reigns with you in the unity of the Holy Spirit, one God, for ever and ever.

Prayer over the Offerings

May God and the Divine Creator accept and sanctify these humble gifts as symbols of the genuine personal offerings we make in commemoration of the Holy Guardian Angels. Through Christ our Light and Saviour.

Communion Antiphon *Ps 138 (137): 1*

In the presence of the Angels I will praise you, my God.

Prayer after Communion

Heavenly Father and God of all Creation, we give thanks for the nourishment of your heavenly gifts of the Bread and Fruits of Eternal Spiritual Life. May our earnest participation together in commemoration of the Holy Guardian Angels bring forth favourable blessings upon our lives, our community and your Holy Apostolic Universal Ecclesia.

XVIII.III – OCTOBER 4

1. **Francis of Assisi** October 4
Memorial

Entrance Antiphon *Psalm 119: 40*

How I long for your Divine maxims! Preserve my life in your righteousness.

Living Testimony: Francis

Lord, make me an instrument of thy peace. Where there is hatred, let me sow love, Where there is injury, pardon; Where there is doubt, faith; Where there is despair, hope; Where there is darkness, light; And where there is sadness, joy. O Divine Master, grant that I may not so much seek to be consoled as to console, to be understood as to understand, to be loved, as to love. For it is in giving that we receive, It is in pardoning that we are pardoned, and it is in dying that we are born to eternal life.

Living Gospel: Francis of Assisi *Francis of Assisi*

Above all the grace and the gifts that Christ gives to his beloved is that of overcoming self. All the darkness in the world cannot extinguish the light of a single candle. Start by doing what is necessary, then what is possible, and suddenly you are doing the impossible. The deeds you do may be the only sermon some persons will hear today. We have been called to heal wounds, to unite what has fallen apart, and to bring home those who have lost their way. Remember that when you leave this earth, you can take with you nothing that have received--only what you have given.

Offertory Antiphon

O God and Divine Creator, by whose gift Saint Francis was conformed to Christ in poverty and humility, grant that, by walking in Francis' footsteps, we may follow your Son, and, through joyful charity, come to be united with you. Through our Lord Jesus Christ, your Son, who lives and reigns with you in the unity of the Holy Spirit, one God, for ever and ever.

Prayer over the Offerings

May God and the Divine Creator accept and sanctify these humble gifts as symbols of the genuine personal offerings we make in commemoration of Francis of Assisi. Through Christ our Light and Saviour.

Communion Antiphon — Mt 5: 3

Blessed are the poor in spirit, for theirs is the Kingdom of Heaven.

Prayer after Communion

Heavenly Father and God of all Creation, we give thanks for the nourishment of your heavenly gifts of the Bread and Fruits of Eternal Spiritual Life. May our earnest participation together in commemoration of Francis of Assisi bring forth favourable blessings upon our lives, our community and your Holy Apostolic Universal Ecclesia.

XVIII.IV – OCTOBER 6

1.

Bruno of Cologne, Priest — October 6
Founder of Order of Carthusians
Memorial

Entrance Antiphon — Psalm 119: 43

Do not snatch the word of truth from my mouth, for I have put my hope in your Divine maxims of Law.

Offertory Antiphon

O God and Divine Creator, who called Saint Bruno to serve you in solitude, grant, through his intercession, that amid the changes of this world we may constantly look to you alone. Through our Lord Jesus Christ, your Son, who lives and reigns with you in the unity of the Holy Spirit, one God, for ever and ever.

Prayer over the Offerings

May God and the Divine Creator accept and sanctify these humble gifts as symbols of the genuine personal offerings we make in commemoration of Bruno of Cologne. Through Christ our Light and Saviour.

Prayer after Communion

Heavenly Father and God of all Creation, we give thanks for the nourishment of your heavenly gifts of the Bread and Fruits of Eternal Spiritual Life. May our earnest participation together in commemoration of Bruno of Cologne bring forth favourable blessings upon our lives, our community and your Holy Apostolic Universal Ecclesia.

2. William Tyndale — October 6

Ordinary

Entrance Antiphon — Psalm 119: 43

Do not snatch the word of truth from my mouth, for I have put my hope in your Divine maxims of Law.

Prayer over the Offerings

May God and the Divine Creator accept and sanctify these humble gifts as symbols of the genuine personal offerings we make in commemoration of William Tyndale. Through Christ our Light and Saviour.

Prayer after Communion

Heavenly Father and God of all Creation, we give thanks for the nourishment of your heavenly gifts of the Bread and Fruits of Eternal Spiritual Life. May our earnest participation together in commemoration of William Tyndale bring forth favourable blessings upon our lives, our community and your Holy Apostolic Universal Ecclesia.

XVIII.V – OCTOBER 9

1. **Denis of Paris,** Bishop, **and Companions,** Martyrs

October 9

Memorial

Entrance Antiphon

Psalm 119: 51

The arrogant judges and lawyers mock me without restraint, but I do not turn from your Divine maxims of Law.

Offertory Antiphon

O God and Divine Creator, who sent Saint Denis and his companions to preach your glory to the nations and strengthened them for their mission with the virtue of constancy in suffering, grant, we pray, that we may imitate them in disdaining prosperity in this world and in being undaunted by any trial. Through our Lord Jesus Christ, your Son, who lives and reigns with you in the unity of the Holy Spirit, one God, for ever and ever.

Prayer over the Offerings

May God and the Divine Creator accept and sanctify these humble gifts as symbols of the genuine personal offerings we make in commemoration of Denis of Paris and Companions. Through Christ our Light and Saviour.

Communion Antiphon

Lk 22: 28-30

It is you who have stood by me in my trials; and I confer a kingdom on you, says the Lord, that you may eat and drink at my table in my kingdom.

Prayer after Communion

Heavenly Father and God of all Creation, we give thanks for the nourishment of your heavenly gifts of the Bread and Fruits of Eternal Spiritual Life. May our earnest participation together in commemoration of Denis of Paris and Companions bring forth favourable blessings upon our lives, our community and your Holy Apostolic Universal Ecclesia.

XVIII.VI – OCTOBER 10

1. **John XXIII**, Pope October 10
Memorial

Entrance Antiphon   Psalm 119: 55

In the night I remember your name, O Lord, and I will keep your Divine maxims of Law.

Living Testimony: John XXXIII

Consult not your fears but your hopes and your dreams. Think not about your frustrations, but about your unfulfilled potential. Concern yourself not with what you tried and failed in, but with what it is still possible for you to do.

Living Gospel: John XXXIII   John XXXIII

The solidarity which binds all men together as members of a common family makes it impossible for wealthy nations to look with indifference upon the hunger, misery and poverty of other nations whose citizens are unable to enjoy even elementary human rights. The nations of the world are becoming more and more dependent on one another and it will not be possible to preserve a lasting peace so long as glaring economic and social imbalances persist.

Offertory Antiphon

O God and Divine Creator who called upon John to be a servant for all the world in convoking the Second Vatican Council to fulfil the Divine Mission of Christ that Christ himself bestowed in trust to the apostles, grant that we may continue the heroic work of John in unifying and renewing the Universal Ecclesia as the Living Body of Christ. Through our Lord Jesus Christ, your Son, who lives and reigns with you in the unity of the Holy Spirit, one God, for ever and ever.

Prayer over the Offerings

May God and the Divine Creator accept and sanctify these humble gifts as symbols of the genuine personal offerings we make in commemoration of Pope Saint John XXIII. Through Christ our Light and Saviour.

Communion Antiphon   Jn 10: 11

The Good Shepherd did sacrifice his own life for his flock.

Prayer after Communion

> Heavenly Father and God of all Creation, we give thanks for the nourishment of your heavenly gifts of the Bread and Fruits of Eternal Spiritual Life. May our earnest participation together in commemoration of Pope Saint John XXIII bring forth favourable blessings upon our lives, our community and your Holy Apostolic Universal Ecclesia.

XVIII.VII – OCTOBER 14

1.   **Callistus I,** Pope and Martyr   October 14
Memorial

Entrance Antiphon   Psalm 119: 67

> Before I was afflicted I went astray, but now I obey your Divine Word.

Offertory Antiphon

> O God and Divine Creator, who raised up Pope Saint Callistus the First to serve the Church and attend devoutly to Christ's faithful departed, strengthen us, we pray, by his witness to the faith, so that, rescued from the slavery of corruption, we may merit an incorruptible inheritance. Through our Lord Jesus Christ, your Son, who lives and reigns with you in the unity of the Holy Spirit, one God, for ever and ever.

Prayer over the Offerings

> May God and the Divine Creator accept and sanctify these humble gifts as symbols of the genuine personal offerings we make in commemoration of Pope Saint Callistus. Through Christ our Light and Saviour.

Communion Antiphon   Lk 22: 28-30

> It is you who have stood by me in my trials; and I confer a kingdom on you, says the Lord, that you may eat and drink at my table in my kingdom.

Prayer after Communion

> Heavenly Father and God of all Creation, we give thanks for the nourishment of your heavenly gifts of the Bread and Fruits of Eternal Spiritual Life. May our earnest participation together in commemoration of Pope Saint Callistus bring forth favourable blessings upon our lives,

our community and your Holy Apostolic Universal Ecclesia.

XVIII.VIII – OCTOBER 15

1. **Teresa of Ávila,** Virgin and Doctor of the Church
Co-founder of Order of Discalced Carmelites
Memorial

October 15

Entrance Antiphon　　　　　　　　　　　　　　　　　　　　　　　　Psalm 42: 2-3

Like the deer that yearns for running streams, so my soul is yearning for you, my God; my soul is thirsting for God, the living God.

Offertory Antiphon

O God and Divine Creator, who through your Spirit raised up Saint Teresa of Jesus to show the Church the way to seek perfection, grant that we may always be nourished by the food of her heavenly teaching and fired with longing for true holiness. Through our Lord Jesus Christ, your Son, who lives and reigns with you in the unity of the Holy Spirit, one God, for ever and ever.

Prayer over the Offerings

May God and the Divine Creator accept and sanctify these humble gifts as symbols of the genuine personal offerings we make in commemoration of Teresa of Ávila. Through Christ our Light and Saviour.

Communion Antiphon　　　　　　　　　　　　　　　　　　　　　　Ps 89 (88): 2

I will sing for ever of your mercies, O Lord;
through all ages my mouth will proclaim your fidelity.

Prayer after Communion

Heavenly Father and God of all Creation, we give thanks for the nourishment of your heavenly gifts of the Bread and Fruits of Eternal Spiritual Life. May our earnest participation together in commemoration of Teresa of Ávila bring forth favourable blessings upon our lives, our community and your Holy Apostolic Universal Ecclesia.

XVIII.IX – OCTOBER 16

1.   **Hedwig of Silesia,** Religious   October 16

Memorial

Entrance Antiphon   Psalm 119: 86

All your Divine maxims of Law are true; help those find justice when persecuted by corrupt judges and lawyers without cause.

Offertory Antiphon

O God and Divine Creator, grant that the revered intercession of Saint Hedwig may bring us heavenly aid, just as her wonderful life is an example of humility for all. Through our Lord Jesus Christ, your Son, who lives and reigns with you in the unity of the Holy Spirit, one God, for ever and ever.

Prayer over the Offerings

May God and the Divine Creator accept and sanctify these humble gifts as symbols of the genuine personal offerings we make in commemoration of Hedwig of Silesia. Through Christ our Light and Saviour.

Prayer after Communion

Heavenly Father and God of all Creation, we give thanks for the nourishment of your heavenly gifts of the Bread and Fruits of Eternal Spiritual Life. May our earnest participation together in commemoration of Hedwig of Silesia bring forth favourable blessings upon our lives, our community and your Holy Apostolic Universal Ecclesia.

XVIII.X – OCTOBER 17

1.   **Ignatius of Antioch,** Bishop and Martyr   October 17

Memorial

Entrance Antiphon   Psalm 119: 96

To all human perfection I see a limit; but your Divine maxims of Law are boundless.

Offertory Antiphon

O God and Divine Creator, who adorn the sacred body of your Church with the confessions of holy Martyrs, grant, we pray, that, just as the glorious passion of Saint Ignatius of Antioch, which we celebrate today, brought him eternal splendor, so it may be for us unending protection. Through our Lord Jesus Christ, your Son, who lives and reigns with you in the unity of the Holy Spirit, one God, for ever and ever.

Prayer over the Offerings

May God and the Divine Creator accept and sanctify these humble gifts as symbols of the genuine personal offerings we make in commemoration of Ignatius of Antioch. Through Christ our Light and Saviour.

Communion Antiphon
Lk 22: 28-30

It is you who have stood by me in my trials; and I confer a kingdom on you, says the Lord, that you may eat and drink at my table in my kingdom.

Prayer after Communion

Heavenly Father and God of all Creation, we give thanks for the nourishment of your heavenly gifts of the Bread and Fruits of Eternal Spiritual Life. May our earnest participation together in commemoration of Ignatius of Antioch bring forth favourable blessings upon our lives, our community and your Holy Apostolic Universal Ecclesia.

XVIII.XI – OCTOBER 18

1. **Saint Luke,** Evangelist — October 18

Memorial

Entrance Antiphon
Psalm 119: 99

I have more insight than all my teachers, for I meditate on your Divine maxims of Law.

Living Testimony:
Is 52: 7

How beautiful upon the mountains are the feet of him who brings glad tidings of peace, bearing good news, announcing salvation!

Offertory Antiphon

O God and Divine Creator, who chose Saint Luke to reveal by his preaching and writings the mystery of your love for the poor, grant that those who already glory in your name may persevere as one heart and one soul and that all nations may merit to see your salvation. Through our Lord Jesus Christ, your Son, who lives and reigns with you in the unity of the Holy Spirit, one God, for ever and ever.

Prayer over the Offerings

May God and the Divine Creator accept and sanctify these humble gifts as symbols of the genuine personal offerings we make in commemoration of Saint Luke The Evangelist. Through Christ our Light and Saviour.

Communion Antiphon — Lk 10: 1, 9

The Lord sent out disciples to proclaim throughout the towns: The kingdom of God is at hand for you.

Prayer after Communion

Heavenly Father and God of all Creation, we give thanks for the nourishment of your heavenly gifts of the Bread and Fruits of Eternal Spiritual Life. May our earnest participation together in commemoration of Saint Luke The Evangelist bring forth favourable blessings upon our lives, our community and your Holy Apostolic Universal Ecclesia.

XVIII.XII – OCTOBER 19

1. **Jean de Brébeuf,** Martyr — October 19
Memorial

Entrance Antiphon — Psalm 119: 100

I have more understanding than the elders, for I obey your Divine maxims of Law.

Living Testimony: Jean de Brébeuf

On receiving the blow of death, I shall accept it from your hands with the fullest delight and joy of spirit. For this reason, my beloved Jesus, and because of the surging joy which moves me, here and now I offer my blood and body and life. May I die only for you, if you will grant me this grace, since you willingly died for me. Let me so live that you may grant me the gift of such a happy death. In this way, my God and Saviour, I will take from your hand the cup of your sufferings and call on your name.

Living Gospel: Jean de Brébeuf — Jean de Brébeuf

My God and my savior Jesus, what return can I make to you for all the benefits you have conferred on me? I make a vow to you never to fail, on my side, in the grace of martyrdom, if by your infinite mercy you offer it to me some day.

Offertory Antiphon

O God and Divine Creator, Through our Lord Jesus Christ, your Son, who lives and reigns with you in the unity of the Holy Spirit, one God, for ever and ever.

Prayer over the Offerings

May God and the Divine Creator accept and sanctify these humble gifts as symbols of the genuine personal offerings we make in commemoration of Jean de Brébeuf. Through Christ our Light and Saviour.

Communion Antiphon — Lk 22: 28-30

It is you who have stood by me in my trials; and I confer a kingdom on you, says the Lord, that you may eat and drink at my table in my kingdom.

Prayer after Communion

Heavenly Father and God of all Creation, we give thanks for the nourishment of your heavenly gifts of the Bread and Fruits of Eternal Spiritual Life. May our earnest participation together in commemoration of Jean de Brébeuf bring forth favourable blessings upon our lives, our community and your Holy Apostolic Universal Ecclesia.

XVIII.XIII – OCTOBER 20

1. **Paul of the Cross, Priest** — October 20

Founder of Congregation of the Passion of Jesus Christ (Passionists)

Memorial

Entrance Antiphon — Psalm 119: 102

I have not departed from your Divine maxims of Law, for you yourself have taught me.

Offertory Antiphon

O God and Divine Creator, may the Priest Saint Paul, whose only love was the Cross, obtain for us your grace, so that, urged on more strongly by his example, we may each embrace our own cross with courage. Through our Lord Jesus Christ, your Son, who lives and reigns with you in the unity of the Holy Spirit, one God, for ever and ever.

Prayer over the Offerings

May God and the Divine Creator accept and sanctify these humble gifts as symbols of the genuine personal offerings

we make in commemoration of Saint Paul of the Cross. Through Christ our Light and Saviour.

Communion Antiphon   1 Cor 1: 23, 24

We proclaim Christ crucified; Christ, the power of God and the wisdom of God.

Prayer after Communion

Heavenly Father and God of all Creation, we give thanks for the nourishment of your heavenly gifts of the Bread and Fruits of Eternal Spiritual Life. May our earnest participation together in commemoration of Saint Paul of the Cross bring forth favourable blessings upon our lives, our community and your Holy Apostolic Universal Ecclesia.

XVIII.XIV – OCTOBER 22

1.   **John Paul II The Great,** Pope   October 22

Memorial

Entrance Antiphon   Psalm 119: 106

I have taken an oath and confirmed it, that I will follow your righteous laws.

Living Testimony: John Paul II The Great

Ask yourselves, young people, about the love of Christ. Acknowledge His voice resounding in the temple of your heart. Return His bright and penetrating glance which opens the paths of your life to the horizons of the Church's mission. It is a taxing mission, today more than ever, to teach men the truth about themselves, about their end, their destiny, and to show faithful souls the unspeakable riches of the love of Christ. Do not be afraid of the radicalness of His demands, because Jesus, who loved us first, is prepared to give Himself to you, as well as asking of you. If He asks much of you, it is because He knows you can give much.

Living Gospel: John Paul II The Great   John Paul II The Great

Faith and reason are like two wings on which the human spirit rises to the contemplation of truth; and God has placed in the human heart a desire to know the truth- in a word, to know himself- so that, by knowing and loving God, men and women may also come to the fullness of truth about themselves.

Missale Christus | Proper of Heroes & Saints

Offertory Antiphon

O God and Divine Creator who tasked John Paul with the heroic and virtuous task of beginning the new evangelisation of faith by earnestly living according to the Gospel of Christ, grant us the same passion and courage to commit our lives to Christ and Our Mother Mary. Through our Lord Jesus Christ, your Son, who lives and reigns with you in the unity of the Holy Spirit, one God, for ever and ever.

Prayer over the Offerings

May God and the Divine Creator accept and sanctify these humble gifts as symbols of the genuine personal offerings we make in commemoration of Pope Saint John Paul II. Through Christ our Light and Saviour.

Communion Antiphon — Jn 10: 11

The Good Shepherd did sacrifice his own life for his flock.

Prayer after Communion

Heavenly Father and God of all Creation, we give thanks for the nourishment of your heavenly gifts of the Bread and Fruits of Eternal Spiritual Life. May our earnest participation together in commemoration of Pope Saint John Paul II bring forth favourable blessings upon our lives, our community and your Holy Apostolic Universal Ecclesia.

XVIII.XV – OCTOBER 23

1. **Saint John of Capistrano, Priest** — October 23

Memorial

Entrance Antiphon — Psalm 119: 107

I have suffered much; preserve my life, O Lord, according to your Divine Word.

Offertory Antiphon

O God and Divine Creator, who raised up Saint John of Capistrano to comfort your faithful people in tribulation, place us, we pray, under your safe protection and keep your Church in everlasting peace. Through our Lord Jesus Christ, your Son, who lives and reigns with you in the unity of the Holy Spirit, one God, for ever and ever.

Prayer over the Offerings

May God and the Divine Creator accept and sanctify these

Title XVIII: Proper of October

humble gifts as symbols of the genuine personal offerings we make in commemoration of John of Capistrano. Through Christ our Light and Saviour.

Prayer after Communion

Heavenly Father and God of all Creation, we give thanks for the nourishment of your heavenly gifts of the Bread and Fruits of Eternal Spiritual Life. May our earnest participation together in commemoration of Saint John of Capistrano bring forth favourable blessings upon our lives, our community and your Holy Apostolic Universal Ecclesia.

XVIII.XVI – OCTOBER 24

1. **Saint Anthony Mary Claret, Bishop** — October 24
Founder of Missionary Sons of the Immaculate Heart of Mary
Memorial

Entrance Antiphon — Psalm 119: 108

Accept, O Lord, the willing praise of my mouth, and teach me your Divine maxims of Law.

Offertory Antiphon

O God and Divine Creator, who for the evangelization of peoples strengthened the Bishop Saint Anthony Mary Claret with admirable charity and long-suffering, grant, through his intercession, that, seeking the things that are yours, we may earnestly devote ourselves to winning our brothers and sisters for Christ. Who lives and reigns with you in the unity of the Holy Spirit, one God, for ever and ever.

Prayer over the Offerings

May God and the Divine Creator accept and sanctify these humble gifts as symbols of the genuine personal offerings we make in commemoration of Bishop Saint Anthony Mary Claret. Through Christ our Light and Saviour.

Prayer after Communion

Heavenly Father and God of all Creation, we give thanks for the nourishment of your heavenly gifts of the Bread and Fruits of Eternal Spiritual Life. May our earnest participation together in commemoration of Bishop Saint Anthony Mary Claret bring forth favourable blessings upon our lives, our community and your Holy Apostolic

Universal Ecclesia.

XVIII.XVI – OCTOBER 25

1.   **Our Lady of Universal Wisdom & Light**   October 25
Patron of India
Memorial

Entrance Antiphon   Psalm 119: 109

Though I constantly take my life in my hands, I will not forget your Divine maxims of Law.

Offertory Antiphon

O God and Divine Creator of all the Universe and Existence, grant us through the intercession of our Divine Mother Mary as Our Lady of Eternal Wisdom and Light, the radiance of your continued protection for all women of India; and the good health and good fortune of all families and children of India; and the fulfilment of your Divine Mission of unity of all Christians as the Living Body of Christ. Through our Lord Jesus Christ, your Son, who lives and reigns with you in the unity of the Holy Spirit, one God, for ever and ever.

Prayer over the Offerings

May God and the Divine Creator accept and sanctify these humble gifts in the name of our Divine Mother Mary as Our Lady of Eternal Wisdom and Light, as symbols of the genuine personal offerings we make in honour and respect of the protection for all women of India; and the well being of all families and children of India. Through Christ our Light and Saviour.

Prayer after Communion

Heavenly Father and God of all Creation, we give thanks for the nourishment of your heavenly gifts of the Bread and Fruits of Eternal Spiritual Life. May our earnest participation together in commemoration of our Divine Mother Mary as Our Lady of Eternal Wisdom and Light bring forth favourable blessings upon our lives, our nation and your Holy Apostolic Universal Ecclesia as one united body of wisdom and light.

XVIII.XVII – OCTOBER 27

1. **Armand Jean le Bouthillier de Rancé**
Founder of Order of Cistercians of the Strict Observance (Trappists)

October 27

Ordinary

Entrance Antiphon

Psalm 119: 112

My heart is set on keeping your Divine maxims of Law to the very end.

Offertory Antiphon

O God and Divine Creator, Through our Lord Jesus Christ, your Son, who lives and reigns with you in the unity of the Holy Spirit, one God, for ever and ever.

Prayer over the Offerings

May God and the Divine Creator accept and sanctify these humble gifts as symbols of the genuine personal offerings we make in commemoration of Armand Jean le Bouthillier de Rancé. Through Christ our Light and Saviour.

Prayer after Communion

Heavenly Father and God of all Creation, we give thanks for the nourishment of your heavenly gifts of the Bread and Fruits of Eternal Spiritual Life. May our earnest participation together in commemoration of Armand Jean le Bouthillier de Rancé bring forth favourable blessings upon our lives, our community and your Holy Apostolic Universal Ecclesia.

XVIII.XVIII – OCTOBER 28

1. **Saints Simon and Jude, apostles**

October 28

Feast

Entrance Antiphon

Psalm 119: 116

Sustain me according to your promise, and I will live according to your Divine maxims of Law; do not let my faith be dashed when tested.

Offertory Antiphon

O God and Divine Creator, who by the blessed Apostles have brought us to acknowledge your name, graciously grant, through the intercession of Saints Simon and Jude, that the Church may constantly grow by increase of the peoples who believe in you. Through our Lord Jesus Christ, your Son, who lives and reigns with you in the unity of the Holy Spirit, one God, for ever and ever.

Prayer over the Offerings

May God and the Divine Creator accept and sanctify these humble gifts as symbols of the genuine personal offerings we make in commemoration of Saints Simon and Jude. Through Christ our Light and Saviour.

Communion Antiphon — Jn 14: 23

Whoever loves me will keep my word, says the Lord; and my Father will love him, and we will come to him, and make our home with him.

Prayer after Communion

Heavenly Father and God of all Creation, we give thanks for the nourishment of your heavenly gifts of the Bread and Fruits of Eternal Spiritual Life. May our earnest participation together in commemoration of Saints Simon and Jude bring forth favourable blessings upon our lives, our community and your Holy Apostolic Universal Ecclesia.

XVIII.XIX – OCTOBER 30

1. **John Wyclif** — October 30
Memorial

Entrance Antiphon — Psalm 119: 130

The unfolding of your Divine Word gives light; it gives understanding even to the uneducated.

Prayer over the Offerings

May God and the Divine Creator accept and sanctify these humble gifts as symbols of the genuine personal offerings we make in commemoration of John Wyclif. Through Christ our Light and Saviour.

Prayer after Communion

Heavenly Father and God of all Creation, we give thanks for the nourishment of your heavenly gifts of the Bread and Fruits of Eternal Spiritual Life. May our earnest participation together in commemoration of John Wyclif bring forth favourable blessings upon our lives, our community and your Holy Apostolic Universal Ecclesia.

Title XIX: Proper of November

XIX.I – NOVEMBER 1

1.   **All Saints Day**   November 1
                          Memorial

Entrance Antiphon   Psalm 119: 134

Redeem me from the oppression of tyrants, that I may obey your Divine maxims of Law.

Offertory Antiphon

O God and Divine Creator, Through our Lord Jesus Christ, your Son, who lives and reigns with you in the unity of the Holy Spirit, one God, for ever and ever.

Prayer over the Offerings

May God and the Divine Creator accept and sanctify these humble gifts as symbols of the genuine personal offerings we make in commemoration of All Saints Day. Through Christ our Light and Saviour.

Prayer after Communion

Heavenly Father and God of all Creation, we give thanks for the nourishment of your heavenly gifts of the Bread and Fruits of Eternal Spiritual Life. May our earnest participation together in commemoration of All Saints Day bring forth favourable blessings upon our lives, our community and your Holy Apostolic Universal Ecclesia.

XIX.II – NOVEMBER 3

1.   **Martin de Porres,** Religious   November 3
                          Memorial

Entrance Antiphon   Psalm 119: 135

Make your face shine upon your servant and teach me your Divine maxims of Law.

Offertory Antiphon

O God and Divine Creator, who led Saint Martin de Porres by the path of humility to heavenly glory, grant that we may so follow his radiant example in this life as to merit to be exalted with him in heaven. Through our Lord Jesus Christ, your Son, who lives and reigns with you in the unity of the Holy Spirit, one God, for ever and ever.

Prayer over the Offerings

May God and the Divine Creator accept and sanctify these humble gifts as symbols of the genuine personal offerings

Missale Christus | Proper of Heroes & Saints

we make in commemoration of Martin de Porres. Through Christ our Light and Saviour.

Prayer after Communion

Heavenly Father and God of all Creation, we give thanks for the nourishment of your heavenly gifts of the Bread and Fruits of Eternal Spiritual Life. May our earnest participation together in commemoration of Martin de Porres bring forth favourable blessings upon our lives, our community and your Holy Apostolic Universal Ecclesia.

XIX.III – NOVEMBER 4

1.   **Charles Borromeo,** Bishop   November 4
Memorial

Entrance Antiphon   Psalm 119: 142

Your righteousness is everlasting and your Divine maxims of Law are true.

Offertory Antiphon

O God and Divine Creator, preserve in the midst of your people the spirit with which you filled the Bishop Saint Charles Borromeo, that your Church may be constantly renewed and, by conforming herself to the likeness of Christ, may show his face to the world. Who lives and reigns with you in the unity of the Holy Spirit, one God, for ever and ever.

Prayer over the Offerings

May God and the Divine Creator accept and sanctify these humble gifts as symbols of the genuine personal offerings we make in commemoration of Charles Borromeo. Through Christ our Light and Saviour.

Prayer after Communion

Heavenly Father and God of all Creation, we give thanks for the nourishment of your heavenly gifts of the Bread and Fruits of Eternal Spiritual Life. May our earnest participation together in commemoration of Charles Borromeo bring forth favourable blessings upon our lives, our community and your Holy Apostolic Universal Ecclesia.

Title XIX: Proper of November

XIX.IV – NOVEMBER 10

1. **Leo the Great,** Pope and Doctor of the Church

November 10

Memorial

Entrance Antiphon — Psalm 119: 165

Great peace have they who love your Divine maxims of Law, and nothing can make them stumble.

Offertory Antiphon

O God and Divine Creator, who never allow the gates of hell to prevail against your Church, firmly founded on the apostolic rock, grant her, we pray, that through the intercession of Pope Saint Leo, she may stand firm in your truth and know the protection of lasting peace. Through our Lord Jesus Christ, your Son, who lives and reigns with you in the unity of the Holy Spirit, one God, for ever and ever.

Prayer over the Offerings

May God and the Divine Creator accept and sanctify these humble gifts as symbols of the genuine personal offerings we make in commemoration of Pope Saint Leo the Great. Through Christ our Light and Saviour.

Communion Antiphon — Mt 16: 16, 18

Peter said to Jesus: You are the Christ, the Son of the living God. And Jesus replied: You are Peter, and upon this rock I will build my Church.

Prayer after Communion

Heavenly Father and God of all Creation, we give thanks for the nourishment of your heavenly gifts of the Bread and Fruits of Eternal Spiritual Life. May our earnest participation together in commemoration of Pope Saint Leo the Great bring forth favourable blessings upon our lives, our community and your Holy Apostolic Universal Ecclesia.

XIX.V – NOVEMBER 11

1. **Martin of Tours,** Bishop

November 11

Memorial

Entrance Antiphon — Psalm 121: 2-3

From the Lord deliverance comes to me, the Lord who made heaven and earth. Never will he who guards thee allow thy foot to stumble; never fall asleep at his post!

Offertory Antiphon

O God and Divine Creator, who are glorified in the Bishop Saint Martin both by his life and death, make new, we pray, the wonders of your grace in our hearts, that neither death nor life may separate us from your love. Through our Lord Jesus Christ, your Son, who lives and reigns with you in the unity of the Holy Spirit, one God, for ever and ever.

Prayer over the Offerings

May God and the Divine Creator accept and sanctify these humble gifts as symbols of the genuine personal offerings we make in commemoration of Martin of Tours. Through Christ our Light and Saviour.

Communion Antiphon — Mt 25: 40

Amen, I say to you:
Whatever you did for one of the least of my brethren,
you did it for me, says the Lord.

Prayer after Communion

Heavenly Father and God of all Creation, we give thanks for the nourishment of your heavenly gifts of the Bread and Fruits of Eternal Spiritual Life. May our earnest participation together in commemoration of Martin of Tours bring forth favourable blessings upon our lives, our community and your Holy Apostolic Universal Ecclesia.

XIX.VI – NOVEMBER 12

1. Josaphat Kuntsevych, Bishop and Martyr — November 12

Memorial

Entrance Antiphon — Psalm 121:7-8

The Lord will guard thee from all evil; the Lord will protect thee in danger; the Lord will protect thy journeying and thy home-coming, henceforth and for ever.

Offertory Antiphon

O God and Divine Creator, raise up in your Church the Spirit that filled Saint Josaphat as he laid down his life for the sheep, so that through his intercession we, too, may be strengthened by the same Spirit and not be afraid to lay down our life for others. Through our Lord Jesus Christ, your Son, who lives and reigns with you in the unity of the Holy Spirit, one God, for ever and ever.

Title XIX: Proper of November

Prayer over the Offerings

May God and the Divine Creator accept and sanctify these humble gifts as symbols of the genuine personal offerings we make in commemoration of Saint Josaphat. Through Christ our Light and Saviour.

Communion Antiphon — Mt. 10: 39

Whoever loses his life for my sake, will find it in eternity, says the Lord.

Prayer after Communion

Heavenly Father and God of all Creation, we give thanks for the nourishment of your heavenly gifts of the Bread and Fruits of Eternal Spiritual Life. May our earnest participation together in commemoration of Saint Josaphat bring forth favourable blessings upon our lives, our community and your Holy Apostolic Universal Ecclesia.

XIX.VII – NOVEMBER 13

1. Frances Xavier Cabrini, Virgin

Memorial — November 13

Entrance Antiphon — Psalm 126: 3

The Lord has done great things for us, and we are filled with joy.

Offertory Antiphon

O God and Divine Creator, who called Saint Frances Xavier Cabrini from Italy to serve the immigrants of America, by her example, teach us to have concern for the stranger, the sick, and all those in need, and by her prayers help us to see Christ in all the men and women we meet. Through our Lord Jesus Christ, your Son, who lives and reigns with you in the unity of the Holy Spirit, one God, for ever and ever.

Prayer over the Offerings

May God and the Divine Creator accept and sanctify these humble gifts as symbols of the genuine personal offerings we make in commemoration of Saint Frances Xavier Cabrini. Through Christ our Light and Saviour.

Prayer after Communion

Heavenly Father and God of all Creation, we give thanks for the nourishment of your heavenly gifts of the Bread

and Fruits of Eternal Spiritual Life. May our earnest participation together in commemoration of Saint Frances Xavier Cabrini bring forth favourable blessings upon our lives, our community and your Holy Apostolic Universal Ecclesia.

XIX.VIII – NOVEMBER 15

1. **Albert the Great,** Bishop and Doctor of the Church — November 15
Memorial

Entrance Antiphon — Psalm 128: 1-2

Blessed are all who love and respect the Lord, and who walk in his ways. You will eat the fruit of your labor; blessings and prosperity will be yours.

Offertory Antiphon

O God and Divine Creator, who made the Bishop Saint Albert great by his joining of human wisdom to divine faith, grant, we pray, that we may so adhere to the truths he taught, that through progress in learning we may come to a deeper knowledge and love of you. Through our Lord Jesus Christ, your Son, who lives and reigns with you in the unity of the Holy Spirit, one God, for ever and ever.

Prayer over the Offerings

May God and the Divine Creator accept and sanctify these humble gifts as symbols of the genuine personal offerings we make in commemoration of Saint Albert the Great. Through Christ our Light and Saviour.

Communion Antiphon — Psalm 1: 2-3

One who ponders the Divine maxims of Law of the Lord day and night shall yield fruit in due season.

Prayer after Communion

Heavenly Father and God of all Creation, we give thanks for the nourishment of your heavenly gifts of the Bread and Fruits of Eternal Spiritual Life. May our earnest participation together in commemoration of Saint Albert the Great bring forth favourable blessings upon our lives, our community and your Holy Apostolic Universal Ecclesia.

XIX.IX – NOVEMBER 16

1. **Margaret of Scotland** — November 16
Memorial

Entrance Antiphon — Psalm 133: 1

How good and pleasant it is in the eyes of the Lord when brothers and sisters live together in unity!

Offertory Antiphon

O God and Divine Creator, who made Saint Margaret of Scotland wonderful in her outstanding charity towards the poor, grant that through her intercession and example we may reflect among all humanity the image of your divine goodness. Through our Lord Jesus Christ, your Son, who lives and reigns with you in the unity of the Holy Spirit, one God, for ever and ever.

Prayer over the Offerings

May God and the Divine Creator accept and sanctify these humble gifts as symbols of the genuine personal offerings we make in commemoration of Saint Margaret of Scotland. Through Christ our Light and Saviour.

Prayer after Communion

Heavenly Father and God of all Creation, we give thanks for the nourishment of your heavenly gifts of the Bread and Fruits of Eternal Spiritual Life. May our earnest participation together in commemoration of Saint Margaret of Scotland bring forth favourable blessings upon our lives, our community and your Holy Apostolic Universal Ecclesia.

XIX.X – NOVEMBER 17

1. **Elizabeth of Hungary**, Religious — November 17
Memorial

Entrance Antiphon — Psalm 134: 1

Praise the Lord, all you servants of God who minister in the house of the Lord.

Offertory Antiphon

O God and Divine Creator, by whose gift Saint Elizabeth of Hungary recognized and revered Christ in the poor, grant, through her intercession, that we may serve with unfailing charity the needy and those afflicted. Through our Lord

Prayer over the Offerings

May God and the Divine Creator accept and sanctify these humble gifts as symbols of the genuine personal offerings we make in commemoration of Saint Elizabeth of Hungary. Through Christ our Light and Saviour.

Prayer after Communion

Heavenly Father and God of all Creation, we give thanks for the nourishment of your heavenly gifts of the Bread and Fruits of Eternal Spiritual Life. May our earnest participation together in commemoration of Saint Elizabeth of Hungary bring forth favourable blessings upon our lives, our community and your Holy Apostolic Universal Ecclesia.

XIX.XI – NOVEMBER 22

1. **Cecilia,** Virgin and Martyr — November 22

Memorial

Entrance Antiphon — Psalm 139: 12

O Lord, you have searched my heart and conscience and you know me.

Offertory Antiphon

O God and Divine Creator, who gladden us each year with the feast day of your handmaid Saint Cecilia, grant, we pray, that what has been devoutly handed down concerning her may offer us examples to imitate and proclaim the wonders worked in his servants by Christ your Son. Who lives and reigns with you in the unity of the Holy Spirit, one God, for ever and ever.

Prayer over the Offerings

May God and the Divine Creator accept and sanctify these humble gifts as symbols of the genuine personal offerings we make in commemoration of Saint Cecilia. Through Christ our Light and Saviour.

Communion Antiphon — Lk 22: 28-30

It is you who have stood by me in my trials; and I confer a kingdom on you, says the Lord, that you may eat and drink at my table in my kingdom.

Prayer after Communion

Heavenly Father and God of all Creation, we give thanks for the nourishment of your heavenly gifts of the Bread and Fruits of Eternal Spiritual Life. May our earnest participation together in commemoration of Saint Cecilia bring forth favourable blessings upon our lives, our community and your Holy Apostolic Universal Ecclesia.

XIX.XII – NOVEMBER 23

1.   **Clement I,** Pope and Martyr   November 23

Memorial

Entrance Antiphon   Psalm 139: 3-4

You discern my going out and my lying down; you are familiar with all my ways. Before a word is on my tongue you know it completely, O Lord.

Offertory Antiphon

O God and Divine Creator, who are wonderful in the virtue of all your Saints, grant us joy in the yearly commemoration of Saint Clement, who, as a Martyr and High Priest of your Son, bore out by his witness what he celebrated in mystery and confirmed by example what he preached with his lips. Through our Lord Jesus Christ, your Son, who lives and reigns with you in the unity of the Holy Spirit, one God, for ever and ever.

Prayer over the Offerings

May God and the Divine Creator accept and sanctify these humble gifts as symbols of the genuine personal offerings we make in commemoration of Pope Saint Clement. Through Christ our Light and Saviour.

Communion Antiphon   Lk 22: 28-30

It is you who have stood by me in my trials; and I confer a kingdom on you, says the Lord, that you may eat and drink at my table in my kingdom.

Prayer after Communion

Heavenly Father and God of all Creation, we give thanks for the nourishment of your heavenly gifts of the Bread and Fruits of Eternal Spiritual Life. May our earnest participation together in commemoration of Pope Saint Clement bring forth favourable blessings upon our lives, our community and your Holy Apostolic Universal

Ecclesia.

XIX.XIII – NOVEMBER 24

1.   **John Knox**   November 24
Founder of Presbyterian Church of Universal Ecclesia
Memorial

Entrance Antiphon   Psalm 139: 12

No, darkness is no hiding-place from thee, with thee the night shines clear as day itself; light and dark are one.

Prayer over the Offerings

May God and the Divine Creator accept and sanctify these humble gifts as symbols of the genuine personal offerings we make in commemoration of John Knox. Through Christ our Light and Saviour.

Prayer after Communion

Heavenly Father and God of all Creation, we give thanks for the nourishment of your heavenly gifts of the Bread and Fruits of Eternal Spiritual Life. May our earnest participation together in commemoration of John Knox bring forth favourable blessings upon our lives, our community and your Holy Apostolic Universal Ecclesia.

2.   **Andrew Dung-Lac, Priest, and Companions, Martyrs**   November 24
Memorial

Entrance Antiphon   Psalm 139: 12

No, darkness is no hiding-place from thee, with thee the night shines clear as day itself; light and dark are one.

Offertory Antiphon

O God and Divine Creator, source and origin of all fatherhood, who kept the Martyrs Saint Andrew Dung-Lac and his companions faithful to the Cross of your Son, even to the shedding of their blood, grant, through their intercession, that, spreading your love among our brothers and sisters, we may be your children both in name and in truth. Through our Lord Jesus Christ, your Son, who lives and reigns with you in the unity of the Holy Spirit, one God, for ever and ever.

Prayer over the Offerings

May God and the Divine Creator accept and sanctify these humble gifts as symbols of the genuine personal offerings we make in commemoration of Andrew Dung-Lac and

Companions. Through Christ our Light and Saviour.

Communion Antiphon — Mt 5:10

Blessed are they who are persecuted for the sake of righteousness, for theirs is the Kingdom of Heaven.

Prayer after Communion

Heavenly Father and God of all Creation, we give thanks for the nourishment of your heavenly gifts of the Bread and Fruits of Eternal Spiritual Life. May our earnest participation together in commemoration of Andrew Dung-Lac and Companions bring forth favourable blessings upon our lives, our community and your Holy Apostolic Universal Ecclesia.

XIX.XIV – NOVEMBER 25

1. Catherine of Alexandria, Virgin and Martyr — November 25
Memorial

Entrance Antiphon — Psalm 139:13-14

Author, thou, of my inmost being, didst thou not form me in my mother's womb? I praise thee for my wondrous fashioning, for all the wonders of thy creation. Of my soul thou hast full knowledge.

Offertory Antiphon

O God and Divine Creator, who gave Saint Catherine of Alexandria to your people as a Virgin and an invincible Martyr, grant that through her intercession we may be strengthened in faith and constancy and spend ourselves without reserve for the unity of the Church. Through our Lord Jesus Christ, your Son, who lives and reigns with you in the unity of the Holy Spirit, one God, for ever and ever.

Prayer over the Offerings

May God and the Divine Creator accept and sanctify these humble gifts as symbols of the genuine personal offerings we make in commemoration of Saint Catherine of Alexandria. Through Christ our Light and Saviour.

Communion Antiphon — Lk 22:28-30

It is you who have stood by me in my trials; and I confer a kingdom on you, says the Lord, that you may eat and drink at my table in my kingdom.

Prayer after Communion

Heavenly Father and God of all Creation, we give thanks for the nourishment of your heavenly gifts of the Bread

and Fruits of Eternal Spiritual Life. May our earnest participation together in commemoration of Saint Catherine of Alexandria bring forth favourable blessings upon our lives, our community and your Holy Apostolic Universal Ecclesia.

XIX.XV – NOVEMBER 28

1. **Our Lady of Africa** — November 28
Patron of Africa
Memorial

Entrance Antiphon — Psalm 141: 3-4

Set a watch, O Lord, before my mouth; keep the door of my lips. Incline not my heart to any evil thing, to practise wicked works with men that work iniquity: and let me not eat of their dainties.

Offertory Antiphon

O God and Divine Creator, grant us through the intercession of our Divine Mother Mary as Our Lady of Africa, that all peoples of each generation of Africa may come to know your good works and Divine Truth. Through our Lord Jesus Christ, your Son, who lives and reigns with you in the unity of the Holy Spirit, one God, for ever and ever.

Prayer over the Offerings

May God and the Divine Creator accept and sanctify these humble gifts as symbols of the genuine personal offerings we make in commemoration of Our Lady of Africa. Through Christ our Light and Saviour.

Prayer after Communion

Heavenly Father and God of all Creation, we give thanks for the nourishment of your heavenly gifts of the Bread and Fruits of Eternal Spiritual Life. May our earnest participation together in commemoration of Our Lady of Africa bring forth favourable blessings upon our lives, our community and your Holy Apostolic Universal Ecclesia.

XIX.XVI – NOVEMBER 30

1.

Saint Andrew the Apostle
Feast

November 30

Entrance Antiphon — Psalm 143: 1

O Lord, hear my prayer, listen to my cry for mercy; in your faithfulness and righteousness come to my relief.

Living Testimony: — Mt 4: 18-19

Beside the Sea of Galilee,
the Lord saw two brothers, Peter and Andrew,
and he said to them:
Come after me and I will make you fishers of men.

Offertory Antiphon

O God and Divine Creator, we humbly implore your majesty, that, just as the blessed Apostle Andrew was for your Church a preacher and pastor, so he may be for us a constant intercessor before you. Through our Lord Jesus Christ, your Son, who lives and reigns with you in the unity of the Holy Spirit, one God, for ever and ever.

Prayer over the Offerings

May God and the Divine Creator accept and sanctify these humble gifts as symbols of the genuine personal offerings we make in commemoration of Saint Andrew the Apostle. Through Christ our Light and Saviour.

Communion Antiphon — Jn 1: 41-42

Andrew told his brother Simon: We have found the Messiah, the Christ, and he brought him to Jesus.

Prayer after Communion

Heavenly Father and God of all Creation, we give thanks for the nourishment of your heavenly gifts of the Bread and Fruits of Eternal Spiritual Life. May our earnest participation together in commemoration of Saint Andrew the Apostle bring forth favourable blessings upon our lives, our community and your Holy Apostolic Universal Ecclesia.

Title XX: Proper of December

XX.I – DECEMBER 3

1.   **Saint Francis Xavier,** Priest   December 3
Patron of Asia
Memorial

Entrance Antiphon   Psalm 18: 50

I will praise you, Lord, among the nations;
I will tell of your name to my kin.

Offertory Antiphon

O God and Divine Creator, who through the preaching of Saint Francis Xavier won many peoples to yourself, grant that the hearts of the faithful may burn with the same zeal for the faith and that Holy Church may everywhere rejoice in an abundance of offspring. Through our Lord Jesus Christ, your Son, who lives and reigns with you in the unity of the Holy Spirit, one God, for ever and ever.

Prayer over the Offerings

May God and the Divine Creator accept and sanctify these humble gifts as symbols of the genuine personal offerings we make in commemoration of Saint Francis Xavier. Through Christ our Light and Saviour.

Communion Antiphon   Mt 10: 27

What I say to you in the darkness
speak in the light, says the Lord,
what you hear whispered,
proclaim on the housetops.

Prayer after Communion

Heavenly Father and God of all Creation, we give thanks for the nourishment of your heavenly gifts of the Bread and Fruits of Eternal Spiritual Life. May our earnest participation together in commemoration of Saint Francis Xavier bring forth favourable blessings upon our lives, our community and your Holy Apostolic Universal Ecclesia.

XX.II – DECEMBER 4

1.   **John Damascene,** Priest and Doctor of the Church   December 4

Memorial

Entrance Antiphon   Psalm 145: 1

I will exalt you, my God the King; I will praise your name for ever and ever.

Offertory Antiphon

O God and Divine Creator, grant that we may be helped by the prayers of the Priest Saint John Damascene, so that the true faith, which he excelled in teaching, may always be our light and our strength. Through our Lord Jesus Christ, your Son, who lives and reigns with you in the unity of the Holy Spirit, one God, for ever and ever.

Prayer over the Offerings

May God and the Divine Creator accept and sanctify these humble gifts as symbols of the genuine personal offerings we make in commemoration of Saint John Damascene. Through Christ our Light and Saviour.

Communion Antiphon   Psalm 1: 2-3

One who ponders the Divine maxims of Law of the Lord day and night shall yield fruit in due season.

Prayer after Communion

Heavenly Father and God of all Creation, we give thanks for the nourishment of your heavenly gifts of the Bread and Fruits of Eternal Spiritual Life. May our earnest participation together in commemoration of Saint John Damascene bring forth favourable blessings upon our lives, our community and your Holy Apostolic Universal Ecclesia.

XX.III – DECEMBER 6

1.   **Saint Nicholas of Myra,** Bishop   December 6

Memorial

Entrance Antiphon   Psalm 145: 14

The Lord upholds all those who fall and lifts up all who are bowed down.

Offertory Antiphon

O God and Divine Creator, grant us your mercy and protect us in all dangers through the prayers of the Bishop Saint Nicholas, so that the way of salvation may lie open before us. Through our Lord Jesus Christ, your Son, who lives and reigns with you in the unity of the Holy Spirit, one God, for ever and ever.

Prayer over the Offerings

May God and the Divine Creator accept and sanctify these humble gifts as symbols of the genuine personal offerings we make in commemoration of Saint Nicholas of Myra. Through Christ our Light and Saviour.

Prayer after Communion

Heavenly Father and God of all Creation, we give thanks for the nourishment of your heavenly gifts of the Bread and Fruits of Eternal Spiritual Life. May our earnest participation together in commemoration of Saint Nicholas of Myra bring forth favourable blessings upon our lives, our community and your Holy Apostolic Universal Ecclesia.

XX.IV – DECEMBER 7

1.   **Ambrose of Milan,** Bishop and Doctor of the Church   December 7

Memorial

Entrance Antiphon   Psalm 145: 17

The Lord is righteous in all his ways and loving toward all he has made.

Living Testimony: Sir 15: 5

In the midst of the Church he opened his mouth, and the Lord filled him with the spirit of wisdom and understanding and clothed him in a robe of glory.

Offertory Antiphon

O God and Divine Creator, who made the Bishop Saint

Ambrose a teacher of the Catholic faith and a model of apostolic courage, raise up in your Church men after your own heart to govern her with courage and wisdom. Through our Lord Jesus Christ, your Son, who lives and reigns with you in the unity of the Holy Spirit, one God, for ever and ever.

Prayer over the Offerings

May God and the Divine Creator accept and sanctify these humble gifts as symbols of the genuine personal offerings we make in commemoration of Saint Ambrose of Milan. Through Christ our Light and Saviour.

Communion Antiphon
Ps 1: 2, 3

He who ponders the law of the Lord day and night will yield fruit in due season.

Prayer after Communion

Heavenly Father and God of all Creation, we give thanks for the nourishment of your heavenly gifts of the Bread and Fruits of Eternal Spiritual Life. May our earnest participation together in commemoration of Saint Ambrose of Milan bring forth favourable blessings upon our lives, our community and your Holy Apostolic Universal Ecclesia.

XX.V – DECEMBER 9

1. Juan Diego Cuauhtlatoatzin
December 9

Memorial

Entrance Antiphon
Psalm 146: 5-6

Blessed is he whose help is the Divine Creator, whose hope is in the Lord his God, the Maker of heaven and earth, the sea, and everything in them-- the Lord, who remains faithful forever.

Offertory Antiphon

O God and Divine Creator, who by means of Saint Juan Diego showed the love of the most holy Virgin Mary for your people, grant, through his intercession, that, by following the counsels our Mother gave at Guadalupe, we may be ever constant in fulfilling your will. Through our Lord Jesus Christ, your Son, who lives and reigns with you in the unity of the Holy Spirit, one God, for ever and ever.

Prayer over the Offerings

May God and the Divine Creator accept and sanctify these humble gifts as symbols of the genuine personal offerings we make in commemoration of Saint Juan Diego. Through Christ our Light and Saviour.

Prayer after Communion

Heavenly Father and God of all Creation, we give thanks for the nourishment of your heavenly gifts of the Bread and Fruits of Eternal Spiritual Life. May our earnest participation together in commemoration of Saint Juan Diego bring forth favourable blessings upon our lives, our community and your Holy Apostolic Universal Ecclesia.

XX.VI – DECEMBER 10

1. **Saint Damasus I**, Pope
Memorial

December 10

Entrance Antiphon — Psalm 146: 7-8

He upholds the cause of the oppressed and gives food to the hungry. The Lord sets all prisoners free, and gives new sight to the blind, the Lord lifts up those who are bowed down, the Lord loves the righteous.

Offertory Antiphon

O God and Divine Creator, grant that we may constantly exalt the merits of your Martyrs, whom Pope Saint Damasus so venerated and loved. Through our Lord Jesus Christ, your Son, who lives and reigns with you in the unity of the Holy Spirit, one God, for ever and ever.

Prayer over the Offerings

May God and the Divine Creator accept and sanctify these humble gifts as symbols of the genuine personal offerings we make in commemoration of Saint Pope Damasus. Through Christ our Light and Saviour.

Communion Antiphon — Jn 10: 11

The Good Shepherd did sacrifice his own life for his flock.

Prayer after Communion

Heavenly Father and God of all Creation, we give thanks for the nourishment of your heavenly gifts of the Bread and Fruits of Eternal Spiritual Life. May our earnest participation together in commemoration of Saint Pope Damasus bring forth favourable blessings upon our lives, our community and your Holy Apostolic Universal Ecclesia.

XX.VII – DECEMBER 12

1. **Our Lady of Guadalupe** December 12
Patron of the Americas
Memorial

Entrance Antiphon Rev 12: 1

A great sign appeared in the sky, a woman clothed with the sun, with the moon under her feet, and on her head a crown of twelve stars.

Offertory Antiphon

O God and Divine Creator, Father of mercies, who placed your people under the singular protection of your Son's most holy Mother, grant that all who invoke the Blessed Virgin of Guadalupe, may seek with ever more lively faith the progress of peoples in the ways of justice and of peace. Through our Lord Jesus Christ, your Son, who lives and reigns with you in the unity of the Holy Spirit, one God, for ever and ever.

Prayer over the Offerings

May God and the Divine Creator accept and sanctify these humble gifts as symbols of the genuine personal offerings we make in commemoration of Our Lady of Guadalupe. Through Christ our Light and Saviour.

Communion Antiphon Lk 1: 52

The Lord has cast down the mighty from their thrones, and has lifted up the lowly.

Prayer after Communion

Heavenly Father and God of all Creation, we give thanks for the nourishment of your heavenly gifts of the Bread and Fruits of Eternal Spiritual Life. May our earnest participation together in commemoration of Our Lady of Guadalupe bring forth favourable blessings upon our lives, our community and your Holy Apostolic Universal Ecclesia.

XX.VIII – DECEMBER 13

1. **Lucy of Syracuse,** Virgin and Martyr — December 13
Memorial

Entrance Antiphon — Psalm 148: 2-4

Praise him, all his angels, praise him, all his heavenly hosts. Praise him, sun and moon, praise him, all you shining stars. Praise him, you highest heavens and you waters above the skies.

Offertory Antiphon

O God and Divine Creator, grant that the glorious intercession of the Virgin and Martyr Saint Lucy give us new heart, so that we may celebrate her heavenly birthday in this present age and so behold things eternal. Through our Lord Jesus Christ, your Son, who lives and reigns with you in the unity of the Holy Spirit, one God, for ever and ever.

Prayer over the Offerings

May God and the Divine Creator accept and sanctify these humble gifts as symbols of the genuine personal offerings we make in commemoration of Saint Lucy of Syracuse. Through Christ our Light and Saviour.

Communion Antiphon — Lk 22: 28-30

It is you who have stood by me in my trials; and I confer a kingdom on you, says the Lord, that you may eat and drink at my table in my kingdom.

Prayer after Communion

Heavenly Father and God of all Creation, we give thanks for the nourishment of your heavenly gifts of the Bread and Fruits of Eternal Spiritual Life. May our earnest participation together in commemoration of Saint Lucy of Syracuse bring forth favourable blessings upon our lives, our community and your Holy Apostolic Universal Ecclesia.

XX.IX – DECEMBER 14

1.   **John of the Cross,** Priest and Doctor of the Church   December 14

Memorial

Entrance Antiphon   Psalm 148: 5-6

Let them praise the name of the Lord, for he commanded a new covenant of Light be created. He has set his Trust in place for ever and ever; he gave a Testament that will never pass away.

Offertory Antiphon

O God and Divine Creator, who gave the Priest Saint John an outstanding dedication to perfect self-denial and love of the Cross, grant that, by imitating him closely at all times, we may come to contemplate eternally your glory. Through our Lord Jesus Christ, your Son, who lives and reigns with you in the unity of the Holy Spirit, one God, for ever and ever.

Prayer over the Offerings

May God and the Divine Creator accept and sanctify these humble gifts as symbols of the genuine personal offerings we make in commemoration of Saint John of the Cross. Through Christ our Light and Saviour.

Communion Antiphon   Mt 16: 24

Whoever wishes to come after me must deny himself, take up his cross, and follow me, says the Lord.

Prayer after Communion

Heavenly Father and God of all Creation, we give thanks for the nourishment of your heavenly gifts of the Bread and Fruits of Eternal Spiritual Life. May our earnest participation together in commemoration of Saint John of the Cross bring forth favourable blessings upon our lives, our community and your Holy Apostolic Universal Ecclesia.

Title XX: Proper of December

XX.X – DECEMBER 16

1. **Adelaide of Italy** December 16
Memorial

Entrance Antiphon Psalm 1:1

Blessed is the person who does not guide his steps by ill counsel, or turn aside where transgressors walk, or, where scornful souls gather, sit down to rest

Prayer over the Offerings

May God and the Divine Creator accept and sanctify these humble gifts as symbols of the genuine personal offerings we make in commemoration of Saint Adelaide of Italy. Through Christ our Light and Saviour.

Prayer after Communion

Heavenly Father and God of all Creation, we give thanks for the nourishment of your heavenly gifts of the Bread and Fruits of Eternal Spiritual Life. May our earnest participation together in commemoration of Saint Adelaide of Italy bring forth favourable blessings upon our lives, our community and your Holy Apostolic Universal Ecclesia.

XX.XI – DECEMBER 21

1. **Peter Canisius,** Priest and Doctor of the Church December 21
Memorial

Entrance Antiphon Psalm 3:9

From the Lord all deliverance comes; let thy blessing, Lord, rest upon thy people.

Offertory Antiphon

O God and Divine Creator, who for the defense of Your Word made the Priest Saint Peter Canisius strong in virtue and in learning, grant, through his intercession, that those who seek the truth may joyfully find you, their God, and that your faithful people may persevere in confessing you. Through our Lord Jesus Christ, your Son, who lives and reigns with you in the unity of the Holy Spirit, one God, for ever and ever.

Prayer over the Offerings

May God and the Divine Creator accept and sanctify these humble gifts as symbols of the genuine personal offerings

we make in commemoration of Saint Peter Canisius.
Through Christ our Light and Saviour.

Communion Antiphon — Psalm 1: 2-3

One who ponders the Divine maxims of Law of the Lord day and night shall yield fruit in due season.

Prayer after Communion

Heavenly Father and God of all Creation, we give thanks for the nourishment of your heavenly gifts of the Bread and Fruits of Eternal Spiritual Life. May our earnest participation together in commemoration of Saint Peter Canisius bring forth favourable blessings upon our lives, our community and your Holy Apostolic Universal Ecclesia.

XX.XII – DECEMBER 23

1. **John of Kanty,** Priest — December 23

Memorial

Entrance Antiphon — Psalm 5: 9

Lord, you do lead me with faithful care; reveal a clear path, while I walk beset by challenges.

Offertory Antiphon

O God and Divine Creator, grant that by the example of the Priest Saint John of Kanty we may advance in the knowledge of holy things and, by showing compassion to all, may gain forgiveness in your sight. Through our Lord Jesus Christ, your Son, who lives and reigns with you in the unity of the Holy Spirit, one God, for ever and ever.

Prayer over the Offerings

May God and the Divine Creator accept and sanctify these humble gifts as symbols of the genuine personal offerings we make in commemoration of Saint John of Kanty. Through Christ our Light and Saviour.

Prayer after Communion

Heavenly Father and God of all Creation, we give thanks for the nourishment of your heavenly gifts of the Bread and Fruits of Eternal Spiritual Life. May our earnest participation together in commemoration of Saint John of Kanty bring forth favourable blessings upon our lives, our community and your Holy Apostolic Universal Ecclesia.

XX.XIII – DECEMBER 26

1. **Saint Stephen, the First Martyr**
Feast

December 26

Entrance Antiphon

Psalm 5: 12

For all those who trust in thee there is joy and everlasting triumph; welcome protection they have from thee, true lovers of thy name.

Offertory Antiphon

Grant, Lord, we pray, that we may imitate what we worship, and so learn to love even our enemies, for we celebrate the heavenly birthday of a man who knew how to pray even for his persecutors. Through our Lord Jesus Christ, your Son, who lives and reigns with you in the unity of the Holy Spirit, one God, for ever and ever.

Prayer over the Offerings

May God and the Divine Creator accept and sanctify these humble gifts as symbols of the genuine personal offerings we make in commemoration of Saint Stephen. Through Christ our Light and Saviour.

Communion Antiphon

Acts 7: 58

As they were stoning Stephen, he called out:
Lord Jesus, receive my spirit.

Prayer after Communion

Heavenly Father and God of all Creation, we give thanks for the nourishment of your heavenly gifts of the Bread and Fruits of Eternal Spiritual Life. May our earnest participation together in commemoration of Saint Stephen bring forth favourable blessings upon our lives, our community and your Holy Apostolic Universal Ecclesia.

XX.XIV – DECEMBER 27

1. **John the Apostle and Evangelist**
Feast

December 27

Entrance Antiphon

Psalm 8: 2-3

O Lord, our Master, how the majesty of thy name fills all the earth! Thy greatness is high above heaven itself. Thou hast made even the lips of children and infants vocal with praise.

Missale Christus | Proper of Heroes & Saints

Offertory Antiphon

O God and Divine Creator, who through the blessed Apostle John have unlocked for us the secrets of your Word, grant, we pray, that we may grasp with proper understanding what he has so marvelously brought to our ears. Through our Lord Jesus Christ, your Son, who lives and reigns with you in the unity of the Holy Spirit, one God, for ever and ever.

Prayer over the Offerings

May God and the Divine Creator accept and sanctify these humble gifts as symbols of the genuine personal offerings we make in commemoration of Saint John the Apostle. Through Christ our Light and Saviour.

Communion Antiphon — Jn 1: 14, 16

The Word became flesh and made his dwelling among us, and from his fullness we have all received.

Prayer after Communion

Heavenly Father and God of all Creation, we give thanks for the nourishment of your heavenly gifts of the Bread and Fruits of Eternal Spiritual Life. May our earnest participation together in commemoration of Saint John the Apostle bring forth favourable blessings upon our lives, our community and your Holy Apostolic Universal Ecclesia.

XX.XV – DECEMBER 29

1. Thomas Becket, Bishop and Martyr — December 29

Memorial

Entrance Antiphon — Psalm 8-10

Thou hast put them all under his dominion, the sheep and the cattle, and the wild beasts besides; the birds in the sky, and the fish in the sea, that travel by the sea's paths. O Lord, our Master, how the majesty of thy name fills all the earth!

Offertory Antiphon

O God and Divine Creator, who gave the Martyr Saint Thomas Becket the courage to give up his life for the sake of justice, grant, through his intercession, that, renouncing our life for the sake of Christ in this world, we may find it in heaven. Through our Lord Jesus Christ, your Son, who lives and reigns with you in the unity of the Holy Spirit, one God, for ever and ever.

Prayer over the Offerings

May God and the Divine Creator accept and sanctify these humble gifts as symbols of the genuine personal offerings we make in commemoration of Saint Thomas Becket. Through Christ our Light and Saviour.

Communion Antiphon

Lk 22: 28-30

It is you who have stood by me in my trials; and I confer a kingdom on you, says the Lord, that you may eat and drink at my table in my kingdom.

Prayer after Communion

Heavenly Father and God of all Creation, we give thanks for the nourishment of your heavenly gifts of the Bread and Fruits of Eternal Spiritual Life. May our earnest participation together in commemoration of Saint Thomas Becket bring forth favourable blessings upon our lives, our community and your Holy Apostolic Universal Ecclesia.

Title XXI – Notes

XXI.I – NOTES

1. There are no Notes associated with the Official English First Edition of *Proper of Heroes & Saints* of *Missale Christus*.

Notes

Title XXII – Tables

XXII.I – TABLES

1. There are no Tables associated with the Official English First Edition of *Proper of Heroes & Saints* of *Missale Christus*.

www.ingramcontent.com/pod-product-compliance
Lightning Source LLC
Chambersburg PA
CBHW081946230426
43669CB00019B/2936